Language Management and Its Impact

This book provides a comprehensive account of language management and planning at Confucius Institutes in the UK, implementing an ethnographic approach grounded in language management theory. As a global language promotion organisation, Confucius Institutes have previously been discussed in the literature with respect to socio-political issues, but this volume will shed particular light on their role in shaping and informing Chinese language policy at both the institutional and individual classroom levels. The book focuses specifically on Confucius Institutes in the UK, demonstrating how language teaching practice in these organisations is informed and shaped not only by organisational paradigms but also local language needs and institutional attitudes of host institutions. In turn, Li highlights how these organisations' unique position in a multilingual region such as the UK can offer new insights into language management by illustrating their roles as platforms for both individuals and institutions to become involved in the making and implementation of language policy. This volume will be of particular interest to students and researchers in language policy and planning, language education, applied linguistics, and Chinese linguistics.

Linda Mingfang Li is Principal Lecturer and Subject Group Leader for Chinese, Russian, and Japanese in the Regent's Institute of Languages and Culture at Regent's University London, UK.

Routledge Studies in Applied Linguistics

Grounded Theory in Applied Linguistics Research
A Practical Guide
Gregory Hadley

Project-Based Language Learning with Technology
Learner Collaboration in an EFL Classroom in Japan
Michael Thomas

Metacognition in Language Learning and Teaching
Edited by Åsta Haukås, Camilla Bjørke and Magne Dypedahl

Language Management and Its Impact
The Policies and Practices of Confucius Institutes
Linda Mingfang Li

For more information about this series, please visit: www.routledge.com/Routledge-Studies-in-Applied-Linguistics/book-series/RSAL

Language Management and Its Impact
The Policies and Practices of Confucius Institutes

Linda Mingfang Li

NEW YORK AND LONDON

First published 2019
by Routledge
52 Vanderbilt Avenue, New York, NY 10017

and by Routledge
2 Park Square, Milton Park, Abingdon, Oxon OX14 4RN

Routledge is an imprint of the Taylor & Francis Group, an informa business

© 2019 Taylor & Francis

The right of Linda Mingfang Li to be identified as author of this work has been asserted by her in accordance with sections 77 and 78 of the Copyright, Designs and Patents Act 1988.

All rights reserved. No part of this book may be reprinted or reproduced or utilised in any form or by any electronic, mechanical, or other means, now known or hereafter invented, including photocopying and recording, or in any information storage or retrieval system, without permission in writing from the publishers.

Trademark notice: Product or corporate names may be trademarks or registered trademarks, and are used only for identification and explanation without intent to infringe.

Library of Congress Cataloging-in-Publication Data
A catalog record for this book has been requested

ISBN: 978-1-138-48001-8 (hbk)
ISBN: 978-1-351-06406-4 (ebk)

Typeset in Sabon
by Apex CoVantage, LLC

Contents

Preface vi
Abbreviations vii
List of figures ix
List of tables x

1 Introduction 1

2 Language Promotion Organisations and
  Confucius Institutes in the UK 24

3 Studies on Confucius Institute and
  Language Management 47

4 Chinese Language Management at the
  Institution Level 73

5 Language Management at Confucius Institute Level 95

6 Language Management at Confucius Institute
  Classroom Level 128

7 Conclusions 168

Bibliography 179
Index 191

Preface

First of all, I would like to thank all the participants who took part in the research: directors, teachers seconded from *Hanban* and employed locally, and students studying in the two Confucius Institutes where I conducted the field study.

I am most grateful to professor Li Wei and Professor Zhu Hua, who despite a very busy schedule never failed to provide me timely advice and guidance. It was their encouragement and support that helped me to tide over times when I had to struggle between full-time work, family and many other commitments, and the study. On this, I should also thank Regent's University London and colleagues there for their support and encouragement.

I also owe a great deal to my husband George Xinsheng Zhang, our sons Jialiang Luke Zhang and Jialu Louis Zhang for their continuous support and help so that I could concentrate on my work and research. Without their sacrifice and support, it would not have been possible at all for me even to contemplate the idea of doing this research in the first place.

Finally, I thank Elysse Propesi, who not only encouraged me to turn the research into the current book format but also provided me with the much-needed expertise, advice, and guidance during the process; and Routledge for making my research available to anyone interested in the still being debated but awesome phenomenon of Confucius Institute. The completion of this research is only a beginning, as there are many interesting areas that can be further explored on Confucius Institute. I hope my research contributes, from a fresh perspective of language management, to the discussions on Confucius Institute which seems to have an interesting path ahead.

Abbreviations

ATLAS	qualitative data analysis software (Automatically Tuned Linear Algebra Software)
BCT	Business Chinese Test
BULATS	Business Language Testing Service
CEFR	Common European Framework of Reference for Languages
CELTA	Certificate in Teaching English to Speakers of Other Languages
CI	Confucius Institute
CILT	Centre of Information for Language Teaching for England
CNED	National Centre for Distance Education
DELTA	Diploma in Teaching English to Speakers of Other Languages
DFID	Department for International Development
EC	European Commission
EFL	English as a Foreign Language
ESOL	English for speakers of other languages
FCO	Foreign and Commonwealth Office
GIDS	Graded Intergenerational Distribution Scale
Hanban	Chinese Language Teaching Council International (also known as Confucius Institute Headquarters)
HEI	higher education institution
HSK	Chinese Proficiency Test
HSKK	Chinese Proficiency Speaking Test
IDP	International Development Program
IELTS	International English Language Testing System
IMF	International Monetary Fund
LPP	language policy and language planning
MAXQDA	qualitative data analysis software for Windows and Mac OS X
MOOC	massive open online course
MTCSOL	Master Degree of Teaching Chinese to Speakers of Other Languages

NOCFL	National Office for Teaching Chinese as a Foreign Language
PRC	People's Republic of China
SCILT	Scotland's National Centre for Languages
SDR	Special Drawing Right
SSAT	Special School and Academy Trust
TCFL	teaching Chinese as a foreign language
UCL-IOE	University College London—Institute of Education
UCML	University Council of Modern Languages
UNESCO	United Nations Educational, Scientific and Cultural Organisation
UNICEF	United Nations Children's Fund
WTO	World Trade Organisation
YCT	Youth Chinese Test

Figures

1.1	Number of Confucius Institutes and Confucius Classrooms 2005–2017	11
1.2	Teachers and Volunteers at Confucius Institutes 2005–2017	14
1.3	Distribution of Teaching Materials from the Confucius Institute Headquarters	15
2.1	Number of Confucius Institutes and Confucius Classrooms in the UK 2005–2017	39
2.2	UK and Europe: Number of Confucius Institutes and Confucius Classrooms by 2017	40
2.3	UK's Confucius Institutes and Confucius Classrooms in Europe (by percentage) by 2017	40
3.1	Research Methodologies and Research Instruments	62

Tables

2.1	Main Language Promotion Organisations in the World	25
3.1	Publications on Confucius Institute 2005–2017	48
3.2	Questionnaire Survey Sample, Its Spread and Return	68
3.3	Age Distribution of the Respondents	68

1 Introduction

Background

Confucius Institute, the Rise of China, and Growing Interest in Chinese Language

The development of Confucius Institute has been astonishingly fast over the last ten years. It has grown from just over two dozen in 2005 to 525 Confucius Institutes and about 1,113 Confucius Classrooms in 146 countries by the end of 2016, with some 1.7 million people learning Chinese and 12.72 million attending relevant events in these institutes.[1]

Confucius Institute is often compared with some long-established national language promotion organisations, such as Alliance Française of France, British Council of the UK, Cervantes Institutes of Spain, Goethe-Institut of Germany (Mo, 2009; Zhang and Wang, 2006; Liu and Jiang, 2011), the Japan Foundation, and the Korean Foundation (Tianzhong, 2011; Liu, X. P., 2011). Many such organisations are observed to have stepped up their efforts either by increasing their resources input or by modifying their operation models to compete with the expansion of Confucius Institute. For the former, examples include the Japan Foundation and the Chinese Academy of Taiwan (*Taiwan Shuyuan*), both of which have allocated more funds to increase their presences and profiles overseas (Zhang, 2008; Hisa, 2013). For the latter, Alliance Française and Goethe-Institut are reported to have recently formed partnerships with local universities in China. All this is done with the intent to increase their presence in these countries, as these local universities serve either as their exam centres or learning and teaching centres (Wu, Y., 2009)—a format clearly absent from the traditional approach of their development but characteristic of Confucius Institute in its growth in the last ten years. The impact of Confucius Institute is clear, which is accompanied naturally with a lot of studies on the institute in recent years.

There are a few strands in the study of Confucius Institute. The rapid development of Confucius Institute has been regarded by some as a reflection of the rapid economic development that China has achieved with its double digit economic growth for the last three decades, or of the increasingly important role that China is now playing in international economy and trade as well as international politics (Liu, 2013). Other studies have examined Confucius Institute in terms of its instrumental functions for the Chinese government which uses Confucius Institute as a cost-efficient means to build up the soft power of the country (Chen, 2008; Wu, Y., 2009; Gong, 2013) or to enhance the country's foreign diplomacy in line with the country's increasing importance on the world stage (Wu, Y., 2009; Zhang, 2007). There is also research that has focused on the operational model of Confucius Institute and discussed both the advantages and disadvantages of the joint venture format of the institute (Zhou and Qiao, 2008; Wu, Y. H., 2009; Zhang and Wang, 2006). Very little research, however, has studied Confucius Institute from the perspective of language policy and language planning (LPP), even though language learning and teaching is a primary activity of the institute.

The Confucius Institute initiative, in a way, can be regarded as a continuation of China's language policy since the 1950s, focusing on popularising and teaching Putonghua (common speech) and simplified Chinese characters to all its citizens of all the ethnic groups as well as to those who came to study Chinese in China. Teaching Chinese to speakers of other languages in China, often referred to as *Duiwai Hanyu Jiaoxue* in Chinese with a misnomer translation of "teaching Chinese as a foreign language" (TCFL) in English, only started to gather real momentum and became a university degree programme in the early 1980s, which coincided with the start of the economic take-off of the country. The Confucius Institute initiative in the early 21st century that aimed to deliver Chinese language teaching overseas is very much the result of the demand for Chinese language from abroad and the intention of China to take Chinese language learning and teaching to more people abroad. The purpose is not only to increase the understanding of China and Chinese language by those who are unable to go and learn in China, but also to enhance the positive image and profile of China via more cultural and educational exchanges. As mentioned earlier, the learning and teaching of Putonghua and simplified Chinese characters have permeated the entire half century of teaching Chinese to the speakers of other languages, including the ethnic Chinese whose first language is not Chinese. This change of "location" may appear to be only the place where the learning and teaching of Chinese takes place, however it requires some fundamental changes in almost all aspects of the teaching of the language to be localised so that it can fit in with the local needs and requirements as well as the local environment in terms of local language education policy and practices.

As a process, the localisation did not become an explicit policy of *Hanban* (Chinese National Office for Teaching Chinese as a Foreign Language) until recently when Mme Liu Yandong, chair of the council of *Hanban*, specifically pointed out in her keynote speech at the Tenth

Confucius Institute Conference in Shanghai that localisation of Confucius Institutes was one of the three major challenges and tasks in the next phase of the development of Confucius Institute. In other words, it took *Hanban* the entire decade to make the gradual change of its policy from the initial "popularisation model" (that aimed to standardise all the teaching materials, teaching methods, and assessments in all Confucius Institutes based upon the proven experience and expertise in *Duiwai Hanyu Jiaoxue* accumulated in China) to the current localisation model that takes into consideration the local circumstances and requests as well as the power of the local forces, not only the institutional partners but also students and teachers.

As a matter of fact, the gradual change in *Hanban*'s policy is, to a large extent, the result of the interactions in the past years between *Hanban* and Chinese and local partner universities, as well as the students and teachers in the Confucius Institutes. This very process epitomises not only the development in the study of LPP but also the actual change of China's language policy from initially completely internal to a later international one, from its early date to use language planning and policy from the top down as a solution to fix some perceived problems to the current bottom-up model. In view of the joint venture model Confucius Institute adopted and the equality conscious British environment in which Confucius Institutes operated in the UK, this study of Confucius Institute in the light of the framework of language management theory would throw new light on the working of Confucius Institutes and contribute to the increasing body of knowledge of this joint venture.

What has made the world take note of China is clearly the unprecedented rapid economic development since the 1980s. From mere RMB 367 billion in 1978 to over RMB 74 trillion in 2016, China's GDP grew over 200 times as much because of an average of close to double digit growth (National Bureau of Statistics of China, 2017).[2] China's GDP is now only second to the US, overtaking Italy and France in 2005, UK in 2006, Germany in 2007, and Japan in 2010. Some individuals anticipated that China' GDP could surpass the US around 2027 (Ahmed and O'Neill, 2011).

China's role in the world economy gaining increasing momentum in its importance can also be witnessed in the country's currency and investment. China's currency, the renminbi, was traded offshore and accepted as an SDR currency by the IMF in 2015, taking effect from 1 January 2016. In addition, several country's central banks have included the renminbi as a reserve currency. Meanwhile, one can also witness the growing direct investment that China has made overseas since the beginning of the century. Chinese investment overseas started shortly after the country opened its doors, but up to the early 1990s most investment was in the form of contractual work and export of labour. This changed to investment in manufacturing from the early 1990s till the beginning of this century; since then more and more mergers and acquisitions happened. The amount China invested overseas also grew very fast, from about USD 2 billion in 2000 to over USD 7 billion in the following year when China joined the WTO. It is expected that the amount of China's global stock of outbound foreign direct investment, which includes investing in corporate, acquisitions, and start-ups, will grow from USD 744 billon to as much as USD 2 trillion by 2020 (Financial Times, 2015).[3] It is easy to see that the rate of growth is much faster than that of the GDP, signifying the desire, ambition, and purchase power of Chinese enterprises.

The third change is no other than the growing number of Chinese tourists and students going abroad every year. Talking about the potential impacts that the Chinese tourists could have on the local economy and how her organisation was preparing for attracting more Chinese tourists, VisitBritain chief executive Sally Balcombe said:

> Every 22 additional Chinese visitors we attract supports an additional job in tourism. We want to ensure that we continue to compete effectively in this, the world's biggest outbound market, and ensure that we deliver growth and jobs across the nations and regions of Britain.[4]

If one looks at the number of Chinese students going to study overseas since the beginning of the century, the increase was also equally impressive, from about 50,000 in 2001 to some 544,500 in 2016, of which over 498,000 funded themselves and over one-eighth of the total came to study in the UK.[5]

Similarly, one can also observe that the Chinese language is gaining both in its popularity and in its economic value. It is reported that there are over 100 million people learning and/or using Chinese language outside China, of whom 40 million are Chinese born and living overseas[6] or heritage Chinese learners and users. In a study in 2014, Zhang, G. X. (2014) provided three facts illustrating the increasing use of the Chinese language on the internet and significant financial implications that the use of the language had. The first was the increase in the sheer number of the Chinese language internet users. In the decade between 2001 and 2011, Chinese users grew from 46 million, or 8.8% of the total internet users, to a staggering 510 million, nearly a quarter (24.2%) of the total. In the same period, the number of English users grew from 227 million to 565 million, but its percentage sharply dropped from 44% in 2001 to 26.8% in 2011 with a prediction that Chinese would overtake English as the largest language user group very soon.[7] The second was the increased importance of Chinese in terms of its potential commercial value and economic opportunity.[8] Chinese was among the 13 languages that can realise 90% of global online economic opportunity. And the phenomenal online sales of Alibaba in the last couple of consecutive years on

11 November and the value achieved were testimonials of the increasing economic value that the Chinese language has brought with in terms of online sales.

Moreover, an increasing number of national governments seem to give more attention to the teaching of Chinese, especially in all major English-speaking countries like Australia, Canada, the US, the UK, and recently Ireland. The Australian government made East Asia its priority in the 1990s; a white paper titled "Australia in the Asian Century" published in 2012 reaffirms the importance of learning Asian languages, including Chinese in the age of a rising Asia.[9] In the US, the establishment of the National Security Education Programme (NSEP) shortly after 11 September 2001 soon saw the launch of such language programmes as the Flagship project and Star-Talk, both of which include Chinese.[10] In the UK, the government promised to double the number of Chinese language learners by 2020, following the policy decision made a few years ago to include Chinese as one of the strategically important languages to promote in its education system (Tinsley and Board, 2014). On 4 December 2017, Irish Minister for Education and Skills Richard Bruton launched the government's Strategy for Foreign Languages in Education 2017–2026. The plan sets out a roadmap to put Ireland in the top ten countries in Europe for the teaching and learning of foreign languages, through several measures targeted at improving proficiency, diversity, and immersion. There are 100 actions in the strategy, including the introduction of Mandarin Chinese as a Leaving Certificate subject[11] in 2022.

All the above provides the background for the Chinese government to challenge the current world order and push for a new order with the increasing economic and political influence of the country. This is also clear in some of the recent proposals and strategies that the Chinese government has made: the establishment of the Asian Development Bank, the unrolling of the Belt Road Initiative, and the pledge that the Chinese president made at the recent UN General Assembly and Paris Conference to support development in Africa and the fight against the world climate change.

Chinese Language Teaching and Development of Confucius Institute

The teaching of Chinese to speakers of other languages started in a modest way and organised manner in the mid-1950s, usually to groups of homogenous learners from a few countries in a couple of universities in China. A handful of teachers were also sent out to teach Chinese in some countries. However, the development was slow and static over the next 20 years, even regressive in the ten years of the Cultural Revolution. This period was marked with two characteristics. One was that the teaching was in Putonghua and the simplified Chinese characters, as it was the language policy for all Chinese in the country; the other was that very limited attention was given to research into how to teach Chinese as a foreign language.

The first decade of the 21st century witnessed a huge step forward in TCFL overseas. By the end of 2011, while there were about 235,000 overseas students studying in China, the figure often quoted for the number of people learning Chinese overseas stood at 40 million, with some media even running as high as 100 million![12]

As early as 1995, a joint document was sent from the State Education Commission, the Ministry of Foreign Affairs, the Ministry of Culture, and the Office of the Overseas Chinese Affairs of the State Council to all the Chinese diplomatic services abroad, requiring them to step up and strengthen their work concerning TCFL.[13] This was the first time that TCFL was put on the agenda of the Chinese diplomatic services. Later it became a constant feature in diplomatic activities overseas with an increasing number of Chinese ambassadors attending events organised by local Confucius Institutes. In order to engage TCFL academics and professionals from abroad and encourage them to join the efforts of the TCFL language spread policy, Minister of Education Mme Chen Zhili signed off a decree in March 1999 to set up a Chinese Language and Culture Friendship Prize. The prize intended to reward those who had made an outstanding contribution to the teaching of Chinese, research in Sinology, and the promotion of Chinese culture. Therefore, by the end of the 1990s, all seemed to be ready for the take-off of the new TCFL language policy, which marked a clear shift for the TCFL practice at the beginning of the 21st century.

The first characteristics of this phase of the policy development was the clear policy and practice shift from focusing on TCFL in China to the teaching of Chinese globally, or in Chinese from *Duiwai hanyu jiaoxue* to *Hanyu guoji tuiguang* (promotion of Chinese language internationally). The term *Hanyu guoji tuiguang* first appeared in Professor Xu Jialu's proposal of speeding up and strengthening the work on the promotion of Chinese language teaching internationally to a meeting of the China's National Political Consultative Conference on behalf of the Central Committee of the China Association for the Promotion of Democracy in 2006. In the same year, at a National Conference on the International Promotion of Chinese Language, former Minister for Education Mme Chen Zhili mentioned transformations were needed in six areas in her speech. Two of the six areas were about changes concerning policy. One was to change from the focus of TCFL in China to an all-around promotion of the Chinese language internationally; the other was to push hard on the spread of Chinese language internationally associated with the Three Chinese User Circle analysis, with the inner Circle being the Chinese communities overseas, the second Circle the cultures sharing Chinese characters (e.g. Korea, Japan, and Vietnam), and the third Circle the rest of the world. She also suggested that an effective approach for the Chinese language penetrating into the third Circle was through working with the first two, and through making Chinese either the working language or raising its profile at major international activities and events in China, such as the Olympics in 2008 and World Expo in 2010.[14] In order to implement this language policy, the name of *Guojia Duiwai Hanyu Jiaoxue Lingdao Xiaozu* (National Leadership Group for Teaching Chinese as a Foreign Language) was changed into *Guojia Hanyu Guoji Tuiguang Lingdao Xiaozu* (National Chinese Language Council International). *Hanban*'s full name was changed from NOCFL (National Office of Teaching Chinese as a Foreign Language) to OCLCI (Office of Chinese Language Council International) in the year of 2006. A new two-year master's degree of Teaching Chinese to Speakers of Other Languages (*Hanyu Guoji Jiaoyu Shuoshi*-MTCSOL) was designed and validated in 2007. The number of universities offering MTCSOL increased from an initial 24 in 2007 to 63 in 2009 and 82 in 2011.[15] Motivation and measures taken on TCFL was well captured by some scholars. Guo points out:

> Regarding language planning, the value of TCFL as a new discipline lies in its active and critical role in the promotion of the spread of Chinese. While the selection of language, its standardisation and promotion are the main part of language planning, the spread of that language is to increase the use of the language as widely as possible. Any independent state should have a standard language for communication both domestically or even internationally if it plans to achieve national stability, political unity, and economic development. TCAFL is a concrete measure for the Chinese government to implement her international strategy of the Chinese language spread. If judged from the perspective of international spread, rapid spread of Putonghua in more and more places international signifies not only the continuously improved political status of the country, but also the increasing national power in the world.
>
> (Guo, 2006:13)

The second characteristic of this period of policy development was the birth of the new concept of *Guoji Hanyu* around 2008. *Hanban* promulgated the three key documents on standards concerning the Chinese language syllabus, the language competence, and the qualifications of teachers of Chinese, namely *Guoji Hanyu Jiaoxue Tongyong Kecheng Dagang* (International Curriculum for Chinese Language Education), *Guoji Hanyu Nengli Biaozhun* (Chinese Language Proficiency Scales for Speakers of Other Languages), and *Guoji Hanyu Jiaoshi Biaozhun* (Standards for Teachers of Chinese to Speakers of Other Languages). *Guoji Hanyu* caught the public's attention immediately and it soon became very popular, with such terms springing up one after another—*Guoji Hanyu jiaoxue* (learning and teaching of international Chinese), *Guoji Hanyu jiaoshi* (teachers of international Chinese), *Guoji Hanyu jiaocai* (international Chinese language teaching materials), *Guoji Hanyu Xueyuan* (College for international Chinese or School of Chinese as a Second Language), and new academic journals *Guoji Hanyu* (Chinese Language in the World). The literal translation of the Chinese term *Guoji Hanyu* is "international Chinese", though it does have at least two connotations. One is Chinese being international in terms of geographical coverage, and the other is Chinese being international in terms of varieties or scope of its usage. From the aforementioned policy statements and measures we can tell that it is the first connotation, the geographical coverage that reflects the language spread policy of the Chinese government. This is also evident from a scrutiny of media reports, research studies, and implementation practices of the policy.

There is a prevailing view that the language spread has a great implication for the building of a nation's soft power. Strong language and culture will bring about multiple benefits to a nation in the international arena. Many also share the view that the spread of Chinese helps to spread the Chinese culture, as language and culture are closely associated with each other. Therefore, the teaching of Chinese is not simply about language teaching but also a means to promote cultural and trade exchange, improve the national image and political status, and foster awareness of China (Guo, 2006). This leads to the third characteristic of the development in this period, the creation of Confucius Institutes by the Chinese government as a vehicle to implement its policy of promoting Chinese language worldwide.

The growth in teaching Chinese to speakers of other languages in China coincided with the start of economic take-off after the opening of the country at the end of the 1970s. This was marked with a steadily increasing number of learners coming to study Chinese in China from a far more diverse background and more universities offering such courses. As a result, more conscious effort came about in collaboration, research, and publication of more teaching materials, so much so that the teaching was formally accepted as a branch of academic discipline of applied linguistics, with a first batch of undergraduates admitted in the mid-1980s (Zhang, 2000). Nevertheless, the Chinese language policy in teaching Putonghua and simplified Chinese remained unchanged. The next two decades witnessed a huge development of the subject which mirrored the economic success of the country. The development of Chinese economy and investment overseas, and the rise in the international influence of the country, led to the need to extend the teaching of Chinese overseas, and this was the background against which the Confucius Institute initiative came into being.

Once the policy decision was made, the work was soon underway from 2002, led by the Ministry of Education and the State Leading Group for Teaching Chinese as a Foreign Language. However, first and foremost, the new promotion organisation needed an appropriate name. It was felt such organisation should have a name not only easily identifiable and most representative of China and Chinese culture but should also avoid political connotation and fit in well within the global context of an increasingly multicultural and multilingual world. It was with all these considerations that the name of the renowned ancient Chinese educator Confucius was put forward and subsequently adopted by the Chinese government in 2004.[16] In the same year, the Chinese Bridge Project proposal by the Ministry of Education was approved by the State Council, signifying the guarantee of the government commitment and financial support. The proposal suggested, as a priority, an accelerated process to implement the planned Confucius Institute initiative by way of collaboration with education institutions overseas. Alternatively, a franchising approach could be implemented so Confucius Institutes could reach a respectable number in a short period of time to provide non-credit-bearing Chinese language teaching courses and training for local Chinese language teachers.

The proposed collaborative way of building up Confucius Institutes was highly significant in the subsequent rapid development of Confucius Institutes. First, the involvement of local partner institutions overseas, mostly universities, would make the institute a joint venture, tying in the interest of the local partner and giving them financial incentives and access to various resources. This approach also avoided the possible perception that it was entirely a Chinese organisation. Second, the involvement of the local partner institutions gave the Confucius Institute initiative quick access to the local communities and networks, which would have been very difficult for it to achieve alone. Finally, it was also the involvement of the local partner institutions that made the subsequent rapid development of Confucius Institute possible due to their physical resource contribution such as offices, classrooms, and other venues required for all the planned activities, so it was financially efficient for the money that the Chinese government put in.

There is some confusion in the media with regards to which was the first Confucius Institute—the one in Tashkent, Uzbekistan, with its agreement signed in June 2004, or the one in Seoul, South Korea, which opened in November 2004. However, it was undeniable that the quick adjustment from the Seoul experience to adopt the collaborative model for the future Confucius Institute proved to be a key milestone and made a huge difference in rallying interest from potential overseas partner institutions. By the spring of 2005 dozens of agreements had been signed, and in July of the same year *Hanban* held the first World Chinese Conference in Beijing, at which the first 25 Confucius

Institutes were given the official Confucius Institute plaque. The rate of the development of Confucius Institute in the next two years was such that it took the whole world by surprise, including the director general of Confucius Institute Headquarters, Mme Xu Lin herself. As she revealed in an interview, talking about how she was caught by surprise shortly after she took charge of the *Hanban* in 2004,[17] she disclosed that initially the plan was to set up 100 Confucius Institutes around the world over a period of 10 years. However, 46 Confucius Institutes were set up in the first year alone, and the number already reached 100 in the following year, with more and more overseas institutions applying to join the league. It was clear that the proposed Confucius Institute model was well received.

This unexpected development was both the cause and result of the new policy move by the Chinese government in March 2006, noticeably with the change of the full name of *Hanban* as stated above, though the acronym *Hanban* remained the same. With the new aim to accelerate the progress of the Confucius Institute initiative abroad, *Hanban* aimed to realise the six key transformations as quoted in *Hanban* Annual Report that year:

- From teaching Chinese as a foreign language to international promotion of the Chinese language;
- From inviting people to come and study in China to sending teachers out to teach at the same time;
- From just offering Chinese as a major in universities to offering it to the public in the society;
- From having in the formal education system to spreading it outside the system as well;
- From being only directed by the government to a market operation with the support from the government; and
- From mostly the provision of face-to-face teaching based upon printed materials to online teaching backed with multimedia materials.

These changes were clearly indicated the government policy shift. The first Confucius Institute Conference was very significant in putting the Confucius Institute initiative on a firm footing. Not only the conference was named after the initiative, it also adopted the draft constitution and by-laws of the Confucius Institute in principle, which reaffirmed the collaborative model of the initiative and the three key functions of Confucius Institute. As was mentioned in the speech by Zhou Ji, the Minister for Education at that time, these three key functions were:

- A base for teaching Chinese abroad;
- A platform for education collaboration and exchange; and
- A bridge for economic and cultural exchange.

The question of standards and uniformity regarding how the teaching of Chinese should be organised and delivered in the Confucius Institutes was also mentioned, which signified the needs in the time of fast development, though it did not seem to have attracted much attention at that time. The conference was followed with another wave of new Confucius Institutes, and in April 2007, the Confucius Institute Headquarters (same organisation with *Hanban* with two names) was set up with its first council meeting held, to be followed by a bi-monthly magazine "Confucius Institute" and new office premises. By the end of 2007, the number of Confucius Institutes had reached over 200 in 66 countries. If one looks at it year by year, 2006 and 2007 was the time when the number grew the fastest. The growth of Confucius Institutes and Confucius Classrooms in terms of their numbers and number of countries involved is illustrated in Figure 1.1.

As seen in Figure 1.1, the number of Confucius Institutes and the countries in which they were set up increased by an average of 90 and 25 yearly in 2006 and 2007, respectively. The total number of Confucius Institutes and Confucius Classrooms grew from 25 and 17 in 2005 to 206 and 66 by the end of 2007. The rate was never repeated, as there were only additional 269 Confucius Institutes by the end of 2014, spreading in a total of 126 countries, less than an average of 40 Confucius Institutes and two countries a year. However, there was a fast growth in the Confucius Classrooms, which are essentially miniature Confucius Institutes mostly based in schools. After the first few appeared in 2006, there were only 20 Confucius Classrooms in 2007. But the number has grown to 851 by 2014, at a rate of average of nearly 120 a year. Unlike Confucius Institutes, Confucius Classrooms are highly concentrated (63%) in two

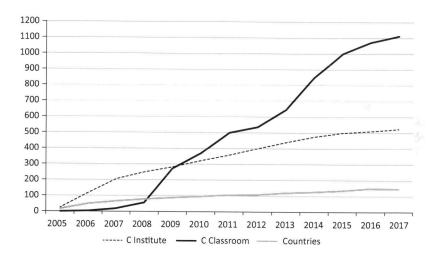

Figure 1.1 Number of Confucius Institutes and Confucius Classrooms 2005–2017

continents, North America (374) and Europe (159). Among those, 356 are in the US and 92 are in the UK, making up about 53% of the total number of Confucius Classrooms at that time. By the end of 2017, of 1,113 Confucius Classrooms worldwide, 501 were in the US and 148 in the UK, rising up to over 58% of the total.[18]

Doubtlessly, the international promotion of Chinese by the Confucius Institute initiative is a huge success as far as the number of the institutions and the geographic coverage are concerned. The chief executive of the International House, a primarily English language schools organisation set up in 1953, said at its annual conference in Prague in 2007 that *Hanban* had achieved in just two years the same growth (by the number of the member institutions) that had taken his organisation over 50 years. What he did not mention was that unlike his organisation, *Hanban* is a government sponsored organisation.

One of the main objectives of the Confucius Institute initiative in the last ten years was to increase the numbers of the institutes and their geographical coverage. This was clearly expounded by Mme Xu Lin, the director general of Confucius Institute Headquarters in an interview in 2012, on talking about the issue of the quality of Confucius Institute which had caused some concern due to its rapid development. She was quoted, "What is the quality for Confucius Institutes at this current stage? Its quality lies in its impact. What is its impact? Its impact is its scale".[19] However, quality and impact may not be regarded to be the same by many others. For instance, few top universities have Confucius Institutes. According to *the* Times Higher Education World Reputation Rankings 2015, of the top 100 universities only 29 have a Confucius Institute partnership. According to the *Guardian* university guide for 2016, among top 20 UK universities only four are involved in Confucius Institute. While there might be many reasons for this seemingly lack of interest from these universities in responding to Confucius Institute initiative, one reason is prominent that the funding from *Hanban*/Confucius Institute Headquarters is not that attractive as these universities are not short of funding as are some universities hosting Confucius Institute.[20]

Another development objective of the Confucius Institute initiative seems to categorise Confucius Institutes so they are "specialised" in certain areas or fields. The first of such special Confucius Institutes include Radio Confucius Institute (2007), Confucius Institute Online (2006), Confucius Institute for Business (2006), Confucius Institute for Traditional Chinese Medicine (2008), Confucius Institute for Physical Education (2008), Confucius Institute for Tourism (2011), Confucius Institute for Research (2011), Confucius Institute for Dance and Performing Arts (2012), and so on.

A third strategic development objective is the increasing emphasis placed upon the localisation of Confucius Institutes and their teaching practices. This change only took place in the recent years as it was increasingly clear that the development of the joint venture cannot overlook the local needs and practices; subsequently the phrase "Confucius Institutes belong to the local community", accompanied by a series of policy changes and more financial support, was released by *Hanban*. For instance, there are increasingly more locally operated teacher training programmes, and some Confucius Institutes also employ "core teachers" locally with generous subsidies from *Hanban*, which will foot the bill for the salaries and benefits of these teachers for an average of seven and a half years, with the initial five years completely paid for by *Hanban* and the second five years shared between *Hanban* and the local host institution.

The rapid development of Confucius Institutes around world has also attracted a lot of attention from academic research to media reports. In the English-language-dominated world, such attention tends to be negative, particularly in media. For example, there are reports on events and incidents with queries about the link of Confucius Institute to the Chinese government, which leads to views that it is being used as a means of propaganda or vehicle to build China's soft power.[21] Incidents include the petition by professors at the University of Chicago in the US that finally ended the university's talk to continue its involvement with their Confucius Institute when the first term came to end;[22] the hiring procedures of local teachers at McMaster University, Canada;[23] and the closure of Confucius Institutes at Pennsylvania State University and the University of Stockholm.[24] As such reports are not completely true because few are based on hard facts, they are not discussed in detail in this study. But reports like these do have an impact on the public in terms of their perception and understanding of Confucius Institute. However, as the Chinese media *China Daily* quoted, *Hanban*/Confucius Institute Headquarters did not expect a chain action or reactions as a result of the previously quoted closures or reports,[25] and Confucius Institutes are still going strong with the number continuing to increase to the all-time high level of the current 500 plus another 1,000 Confucius Classrooms.

Almost all Confucius Institutes offer Chinese language courses and organise China-related cultural activities in accordance with what is laid down in the constitution and by-laws of Confucius Institute. The rapid development of Confucius Institutes in the last ten years has created a huge demand for the supply of qualified Chinese language teachers. *Hanban* currently sends qualified teachers and volunteers to meet the demand. The staff seconded from *Hanban* also includes management staff, such as Chinese directors of Confucius Institutes. A striking figure to note is the gradual increase in the number of local Confucius Institute staff. According to the statistics released in the annual reports of the Confucius Institute Headquarters, the percentage of the Chinese staff from

14 *Introduction*

Hanban decreased from about 50% in 2010 and 2011 to about 30% in 2012 and 2013. It must be noted that while all the seconded Chinese staff tend to work full-time in Confucius Institutes, most of those seconded or employed from the local partner institutions do not. Therefore, the figure for the local staff is more likely to be head counts rather than full-time equivalents. The following Figure 1.2 illustrates the numbers of staff sent by *Hanban* in the past ten years.

Similar rises and falls are also observed in the number of teaching materials that Confucius Institute Headquarters have supplied to all institutions including Confucius Classrooms. There has been a steady fall in supply since its peak time in 2009, as can be seen in Figure 1.3. The main reason for these falls is the gradual emphasis on localisation of individual Confucius Institutes, particularly those with experience and expertise in the teaching of Chinese language. They have been increasingly encouraged and supported by *Hanban* to train their own teaching staff and develop their own teaching materials.

There have been debates on the importance of localisation of Confucius Institutes from its very early days (Wan, 2009; Zhang, 2012). The promotion of Chinese was seen and understood to spread the Chinese language and culture, and this was true, as one of the goals set in the Confucius Institute Development Plan 2012–2012 was to "make the Chinese one of the languages widely studied and extensively used by the people of the world". However, such an aim can only be attained if the teaching is effective. Apart from the issue of suitability, there is the issue

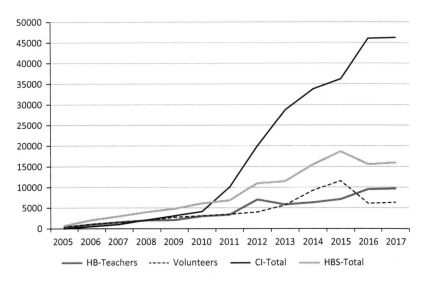

Figure 1.2 Teachers and Volunteers at Confucius Institutes 2005–2017

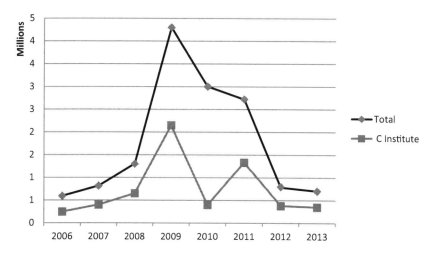

Figure 1.3 Distribution of Teaching Materials from the Confucius Institute Headquarters

of gradual localisation of both teachers and teaching materials in Confucius Institutes. The constant turnover of teachers can hardly guarantee continuity and stability of the teaching team, thus adversely affecting the quality of teaching, and the teaching materials developed in a context with cross-cultural communication in mind can hardly meet the needs in the intercultural context (Ji and Zeng, 2009). In addition, there is the issue of how the teaching is delivered in terms of what methodologies are used, how the teaching is assessed and for what purposes.

While all Confucius Institutes teach Chinese, there is a great variation among them in terms of who teach the language courses and what course books are used for the teaching. This depends largely on if the local partner institution has existing institutional policy and practices concerning the teaching of Chinese, even though the initial version of the constitution and by-laws says that it is the Chinese director who is responsible for the teaching of Chinese language. Therefore, on one end of the spectrum, in places where there is hardly any teaching of Chinese, Confucius Institutes are completely manned with *Hanban* teachers, and using the teaching materials supplied by *Hanban*. On the other end, where there is a long tradition in teaching Chinese language, teaching materials from *Hanban* may be hardly used, and the local partner institutions tend to rely on their own teachers and teaching materials instead *Hanban's*. In the latter case, Confucius Institutes may only have a rather limited presence of *Hanban* teachers, and if they teach, the teaching is confined to the non-degree level.

This Study and Its Contributions

Research Questions and the Needs for the Study

Confucius Institute is described primarily as a Chinese language promotion agent, providing a platform of learning Chinese and Chinese culture as well as facilitating exchange and mutual understanding. The teaching in Confucius Institutes is in Putonghua and simplified Chinese characters. Whatever other "official" functions or intentions that Confucius Institutes may be perceived to have (as the institutes are partially funded by the Chinese government), its primary focus in teaching Chinese and the way it operates as joint ventures between the Chinese and local partner institutions determine to a large extent what they are able to do. This has been neglected by most of the research on Confucius Institute.

Unlike most other existing research, the present study looks at the language policy concerning Chinese as observed through working in Confucius Institutes in the UK. The focus of this study is to examine and, in a sense, also to "assess" how the international Chinese language policy of *Hanban* is being implemented in the local British Confucius Institutes. Therefore, the primary research question for this study has three sub questions at three levels: (1) how the Chinese government language policies have evolved with regard to the teaching of Chinese language as a foreign language overseas along with the initiative of Confucius Institute; (2) how China's central language policies concerning the learning and teaching of Chinese have been interpreted and incorporated into the policy statement, if any, by the partner institutions; and (3) what the actual learning and teaching practices are like in the classrooms of Confucius Institutes with regard to the Chinese language policy. Answers to these questions would first lead to a better understanding of the development of China's language policy, which provides the background and context for the initiative of Confucius Institute. Since it is the implementation and results of the language policy that really matter as compared to the mere statements, answers to questions (2) and (3) could shed light on how the Chinese language policy manifests and even modify itself at the two key levels in the system: the institutional level involving the Chinese and local joint venture partners, and the classroom level in Confucius Institutes involving teachers and students.

The purposes of this study are both exploratory and evaluative. It is exploratory as this study intended to examine and investigate the learning and teaching of Chinese language in the Confucius Institutes. It is evaluative as this study intended to assess Chinese language teaching and how it reinforced or diverted from the international Chinese language policy of *Hanban*. It will shed new light on how the various agents of Confucius Institutes reformulate and interact with the central Chinese language policy, making unique contributions to our knowledge and understanding of the role of Confucius Institute in the management of Chinese language overseas.

There are multiple needs for such research. First and foremost, little existing research has looked into the Chinese language learning and teaching in Confucius Institutes, neglecting the primary function of the institutes. Second, little research has studied Confucius Institutes from the perspective of language policy, forgetting that the practice in any language institute is an integral part of the relevant language policies and practices. Third, in addition to helping with the understanding of how Confucius Institutes are operating with regards to teaching, Confucius Institutes themselves also need to reflect on their teaching practices as they are different from that of *Duiwai Hanyu Jiaoxue* in China. Many Chinese researchers and scholars used to treat Confucius Institutes just like an extension abroad of their practices of *Duiwai Hanyui Jiaoxue* in China. If Confucius Institutes are serious about long-term sustainable development in offering Chinese language, it is important that they understand how Chinese language could best be learned and taught to meet both the local needs and the objectives of the institutes.

Significance of This Study and Its Contributions

This study helps to fill in gaps in research on Confucius Institutes and is significant in a number of ways. The significance of this study is also enhanced by both theoretical contributions this study could make to Confucius Institutes and practical implications that this study has for the learning and teaching of Chinese in Confucius Institutes.

Most of the research on Confucius Institute tend to focus on its political intentions, activities abroad and instrumentation to build China's soft power. Few seem to have touched upon the individuality of each Confucius Institute and how its Chinese language teaching reflects and interacts with the Chinese language policy. This is what this research set to investigate. The study took ethnography as a methodological approach with a field study of two case Confucius Institutes using a combination of research instruments to collect data, which were subsequently analysed and discussed in the light of language management theory.

Theoretically the significance of this research lies in the fact that it is one of the first studies of Confucius Institutes from the academic perspective of language policy and planning, and it is the first to analyse and discuss the research findings of Confucius Institute in the light of the framework of language management. The study has taken a step forward regarding language management theory in that it is the first to use it to examine Confucius Institute as a national language promotion organisation with its multiple agents and stakeholders. The perspective of language policy and planning is relevant in that the primary function of Confucius Institute is Chinese language teaching. Confucius Institute, like other mentioned similar organisations, would not be a language promotion body without Chinese language learning and teaching. Even if language is just a tool, there is still the need to understand how the language learning and teaching is carried out and how it fulfils the overall objectives of the institutes. The perspective of language policy and planning and the use of language management theory also help to focus on how the joint ventures format impact on the primary activity of language learning and teaching in the institutes. The focus also helps to understand the interactive process of the collaborative model between *Hanban*/Confucius Institute Headquarters and various institutional and individual agents involved in the making and implementing of the local language policy concerning Chinese language learning and teaching in the institutes, and how the process affects the change or modification of the policy at the level of headquarters.

UK leads Europe in terms of the history and the number of Confucius Institutes. The first British Confucius Institute appeared in 2005 which was the second in Europe (the first one has now stopped its operation). UK is also the home for many first specialised Confucius Institutes in the world, such as Confucius Institutes for business, schools, Chinese medicine, dance and performing arts, and publication.

Thus the last, but certainly not the least, aspect of the significance of the study is that it is the very first in-depth and systematic study of Confucius Institutes in the UK where the development of Confucius Institutes outpaces almost all the other countries in the world. Therefore, by way of analysing the Confucius Institutes in the UK, this research will provide insight into the working of Confucius Institutes not only in the UK but also in the world. These insights will complement discussions and reports that often appear in many media across the world.

On the practical level, the significance and contributions of this study lie in that the research has a range of practical implications for learning and teaching Chinese in general and for Confucius Institutes in particular. As Chinese language learning and teaching is more widely spread across the world, and it is the core activity of Confucius Institutes, understanding of how learning and teaching take place in local institutes is crucial for ensuring that learners can have an efficient and enjoyable experience. As far as learning is concerned, Confucius Institutes need to have a clear understanding of how their learners learn Chinese so that they could be in a better position to help them. As for the teaching, Confucius Institutes need to work out what and how to teach based upon the knowledge of how their learners learn and what they wish to learn. The findings of the study will have some very practical implications concerning learning and teaching of Chinese in Confucius Institutes, and the study hopes that its findings would promote best practices in this regard for Confucius Institutes as well as other institutions that offer Chinese language courses.

In a sense, the results of this study also have direct relevance and implications for *Hanban*/Confucius Institute Headquarters regarding both its policies and practices concerning the learning and teaching of Chinese in its Confucius Institutes. The findings and the conclusions of the study will be presented to *Hanban*/Confucius Institute Headquarters and could have profound impacts, if taken seriously, in terms of the ways in which the teaching of Chinese is organised and delivered in its classrooms, the teachers' beliefs and their behaviours, the use of resources, and collaborations between various local Confucius Institutes throughout the world.

Theoretical Framework and Research Methodologies

LPP and Language Management

As mentioned earlier, this study will approach Confucius Institute in terms of its primary function as a national language promotion organisation and from the theoretical perspective of LPP, more specifically language management, a framework recently developed and updated by Bernard Spolsky (2004, 2009) based upon the work by people such as Cooper and Ricento before him.

The choice of LPP as the theoretical perspective to study Confucius Institute is primarily because the Confucius Institute initiative corresponds well with LPP in terms of its functions and purposes. Confucius Institute has a clear mission to popularise the learning and use of Chinese language in parts of the world where it can address the issue of absence of the due presence of the Chinese language, so the instrumental and utilitarian nature of the Confucius Institute policy initiative is as self-evident as expected by language policy and planning in the early days (Haugen, 1959). The study of LPP in the West changed from this centralised problem-solving approach in the 1960s to a more democratic orientation that tended to look at the language learning and teaching as a human right in the 1980s, and then to the current consensus that all the stakeholders in the language policy and planning play a certain role in the shaping and working of the relevant language policy. This is an approach that reflects the multicultural and multilingual tendency of most of the societies in the world today characterised by its multi-polar power structure and a changing world order. The findings of this study suggest that this is what has happened to Confucius Institutes too over the last ten years, as the Confucius Institute policy has changed from a more centralised one to the present one that stresses the importance of localisation of all aspects concerning the learning and teaching of Chinese language.

The multiple agents involved in the operation of Confucius Institutes come as a result of its one distinctive feature when compared with other similar language promotion organisations—they are joint ventures operating abroad. Apart from a very few, most of the 134 countries and regions in which Confucius Institutes operate are multilingual and multicultural societies with decentralised power structures, from Australia in the South to Norway in the North, from Argentina in Latin America to Zimbabwe in Africa. In these countries and regions, language policy and planning are very complicated processes managed by various stakeholders. Therefore, the application of language management theory is appropriate in a language spread situation like Confucius Institute, involving many agents across different cultural, social, and political boundaries. Confucius Institutes present a very complex and versatile task for study and analysis that only language management can help untangle some of the myths, especially when concerning motivation and beliefs of the learners and teachers, overt and covert institutional language policy statements, and the practices of all the agents concerned.

Ethnographical Approach and Research Instruments

Since almost all Confucius Institutes follow the format as joint ventures between *Hanban*/Confucius Institute Headquarters, a Chinese university (sometimes more than one), and a local university (or educational organisation) abroad, this seemingly similarity often covers the reality that rarely are two Confucius Institutes the same as their partner institutions are different. It is this very feature of Confucius Institutes that suggests a qualitative approach would be more adequate for any in-depth study of Confucius Institutes. Therefore, this study has decided to use two individual but quite representative Confucius Institutes as case Confucius Institutes for an ethnographic study.

As a methodology, ethnographic study was first widely used in anthropology to study in detail a social phenomenon in its organic nature, and it often focuses on individual cases that constitute an organic part of the whole picture (Patton, 2015; Hymes, 1964). This methodology was later used in many disciplines of social sciences and education (Silverman, 2004; Black, 2001; Heller, 2011). Although quantitative research has been popular in the last few decades, and at times has even dominated the social sciences and education research, qualitative ethnographic studies have regained momentum in the last ten years or so, particularly in education where quantitative research is regarded as lack of depth in fully exploiting or expounding the reasons behind an observed social phenomenon. Regarding research on Confucius Institutes, while only a limited number are on actual Chinese language learning and teaching, even fewer study it ethnographically, so research in this area remains weak not only in numbers but also in depth.

Ethnographic studies require collecting field study details before analysing them in any chosen theoretical framework. The instruments used most often are observation and interview. As this research studies the learning and teaching of Chinese in Confucius Institutes, the primary venue for data collection is classrooms, which enable the researcher to observe both the students and teachers who are the real key players at the grass-roots level with regards to the language policy. To complement the observed data, this study also uses semi-structured interviews. These are aimed at obtaining in-depth information concerning all major aspects related to learning and teaching from students, teachers, and directors or managers of the two Confucius Institutes, as such data will help illuminate questions observed in the classrooms, thus achieving a better understanding of the issues under study. In addition, this study employs a student survey questionnaire. It is designed to solicit information to produce a general snapshot profile of the students in the two Confucius Institutes and how they view their learning in the Confucius Institutes.

Structure of the Book

This book consists of seven chapters. After this introductory chapter, Chapter 2 provides a brief account of some established language promotion organisations and the development of Confucius Institute in the UK to set the scene for the purposes of this study. Chapter 3 reviews the study of language planning and policy, both in the West and in China. It delineates how the study of language policy has evolved from the early days, when language policy and planning was used as a tool to address the perceived social problem of lack of proficiency, to the present day, when it becomes a platform to examine how individuals and institutions are involved in the making and implementation of a language policy in the societies. It also reviews some of the relevant research on Confucius Institute before setting out what this research aims to study and achieve. The following three chapters report on the main research findings of the field study, and analyses and discusses these findings in the light of language management theory. Chapter 4 examines the language management in terms of the interactions between the institutional players and subsequent local policies at the institutional level. Chapter 5 looks into the language management with regards to the operation of Confucius Institute, and Chapter 6 scrutinises the language management from the perspectives of the two main individual agent groups: the students and teachers.

Finally, Chapter 7 mainly draws some conclusions from the findings of the study and their analyses and discussions. It starts with a recap of the research questions, findings, and contributions. After presenting the conclusions, it mentions some limitations with the current research. Then it suggests some potential topics for future research on Confucius Institutes, focusing on Chinese language learning and teaching of Confucius Institutes as part of language management, the research efforts that this study has started but has not yet been able to explore in more depth due to various constraints.

Notes

1. *Hanban*. Confucius Institute annual development report: http://www.hanban.org/report/index.html
2. National Bureau of Statistics of China. *China Statistical Yearbook*: www.stats.gov.cn/tjsj/ndsj/2017/indexeh.htm
3. Anderlini, J. China to become one of world's biggest overseas investors by 2020: https://www.ft.com/content/5136953a-1b3d-11e5-8201-cbdb03d71480
4. Khomam, N. VisitBritain aims to attract Chinese tourists with new names for landmarks: www.theguardian.com/uk-news/2015/feb/16/visitbritain-mandarin-names-uk-landmarks-chinese-tourists
5. Ministry of Education of the People's Republic of China. 2016 Statistics on the number of people studying overseas (2016 年度我国出国留学人员情况统计): http://www.moe.gov.cn/jyb_xwfb/xw_fbh/moe_2069/xwfbh_2017n/xwfb_170301/170301_sjtj/201703/t20170301_297676.html
6. Centre for China and Globalisation. 2016 Report on Development of World Overseas Chinese Entrepreneurs: http://en.ccg.org.cn/wp-content/uploads/2016/12/2016-Report-on-Overseas-Chinese-Enterpruners.pdf
7. Kushinka, M. Internet users by region and language: www.redlinels.com/2012/05/29/internet-users-by-region
8. CSA Research. What languages matter most online: http://ow.ly/i/OGva
9. Australian government. Australia in the Asian Century, White Pape: http://pandora.nla.gov.au/pan/133850/20130914-0122/asiancentury.dpmc.gov.au/white-paper.html
10. National Security Education Program. Mission and Objectives: www.nsep.gov/content/mission-and-objectives
11. Department of Education and Skills. Languages Connect: Ireland's Strategy for Foreign Languages in Education 2017–2026: www.education.ie/en/Schools-Colleges/Information/Curriculum-and-Syllabus/Foreign-Languages-Strategy/fls_languages_connect_strategy.pdf
12. Li, Z. W. 100 million foreigners keen to learn Chinese (一亿外国人热衷学汉语): http://paper.people.com.cn/rmrbhwb/html/2011-11/28/content_967578.htm
13. Zhang, D. X. New development in teaching Chinese as a foreign language (对外汉语教学新发展): www.pep.com.cn/xgjy/hyjx/dwhyjx/jxyj/hjlw/201009/t20100901_852764.htm
14. Li, Y. M. Language of powerful states and powerful language states (强国的语言和语言强国): https://wenku.baidu.com/view/dd9099385627a5e-9856a561252d380eb629423b5.html
15. *Hanban*. MTCSOL. On MTCSOL programme (关于MTCSOL (汉语国际教育硕士专业学位)): http://english.hanban.org/node_9904.htm
16. Xinhua net. Overview of overseas Confucius Institutes (海外孔子学院概况): http://news.xinhuanet.com/newscenter/2006-04/29/content_4491339.htm
17. Xu Lin, Director of *Hanban*: Confucius Institute at a critical junction (国家汉办主任许琳: 孔子学院正处在一个关键路口): www.chinaqw.com/hwjy/2015/06-23/54175.shtml
18. *Hanban*. Confucius Institute/Classroom: http://english.hanban.org/node_10971.htm
19. Watch, Oriental Weekly. The American incident tests the vitality of Confucius Institute (美国事件验证孔子学院生命力): http://style.sina.com.cn/news/p/2012-06-12/094797685.shtml
20. Marcus, J. West's universities reconsider China-funded Confucius Institute: www.timeshighereducation.com/news/wests-universities-reconsider-china-funded-confucius-institutes/2002870.article

21. Sudworth, J. Confucius institute: The hard side of China's soft power: www.bbc.co.uk/news/world-asia-china-30567743
22. Statement on the Confucius Institute at the University of Chicago: https://news.uchicago.edu/article/2014/09/25/statement-confucius-institute-university-chicago
23. Bradshaw, J. & Freeze, C. McMaster closing Confucius Institute over hiring issues: www.theglobeandmail.com/news/national/education/mcmaster-closing-confucius-institute-over-hiring-issues/article8372894/
24. Volodzko, D. China's Confucius Institutes and the Soft War: http://thediplomat.com/2015/07/chinas-confucius-institutes-and-the-soft-war/
25. *Hanban*. Closing of Confucius Institute in Sweden not to trigger ripple effect: www.chinadaily.com.cn/china/2015-01/13/content_19306747.htm

2 Language Promotion Organisations and Confucius Institutes in the UK

Since the establishment of the first Confucius Institute, its rapid development is widely seen as a result of the Chinese government's efforts to build the country's soft power in line with its fast-growing economic and political might in the world arena. However, a national language promotion organisation like Confucius Institute is not uncommon. This chapter consists of four sections. The first section examines the operation of three major European language promotion agencies. The second section reviews briefly the development of Confucius Institutes and Classrooms in the UK. The third section gives some comparisons between these language promotion organisations and discusses characteristics they share. The final section is a summary, with the point that there is not much existing research on Confucius Institute in the light of language policy and planning, and the theory of language management can provide an adequate framework for such an attempt.

Similar Language Promotion Organisations

There have been several similar organisations that are charged with the primary task to promote a particular language and culture, such as British Council (English) and Alliance Française (French). It seemed to be purely by coincidence that in 2005, when the first batch of 27 Confucius Institutes was established, British Council, along with the other five institutions (Alliance Française, Società Dante Alighieri, Goethe-Institut, the Instituto Cervantes, and the Instituto Camões), shared the Prince of Asturias Award of that year for their outstanding achievements in communications and the humanities. Table 2.1 displays some main language promotion organisations in the world.

Before examining some major European language promotion organisations, it is worthwhile mentioning *Taiwan Shuyuan*. The first *Taiwan Shuyuan* was opened in 2011 in New York and was followed by two in Houston and Los Angeles, respectively.[1] *Taiwan Shuyuan* was quoted to "focus on promoting understanding of Taiwan, as well as sinology research, Taiwan's multicultural experience, and Mandarin teaching

Table 2.1 Main Language Promotion Organisations in the World

Country	Organisation
France	Alliance Française
Germany	Goethe-Institut
Italy	Società Dante Alighieri
Japan	Japan Foundation
Korea	Sejong Institute
Portugal	Instituto Camões
Russia	Russkiy Mir Foundation
Spain	Instituto Cervantes
UK	British Council
US	Amerika Haus

service".[2] It was clear that the newly founded *Taiwan Shuyuan* has as its primary task the promotion of the understanding of contemporary Taiwan in the wider context of Chinese culture, through a network to be built around the world. Although there was an ambitious plan to expand the network, the actual development was modest. According to a foreign policy report of the Taiwanese authority in 2013,[3] the number of *Taiwan Shuyuan* still remained unchanged as two years ago when the three were founded in the US, with contacts set up in 64 countries. On *Taiwan Shuyuan*'s website,[4] only 11 physical centres are listed—three in Asia, five in Europe and three in America—most of which appear in the name of Cultural Centre, with many located in the cultural division of the Taiwanese representative office. Regarding the Chinese language, *Taiwan Shuyuan* promotes the teaching of Mandarin with traditional Chinese characters, but its teaching seems to be confined to some local community schools or centres that have links with Taiwan rather than with any distinctive programmes with dedicated staff and organisation. As *Taiwan Shuyuan* is relatively young, more study will be needed to follow its development path and to compare it with Confucius Institute.

In the following sections, only three major organisations will be discussed as these three are more influential in the field of language and cultural promotion. These are British Council, Alliance Française, and Goethe-Institut. The review will touch upon the following aspects: a brief historical review of their development; management and funding; language courses and cultural activities; and teachers, students, and assessments.

British Council

According to its Annual Report 2013–2014, in the year of its 80th anniversary British Council was operating in more than 100 countries around the world with an annual turnover of almost GBP 865 million, and about 11 million people visited its events. As for English language teaching, it had 83 teaching centres in about 50 countries with 388,000 learners, and 2.6 million candidates took the English language examinations that it organised in the various centres all over the world (British Council, 2015).

A Brief History

British Council was initially established as "British Committee for Relations with Other Countries" in 1934 at the request of business community to promote English language teaching and British culture abroad (Phillipson, 1992). The name changed to "British Council for Relations with Other Countries" in the following year, and in 1936 it was officially shortened to "British Council". The initial funding of British Council came from private companies, but soon the government got involved and an annual funding was established through the Foreign Office. The 1940 Royal Charter set the objectives of the organisation as to promote "abroad a wider appreciation of British culture and civilisation, encouraging cultural, educational and other interchanges between the United Kingdom and elsewhere".[5] British Council is known to have three main business strands: the English language, the arts, and education and society.

The development of British Council can be roughly divided into four stages: the initial stage from 1934 to 1953, when it was more focused on cultural activities; the development stage from 1954 to 1976, when it refocused on promoting English language; the consolidation stage from 1977 to late 1990s, when it readjusted its strategy to meet the challenges posed by the dramatic and rapid global changes in the late 1980s; and finally the new era stage since 2000, when Europe is becoming increasingly multilingual and the world an increasingly globalised economic and complex political reality.

During the first decade between the mid-1930s and 1940s, the government involved British Council in the activities "designed to combat German and Italian propaganda" (Phillipson, 1992:137) by setting up cultural centres, donating books, offering scholarships, and supporting British schools, including providing help to students coming to study in the UK. In the second decade after the WWII, British Council became more involved in promoting activities with commercial interest due to lack of long-term decision on the part of the government and a continuous decrease in the government funding, as well as to political instability which led British Council to pull out its operation from a number of countries across the world, such as Poland in Eastern Europe, China in the Far East, Cyprus and Greece in the Mediterranean, Jordan and Syria in the Middle East, and Egypt in Africa. Therefore, there was an urgent need for British Council to secure its long-term future with a clearly defined goal and development strategy.

The second stage of British Council's development started with the shift of its focus to the teaching of English language because of the recommendations by a number of government reviews—first the Independent Committee of Enquiry in the Overseas Information Services of April 1954 (also known as the Drogheda Report), and then the Official Committee on the Teaching of English Overseas in 1956. The former pointed out that the teaching of English by British Council would be highly beneficial for trade overseas, and to secure English as the language of science and technology and as a lingua franca, while the latter stressed that there were opportunities in teaching English by British Council in increasing the use of the language as the main second language in most parts of the non-English speaking world (Benesche, 2001). Many British teachers were sent overseas. British Council was also involved in teacher training overseas while many teachers were brought to the UK to be trained in the universities. The year 1965 saw the first proficiency test of English language for studying in the UK, which was the forerunner of the IELTS (International English Language Testing System). British Council's work in the two decades contributed to the rapid development of the teaching of English worldwide, including bilateral cooperation programmes. All this helped to lay a solid foundation for establishing English as a lingua franca internationally. While the teaching of English had become an important source of income for British Council, a government review in 1977 (the Berrill Report) suggested that it was no longer a government priority as teaching English was using public money to promote the interest of private sector (Benesche, 2001:31) and called for the abolition of the organisation and end of its overseas operation.

Consequently, the third stage of British Council's development started off with some difficult years marked with reduced government funding and a sharp reduction of British Council's overseas operation and closure of two-fifths of its UK regional offices in the early 1980s. But a succession of important events in the late 1980s and early 1990s, such as the fall of the Berlin Wall, the dissolution of the Union of Soviet Socialist Republics, the birth of the European Union, and the continued rapid economic growth in the Asia and Pacific region, especially in China, brought about renewed demand for English language across the world and new demand for British know-how in management. This led to another round of fast expansion of British Council's overseas operation with increased government funding. However, British Council by then had learned how to maintain its operation with multiple funding sources and engaged in more income generation activities. It also knew how to readjust its strategies in a timely manner so as to ensure that it could achieve its sustained long-term development.

The 21st century started with many new challenges politically, economically, culturally, and environmentally—more than ever before. In face of this, British Council reoriented itself in line with its strategy and introduced some large-scale programmes. While English language teaching and testing remained an important aspect of its work as the demand for English as a lingua franca was stronger than ever before, British Council has become far more active not only in its traditional areas of promoting cultural exchange and understanding through arts, school networking, and all aspects of education, but also in a much wider range of areas with many projects concerning climate change, human rights and justice, social development, and so on both in Europe and around the world. The projects aim to raise the public awareness of cultural diversity and of the importance of mutual tolerance and understanding for living in the world today. The work of British Council is not restricted in the 100-plus countries where it has a physical presence, but far more beyond, with online programmes that were used by about 73 million website users in 2013–2014 (British Council, 2015).

Management and Funding

British Council is a charity, but it is also a "public corporation and an executive non-departmental public body" sponsored by the Foreign and Commonwealth Office with its own operational independence. However, as it uses the public fund, it means that it is under the public auditing as well as the usual scrutiny of a charitable organisation. Its management, led by a chief executive, is held accountable to the board, which consists of a group of distinguished personnel, many of whom also head specialised committees. The organisation is managed on two dimensions, operations and regions, and its regional heads are often seen as "diplomats" as they are based in the cultural and education section of the local British embassies or consulates. British Council has the reputation as

> a high-quality provider with expertise in economic development, education management and reform, human rights and justice, public administration and reform, social development, and technical and vocational education and training.
>
> Examples of this expertise includes the DFID (Department for International Development) funded police training and development project in Sudan, the UNICEF (United Nations Children's Fund) funded releasing potential in schools in Iraq and the EC (European Commission) funded social security reform co-operation programme in China.[6]

Most of its activities and operations are carried out in partnership with a range of organisations from multinationals and businesses to government departments, non-government organisations, universities, and schools. For example, the established IELTS examination is a case of nearly 30 years' collaboration with the Cambridge ESOL (English for speakers of other languages) and IDP (International Development Program)

Australia, and it is now the largest English examination in the world. According to its 2013–2014 Annual Report, British Council employs over 8,000 staff, about 2,000 of whom are engaged in activities related to the English language.

While still supported with public money, the reliance on the government funding has been steadily reduced. As a result, British Council has to rely on multiple funding sources, including bidding and managing contracts and projects from governments or other organisations. If one looks at the balance sheet figures of the British Council's Annual Reports for 2003, 2009, and 2013, the percentage of the government grant has come down steadily from 37.6% to 30% and 20%, respectively. In 2017, the government grant was reduced to 14.7%. What is worth noting here is that a most important revenue generating stream is undoubtedly English language activities, which includes the teaching of English, training of language teachers, examination administration, and so forth, with the income level steadily rising in the same period from 36% to 55% and 72% of the total earned revenue, respectively. This was achieved under the circumstance that the staff level working in the English language remained more or less unchanged during the same period in the last ten years. In other words, the team has been improving its efficiency all the time.

Courses, Teachers, and Assessments

It is not quite clear that since when the English language started to be offered as demanded rather than provided as was the case with most of the language and cultural promotion agencies. However, British Council seems to be engaged in the provision of English language teaching in three ways: face-to-face teaching in its 82 language centres or schools in 49 countries across the world; online English language courses and learning materials; and finally, by collaborating with education organisations or other institutions of all levels, both public and private, at home and abroad. With regards to the means of teaching, the latter two have produced far more impact than the first as they can reach a much wider audience, particularly the online courses and materials which are available anywhere, anytime, and by anyone with internet access.

The courses that British Council offers at its language centres or schools are usually the Common European Framework of Reference for Languages (CEFR) referenced and clearly stated in places where the CEFR is understood, for example in its school in Paris, France; but may not necessarily be explicitly stated in places such as its school in Algiers, Algeria. The labels of the level descriptors that British Council uses are non-technical and easy to follow. The terms used for the six levels are Beginner and Elementary (or Elementary 1 and 2) for A1; Pre-intermediate (which can include 1 and 2) for A2; Intermediate for B1; Upper intermediate for B2,

Advanced for C1, and Mastery for C2. Intermediate level and above may consist of a couple of sublevels where needed, just as is the case with the lower level A. British Council started to create an innovative English language course online, which was launched in mainland China in 2007; the trial also included Hong Kong. It soon had some 30,000 users. After years of continuous development, the online course Learn English Online[7] is a huge success and has a range of different courses for adults, children, and business people, making use of the latest online and mobile technologies with its own apps, interactive games, podcasts, and audio and video materials. The courses are even available on MOOCs (massive open online courses), radio, and social media such as Facebook, Twitter, and YouTube. In 2013–2014, the online users total about 73 million, as compared to some 333,000 students learning face-to-face in its 83 centres all over the world.

There seem to be no prescribed printed course books for the language courses that British Council offers, primarily because there is so much material that the centres and their teachers can choose from. As part of collaboration, British Council does provide a lot of expertise and support when and where needed to help develop locally demanded materials. This is usually in printed matter, as it has a team of more than 2,000 experienced English as foreign language teaching professionals, including teachers, teacher trainers, assessment experts, and consultants on the learning and teaching of English language in the multilingual and multicultural age and environment. British Council is involved in providing accreditation to English language schools in the UK. It also delivers qualifying tests such as CELTA (Certificate in Teaching English to Speakers of Other Languages) and DELTA (Diploma in Teaching English to Speakers of Other Languages) for the teachers of English and administers, and IELTS for those who need the qualifications to study and work in an English-speaking environment. According to British Council's own estimate, the UK's English language teaching market is worth about GBP 2 billion annually and as many as some 2.6 million candidates take IELTS worldwide, generating around GBP 70 million in earnings each year for the UK examination boards. However, promoting English language is not just about making money, more importantly it is seen as a vehicle to serve for more profound impact that British Council intends to achieve, as British Council states on its website:

> By teaching English, changing the way we see each other through the Arts, offering international education opportunities and sharing the UK's ways of living and organising our society, we create opportunity, trust, prosperity and security for the people of the UK and the many other countries we work in around the world.
>
> (British Council Web statement)

Alliance Française

Alliance Française is a renowned non-profit organisation with a long history which focuses on promoting French language and culture around the world. Today it runs a network of 850 establishments in 136 countries on all five continents. Each year, about 500,000 people attend courses provided by Alliance Française to learn French, and more than six million people participate in the cultural activities that Alliance Française organises all over the world.[8]

A Brief History

Alliance Française, a not-for-profit organisation with its status conferred by the relevant government law of 1901, was created in Paris in 1883 by a group of eminent individuals, including scientists, diplomats, businessmen, and well-known writers (e.g. Jules Verne, the author of *Around the World in Eighty Days*). While it is widely known that the organisation was aimed to actively promote French language internationally (which in those days really meant "in the colonies and foreign lands"), little was mentioned about the fact that its birth was also part of the efforts to continue to extend and preserve the influence of the French language and culture a decade after the bitter Franco-Prussian War (1870–1871), for the war had not only ended France's dominance in continental Europe but also greatly hurt the nation's pride as a result of Germany's annexation of Alsace-Lorraine. Alliance Française was from the start in favour of respecting civilisations, not just the French one (Bruézière, 1983:239), and all the member institutes enjoy a great deal of "autonomy" as long as they share the passion and mission of the association. Ever since its earliest days, all Alliances Françaises work towards three essential tasks: (1) offering French classes for all, both in France and abroad; (2) spreading awareness of French and Francophone cultures; and (3) promoting cultural diversity and valuing all cultures.[9]

In the two years following the formation of the association, Alliance Française was soon set up in Paris, Barcelona, Mauritius, and Mexico, to be followed by Rio de Janeiro in 1886, India in 1889, and Melbourne in 1890. By the 1890s, Alliance Française existed in all parts of the world. There was also a great deal of cooperation with the French government in terms of organising cultural activities overseas, and for this the Alliance was given the status of "public utility" in 1896, enabling it to access government funding in this regard. Therefore, Adamson mentioned that Alliance Française was indeed quite difficult to define clearly with regard to its nature, as it is an organisation both private (non-profit) and government funded, both French and foreign (2007:55).

However, the development was very slow in the first half of the 20th century, due to a number of reasons, particularly the Second World War which forced Alliance Française to move its headquarters to London in 1943 when Paris was occupied by Nazi Germany. The speed of development started to pick up in the second half of the 20th century, largely due to the changing geo-political scene of the world and that the government recognised the important role Alliance Française could play in maintaining French influence. As explicitly said in a speech by Charles de Gaulle, it was by forging relationships between the French and others based upon free and moral grounds that the French could extend their cultural influence on the benefit of all, and it was for that relationship that Alliance Française was born, to live and to continue.[10] Since then all French presidents have been the honorary presidents of the Alliance. In 2013 President François Hollande held a celebration to mark the 130th anniversary of the Alliance.[11] In 1983, Alliance Française was established in 80 countries, and by 1999, they were in 138 countries (including France), with 1,135 committees and some 372,000 students.[12] It is interesting to observe that in the last 15 years or so, the numbers of Alliance Française and countries where they operate have changed little, but the number of learners has increased by some 34%. In 2007 the Alliance was reorganised when the Alliance Française Foundation was created (the Foundation is separate from the Alliance) to take charge of the development work of the Alliance as well as the cultural activities.

Management and Funding

By nature, all Alliances Françaises are "free associations of free men and women". Alliance Française, from its very beginnings, has adopted three main principles: a non-governmental and independent organisation; culture and cultural exchanges among the peoples preferable to conflict and war; and a local not-for-profit organisation operating autonomously in the local juristic system.

This has determined the franchising nature of all local Alliances Françaises which have shared values as the basis for all their actions as well as their commitments that are the love of French language and interest in Francophone culture and cultural diversity. The brand of Alliance Française is owned by the Paris centre, which also serves as the headquarters of the entire Alliance Française organisation. Each Alliance Française outside Paris is essentially a local and independently run franchise, with its own committee and president.

The creation of Alliance Française Foundation marks a major change in Alliance Française and enables it to focus its own resources more on language teaching. The Foundation takes charge of coordinating and developing Alliance Française network, offering professional evaluation, training, and consultancy services, as well as organising cultural diversity programmes that usually operate at a loss. Therefore, the move was in a way compelled by the increasing financial difficulty and challenges faced by Alliance Française in terms of its principles of independence. Though the separation led to more government involvement with financial and human resources support for the cultural activities that Alliance Française was involved in, it also allowed the Alliances to maintain their independence in their language teaching activities to meet the local needs. This is best illustrated in the case of Alliance Française London offering commercial courses as early as in 1894, and many of its presidents and council members were also associated with businesses. Today the language revenue is about one-third of the entire budget of the Alliance and the dependence of the organisation on alternative funding sources is obvious.

Each Alliance is usually managed by a director, appointed and sent by the Alliance head office. An interesting thing to observe is that the Alliance seems to pay more attention to the regional synergy and have held several regional conferences in the recent years, with the first one for the African region in Nairobi in 2009, then in Brussels in 2010 for Europe, Rio in 2011 for Latin America, and in Bangkok in 2012 for Asia and Oceania. Such conferences not only provide an ideal forum for the head office to transmit messages in an open and transparent manner and a platform for the regional branches to meet and share their experiences and resources, but they have also changed the single individual linear way that the Alliance used to "manage" its branches in the past.

Courses, Teachers, and Assessments

French language courses are not offered in a uniform format in all the Alliance branches as far as the length of a course and the total number of hours required for certain levels are concerned. However, they all seem to be linked to the standardised level descriptors set across the entire Alliance network by the organisation and designed with regards to the CEFR, but the time needed to study for these levels vary from place to place. For example, one can learn French from scratch part-time and complete the study at B1 level in 330 hours in Alliance London, UK;[13] the same level will require 495 hours over five months with 25 hours a week of intensive study or a total 655 hours with 12.5 hours a week over ten months in Alliance Nanjing;[14] and 800 hours with ten hours a week over a period of one year in Alliance Beijing.[15] While it is not common, sometimes a local Alliance may put on other language or related courses to meet the local needs so it is perceived to be local.[16]

The Alliance branches have a range of French course books at their disposal, and new course books are usually related to the CEFR levels. For instance, the textbooks *Alter Ego* 1–5 published between 2005 and 2010 and *Version Originale* 1–4 published between 2009 and 2012 are both linked to the CEFR levels, from A1 to C2 and from A1 to B2, respectively. While these books may not have been designed with specific learners from certain cultural and linguistic backgrounds in mind, the Alliance nowadays appears to be much more aware of the need to "adapt" the learning materials to meet local requirement. The Alliance China mentions on its website that efforts are underway to provide for China specially adapted versions of the textbooks *Alter Ego* to be used in all Alliances Françaises in China.[17] In addition, the teachers in various local branches are often engaged in the compilation of supplementary materials to go with the selected textbook when such needs arise. Training is also being provided in the use of certain teaching materials with the help of the Alliance head office.

Most of the teachers are French native speakers, although non-native speakers and local teachers are also employed. All the teachers have teaching qualifications such as DAE-FLE (Diplôme d'Aptitude à l'Enseignement du Français Langue Étrangère) which the Alliance created with the National Centre for Distance Education (CNED) and requires ten months' study. Another teaching qualification DPAFP-FLE (Diplôme Professionnel de l'Alliance Française Paris ile-de-France en Français Langue Étrangère) normally requires five months' study on site in Paris. The Alliance Paris also serves as a central teacher training centre, though many Alliances also offer teacher training opportunities, especially workshops and distance learning. Over 2,000 teachers receive such training every year. The Alliance Paris is awarded a top QFLE label (Qualité français langue étrangère) for high-quality French language teaching by a joint commission comprising three government ministries: education, culture, and foreign affairs.

Goethe-Institut

"The Goethe-Institut brings the German language to the world". This slogan on the institute's website represents what Goethe-Institut is about. However, that is not quite the complete picture. Through a network of 160 Goethe-Instituts in 94 countries (12 in Germany), with many alliances and partners, Goethe-Institut also provides information and organises activities on the culture, language, and other general aspects of Germany,[18] almost acting as a cultural and educational ambassador for the country.

A Brief History

Goethe-Institut, founded in 1951 in Munich, was part of Germany's efforts to gain back the trust that the country had lost due to its role in World War II. It was initially established as a dedicated professional organisation to provide training to teachers of the German language from abroad. The institute soon ran German language courses for speakers of other languages in Germany as well. It was in the following year that its first overseas branch was set up in Athens, Greece. The teaching of German to learners from overseas led to the need for the institute to develop its own teaching materials, *Schulz-Griesbach*, a classic textbook in the history of Goethe-Institut. The initial success was very encouraging, and the institute also realised that language alone would not be able to achieve the kind of mission it was tasked with. Therefore, in 1953, the role of the Institute expanded to include providing programmes of cultural events to accompany courses. This new "addition" has remained as a focus with the Goethe-Institut ever since, as one can see from the following current mission statement:

> We promote knowledge of the German language abroad and foster international cultural cooperation. We convey a comprehensive image of Germany by providing information about cultural, social and political life in our nation. Our cultural and educational programmes encourage intercultural dialogue and enable cultural involvement. They strengthen the development of structures in civil society and foster worldwide mobility.[19]

There were a couple of periods in the history of Goethe-Institut when it developed quickly in terms of numbers. The first peak was the decade following the establishment of the first institute in 1951, with 54 offices opened abroad and 17 in Germany (Bach, 2011). The second peak was after the fall of the Berlin Wall in 1989, when there was a need as well as an opportunity for expansion in Eastern European countries, which continued into the 1990s with several institutes and office being opened in Warsaw, Prague, Krakow, Budapest, and Moscow. In 2001 Goethe-Institut merged with Inter Nationes, a similar institution in terms of history (also founded in 1951) and nature (also largely founded by the government but legally independent), but mainly charged with the promotion of German culture overseas. Since then the institute is increasingly turning towards the Middle East, Africa, and Asia where, as its president said, there are more challenges as well as opportunities.

Management and Funding

Goethe-Institut is a German not-for-profit organisation running from its headquarters in Munich. With a board of trustees and directors consisting of eminent external figures, government, and its own staff representatives, the institute is managed by a team of executives with an appointed secretary general as the head of the operation. The head office has various functional departments, such as language, culture, finance, human resources, and so on, but the management also has a second layer made up of 13 regions over the world with Germany itself as one of the regions based at the head office. Typically, the director of each institute is appointed and sent by the head office.

The institute has always been defined as a voluntary organisation, but with most of its funding from the government and fulfilling cultural exchange and promotion functions on behalf of the government, its independence remained as a question till 1976 when a formal agreement was drawn up and signed between the foreign office of the federal government and the institute. The Articles of Association and the Agreement clearly define its independent status as a non-profit charity, with tasks delegated by the government supported with funding to work as a cultural agent of the country overseas. The government funding is important to the institute (Zhang and Wang, 2006), but Klaus-Dieter Lehmann, the current president of the institute, clarifies this by saying:

> We are not a state-owned enterprise. We are an independent legal entity. Two-thirds of our budget is provided by the German parliament and one third comes out of our own profits. But we are entirely autonomous with respect to the content of our programs. That is recognized around the world and it is what we draw our credibility from.
>
> (Bach, 2011)

Lehmann was right about the government grant. According to the 2014 annual report[20] of the institute, of the total revenue of EUR 351 million, EUR 208 million (59%) was government grants, EUR 121 million (34%) came from teaching, and the remaining EUR 22 million (7%) from other sources. With regards to the institutional organisation, in addition to full-fledged institutes, Goethe-Institut operates through a network of a large number of subordinated institutions including cultural societies, Goethe Centres, reading rooms and libraries, language learning centres, and examination centres. It is quite clear that apart from the government grant, the provision of German language courses is the main source of income for the institute.

Courses, Teachers, and Assessments

Goethe-Institut has set up a uniform framework of course levels in line with the CEFR which has three main levels consisting of two sublevels each. While courses may be offered in different formats, intensive in a short period of time or extensive over a longer period, there is a notional number of hours needed for completing each course level. However, it also suggests the amount of course hours varies from one region to another and appears to be associated with the venue where the learning and teaching of German takes place. For example, more hours of learning are required for Chinese learners of German in Shanghai, who need to study 160 hours for A1 courses, while English learners of German in London only need to do half of that amount for completing the same level. Where accelerated intensive German courses are offered, it is expected that these Chinese learners of German should have a good command of English.[21]

Goethe-Institut has a range of approved or recommended materials for individual institutes or centres to choose from. All the main course books appear to have been developed by native German-speaking specialists with most of the contents and situational scenes set in Germany, although they do reflect the change of times over the years, with some intercultural elements incorporated to mirror the growing multilingual nature of the society in Europe. The local teachers are also engaged in either developing or sourcing supplementary materials to meet the local needs, as is the case with several centres across China. There has also been talk of either modifying existing materials or developing more tailor-made materials for Chinese learners of German.

There is a clear change in the composition of the teachers in Goethe-Institut worldwide. One may still find a lot of native German-speaking teachers in many of the institutes in Europe, but it is common elsewhere that many local teachers with adequate training and experiences are employed to teach at the institutes, usually with the given syllabuses and materials, and many work on a part-time basis. These teachers, like other teachers of German in the host country, can also apply for sponsorship to attend professional development programmes which the institute organises worldwide. These programmes are available not only to the institute's own teachers, but also to teachers of German in general, and they can be held in Germany, in the host country, or via distance learning.[22]

Assessment of the courses at the institute are both formative and summative, and learners can choose what to do according to their needs since the courses are all designed with regard to the CEFR. There is a range of formal qualifications as proof of learners' linguistic competence, from lower levels for young learners to the whole range for students and mature learners. The institute also has its own certificate (Goethe-Zertifikat) as an evidence of language ability, which is recognised throughout Germany. The learners can also take external proficiency tests at comparable level should they like to, for example BULATS for business German and Test Daf for B2 and C1 levels, and GDS for C2 level as proof of general German proficiency to function in a German-speaking environment.

Confucius Institute and Its Development in the UK

Chinese Teaching in the UK

The UK has a long history in the teaching of Chinese, which can be traced back to the formally established first professor of Chinese in the

University of London in 1837, followed by two more professorships in Oxford and Cambridge, respectively. In 1916, the School of Oriental Studies was established as a constituent college of the University of London. Like many other European countries, the British tradition of teaching Chinese also started with the missionaries. Robert Morrison, who was most famous for his translation of the Bible into Chinese and the compilation of perhaps the first dictionary for the English-speaking learners of Chinese—*A Dictionary of the Chinese Language* (which came out in 1819)—had acquired both Cantonese and Mandarin in the early years when he served as a missionary in Macau. He taught Chinese evening classes in London between 1824 and 1825 when he was briefly back in England from his missionary service.

However, rapid development of Chinese language teaching in the UK is a recent phenomenon, largely taking place in the last 10 to 15 years. In the school sector, Chinese language courses have now found their way into about a third of the schools, as compared to only handful in the early 2000s (Tinsley and Board, 2014). Most students learning Chinese are no longer the Chinese heritage students. In the higher education sector, in addition to the half dozen or so universities that offer Chinese major degree programmes, over 40 universities offered Chinese as part of their degree programmes in 2015 according to UCAS (University and College Admission Service). This number does not include Chinese courses offered by university language centres as part of the Institution-Wide Language Programme (IWLP). A recent survey by UCML-AULC (2014) shows that 88% of the institutions that responded offer Chinese language, as compared to only 16% in a survey in 1999. Chinese lists in 4th place by popularity after three European languages. Similarly, the Chinese community schools (recently termed as complementary schools) have also witnessed an increase in their number of students, particularly those from non-Chinese families in the local communities (Tinsley and Board, 2014). In addition, there are now numerous language schools that offer non-credit-bearing Chinese language courses of all kinds. Among them are most of the 29 Confucius Institutes that have been set up in the UK since 2005.

The Development of Confucius Institutes in the UK

According to the Confucius Institute Headquarters, by the end of 2017 there were 29 Confucius Institutes and 148 Confucius Classrooms in the UK, as can be seen in Figure 2.1. These figures represent 5.5% and 13% of the total numbers of Confucius Institutes and Confucius Classrooms in the world, respectively. As a matter of fact, UK stands out quite prominently in many ways in terms of its development concerning Confucius Institutes.

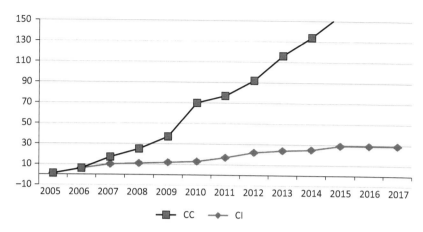

Figure 2.1 Number of Confucius Institutes and Confucius Classrooms in the UK 2005–2017

First, the UK was one of the earliest countries to act in response to the initiative of Confucius Institute. The London Confucius Institute, the first in the UK, was among the first batch of 25 Confucius Institutes awarded in 2005. In the following year, another five Confucius Institutes were set up, bringing the total to six in a single country when there were only 122 in a total of 49 countries worldwide.[23] While this may not seem much, the number of Confucius Institutes within the UK was more than twice the global average, which was 2.4 Confucius Institutes per country at that time, ranking only after the US (16) and Germany (eight).

Second, UK has witnessed fast growth in terms of the numbers of the Confucius Institutes and the Confucius Classrooms, not only in the global context but also in the European context, as indicated in Figure 2.2.

If one looks closely at these numbers, it is easy to see that the total number of the Confucius Institutes and the Confucius Classrooms in the UK amounts to 142, as compared to the total of 370 in the whole Europe in 2014, with 253 spreading out in another 38 countries. In other words, the UK has a total of 142 Confucius Institutes and Confucius Classrooms when the average number of the Confucius Institutes and the Confucius Classrooms stands at fewer than 10 in each country for Europe.

The figure can also be interpreted in terms of percentage, as in Figure 2.3. The UK alone has nearly 17% of the Confucius Institutes and over 48% of the Confucius Classrooms of the total in Europe.

Third, British universities play a very important role in the development of Confucius Institutes and Confucius Classrooms in the UK. All the Confucius Institutes in the UK are partnered in one way or another with local British universities. There were two school-based Confucius

40 *Language Promotion Organisations*

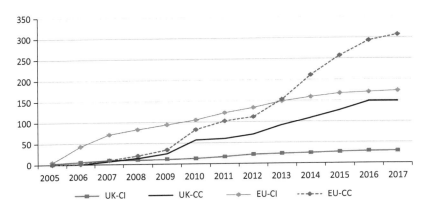

Figure 2.2 UK and Europe: Number of Confucius Institutes and Confucius Classrooms by 2017

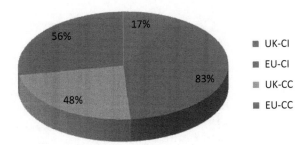

Figure 2.3 UK's Confucius Institutes and Confucius Classrooms in Europe (by percentage) by 2017

Institutes, the one at SCILT (Scotland's National Centre for Languages) and SSAT (Special School and Academy Trust), but they both have recently moved and become integrated into universities. Moreover, the overwhelming majority of the Confucius Classrooms are linked local Confucius Institutes rather than having a direct agreement with Confucius Institute Headquarters. Of the 41 UCAS-listed universities that offer Chinese programmes, 16 host Confucius Institutes on their campus. This level of involvement of the British universities in the development of Confucius Institutes and Confucius Classrooms may well reflect the importance of China and the Chinese language for British universities and their students. It also reflects the great British pragmatic tradition.

Lastly, the UK takes lead in many ways in spearheading new development of Confucius Institutes (i.e. Confucius Institute for special purpose). One can see that the UK has set several "firsts" in this regard in the entire family of Confucius Institutes. Between 2006 and 2008, there emerged the first Confucius Institute for Business (at London School of Economics), the first Confucius Institute for Traditional Chinese Medicine (at South Bank University), the first Confucius Institute for Schools (first at SSAT and now at UCL-IOE), and recently the first Confucius Institute for Dance and Performing Arts (at Goldsmith College, University of London).

Teaching of Chinese in Confucius Institutes in the UK

All the Confucius Institutes in the UK are engaged in the teaching of the Chinese language and culture in one way or another. Few of them are also involved directly in accredited programmes in the host universities due to the quality assurance requirements of the British universities. Typically, three main types of operations can be identified.

The first type is that Confucius Institute is fully involved in the teaching of Chinese language courses, from the design of the courses to the full delivery of the courses. This is usually true of the universities which did not have any or little experience or expertise in the teaching of Chinese before they had Confucius Institutes. While such Confucius Institutes can claim all the help they have given to the programmes, they are not a recognised institutional partner on any of the accredited courses or programmes, which also means a huge financial advantage for the local universities concerned. For Confucius Institutes that operate in this manner, the Chinese director usually takes the full responsibility of running the Chinese language courses with a team of teachers sent from *Hanban* and some employed locally. These Confucius Institutes also tend to use the teaching materials supplied by the headquarters, as the teachers sent from *Hanban* are familiar with them, and what's more, the materials are even free or at a very low cost to the students.

The second type is that Confucius Institute is only involved in the teaching of the existing Chinese language courses of the host university. So the Confucius Institute *Hanban* teachers usually teach alongside the local teachers, delivering a given syllabus but most likely under the supervision of the local course leaders, and are subject to the institutional quality assurance procedures. Many universities use locally developed teaching materials, and even for those universities that use China produced teaching materials recommended by *Hanban*, it is most likely that adjustments are made to ensure they meet the needs of the students (Ji and Zeng, 2009). The host universities obviously welcome such contributions, as they bring in extra resources and financial benefits.

The last type is usually in the form of non-credit-bearing Chinese language courses such as evening or weekend classes open to the university students as well as the public. This is obviously the decision of the host university. While the host university wishes to have the association with Confucius Institute for the benefits it brings, it may also have range of other considerations such as potential conflict of interest, particularly the financial interest between Confucius Institute and the university in the offering of the Chinese language courses. Confucius Institutes operating in this environment usually do not get a lot of support from the host university, let alone fully integration. The teaching is done by both teachers from China and locally, but teaching can also be varied as it falls into the "other" category, thus very little requirement or work regarding quality control when compared to the accredited courses.

Comparisons and Discussions of Language Promotion Organisations

All three aforementioned organisations claim to be international and independent charities tasked with the mission to promote their languages and cultures as well as cultural exchange worldwide. While they have different histories and approaches, they do share the following characteristics in terms of the nature and modes of their operations.

More Cultural Promotion Organisations Than Language Schools

All three organisations are partially funded by the relevant governments on a regular basis, which means that they are, to a certain extent, public organisations by nature and answerable to public scrutiny and taxpayers like any government organisation. The main reason for their access to government funding lies in their missions: the promotion of the language and culture of the country that the government represents. As a matter of the fact, it is the promotion of the culture that the government is keener to get involved in, as it helps to promote the national interest or the soft power of the nation. Therefore, these organisations are also perceived to be associated with the government, and sometimes they do physically base in the cultural or educational section of the embassies or consulates abroad. Their legal status as an independent charity gives them the needed shield from any possible direct "interference" from the government and gives the public a perception that they are not directly affiliated to the government, so they are not the instruments of the government policy. This is particularly so when French and German governments have their own cultural promotion agencies. In a way, the teaching of language in these organisations can be regarded as a means to serve the ultimate purpose of promoting the culture, as this was clearly stated by British Council earlier on. If it was just about the language teaching, these organisations would have been like commercial language schools whose focus is primarily financial returns. A great advantage for them is the access to the government funding and wider access to the international language market. This also makes it possible for these organisations to be the most influential language providers, trainers, accreditation-awarding and standard-setting bodies in the field.

On a Path From Colonial to Multicultural and Multilingual Age

All the three languages are based in Europe and, due to historical reasons, all of them had a colonial past, which in a way accounts for not only the geographical base but also the political, socio-cultural, and economic influence that already exists. It was not until the age of increasing economic globalisation on the one hand and the political unification with the birth and expansion of the European Union characterised by multiculturism and multilingualism on the other hand that cultural exchange and diversity move higher up on the agenda of these organisations. This change is necessitated by both the public awareness and demand along with change of the social and economic equilibrium. One most noticeable change is the way many of the relevant cultural activities are planned and organised nowadays. Regarding the language teaching, it is still quite Euro centric, from the inception of the CEFR to the teaching of these languages, the training of the language teachers, and the compilation of the relevant teaching materials. While it is true that the language teaching and teacher training are provided to meet the local demands, it is still rare that these organisations make conscientious efforts to "localise" and tailor their teaching and teacher training to make them effective based upon the consideration of how the "targeted" learners learn these languages. This is against the background that many education institutions of the European countries receive a lot of international students. There is a growing recognition that international students from different linguistic and cultural backgrounds learn these European languages quite differently too.

Multiple Funding With Central Management

In addition to their legal status, being independent also means that these organisations rely on multiple funding sources and with increasing needs and abilities to generate additional revenue to fulfil the stated missions of the organisations. It is without exception that such language provision does not only manage to make ends meet, but also generates a margin (not called "profits" since they are charities) to subsidise other activities, particularly the cultural activities which are in general loss making. This is because these languages are so-called commodity languages, the languages that have so much demand for them that they can be offered on a fee-paying basis at a market rate. In many ways, the influence of these languages is attributed to the past legacy or the present power of the countries they are associated with. In terms of management, all three organisations have a centralised structure even though Alliance Française says that its local branches are autonomous, which is true only in the sense that these branches are cost centres with their own governance and management structure. For the guidelines and the funding for key cultural events of the three organisations, they all come from the head office, and some may argue that they come directly from the relevant government office in the case of British Council.[24] Additionally, the language teaching, teacher training, and examinations are also no exceptions, with prescribed general frameworks of teaching, standards, and requirements, the practitioners are left with only limited autonomy of choice in terms of delivery methods and materials.

Partnership as a Prevalent Model of Operation to Maximise the Impact

While it is not clear since when partnership became a dominant model of operation, it is very clear that all three organisations have resorted to this model for their operations, both at home and abroad. This is especially the case in the last 20 years or so. As it focuses its effort on inter-governmental and inter-institutional collaborative projects, British Council does not have any teaching centre in China, and all its offices are operating in collaboration with a wide range of partners, looking after the interest of British Council in the entire neighbouring area rather than just the city where they are based. With Alliance Française and Goethe-Institut, almost all their new language centres in China are in some forms of partnership with local organisations, though their preference seems to be local universities. Looking at the way that these three organisations are funded, partnership is perhaps the only way that makes it possible for them to expand their operation fast, as there is greater economic efficiency compared to working on their own.

It is interesting, therefore, to examine in this context the development and research on Confucius Institute, which has obviously adopted a different model regarding its expansion, though its language teaching and culture activities are very similar to the language promotion organisations discussed earlier. However, the focus of this study is on language learning and teaching in Confucius Institute as a demonstration of the relevant language policy.

Summary

While there are other major national language promotion organisations on an international scale, such as British Council, Alliance Française, and Goethe-Institut, Confucius Institute differs from them in at least the following three aspects. First, it is a joint venture involving several institutional partners, a model that some others now also use, such as

Alliance Française, but not in a similar manner or on a similar scale. The management of Confucius Institute is a shared responsibility of the partner institutions. This also means that the performance of individual Confucius Institute may depend to a large extent on the actual relationship between the foreign and Chinese directors and between the partner institutions. Second, Confucius Institute is first and foremost still a language promotion organisation, although the promotion of Chinese culture is part of its remit. Because of the joint-venture nature of Confucius Institute, cultural activities may sometimes take longer time to negotiate and coordinate between all the partner institutions with regards to their purposes and funding. Cultural activities cost money. Finally, there is a huge support, especially resources from the Chinese government in the development of Confucius Institute, while the other three organisations generate a substantial amount of income through their teaching. The Chinese government funding explains how it is possible that Confucius Institute has developed so quickly. As the Chinese language is not yet a real commodity language, it will be years before Confucius Institute can balance its books through its language teaching operation, like British Council has.

It is quite clear that there have been some policy shifts on the part of *Hanban* in the last few years, for instance Confucius Institute is now encouraged in recruiting and training local staff and developing local materials to meet the local needs with its language learning and teaching activities. Supply of teaching materials from *Hanban* has eased off, and funding is made available from *Hanban* for Confucius Institutes to hire local teachers. Such policy change may well be based upon the realisation and awareness that in today's multilingual and multicultural societies, the over-emphasis on or promotion of a particular language and culture without adequate heed to the local needs may hinder the future development of Confucius Institute. The question is, in this context, how the Chinese language policy is implemented in individual Confucius Institute with regards to the roles of all the relevant stakeholders, and above all, from the point of views of the learners and teachers who are active agents of any language policy and its management (Spolsky, 2009). The next chapter will look at the theory of language management and studies and how it can be applied to the study of Confucius Institutes.

Notes

1. *The China Post*. Taiwan academies open in 3 US cities: https://chinapost.nownews.com/20111016-115561
2. Pang-White, A. Gaining a better understanding of Taiwan: www.scranton.edu/academics/ignite/issues/2012/spring/understanding-taiwan.shtml
3. Taiwan. Foreign Policy Reports: www.mofa.gov.tw/en/News_Content3.aspx?n=4BAF9BD5400A05D9&sms=BA5E856472F10901&s=AD2C0693F4D93654

4. Taiwan Academy: http://english.moc.gov.tw/dir/index.php?sn=2720
5. The objectives of British Council are quoted in the 1940 Royal Charter as to (a) promote cultural relationships and the understanding of different cultures between people and peoples of the UK and other countries; (b) promote a wider knowledge of the UK; (c) develop a wider knowledge of the English language; (d) encourage cultural, scientific, technological, and other educational cooperation between the UK and other countries; or (e) otherwise promote the advancement of education: www.britishcouncil.org/about/our-status
6. British Council. https://solas1.live.solas.britishcouncil.net/about/timeline
7. British Council. Learn English: http://learnenglish.britishcouncil.org/en/
8. France's overseas cultural network: www.diplomatie.gouv.fr/en/french-foreign-policy/cultural-diplomacy/france-s-overseas-cultural-network/
9. The Alliance Française, at the heart of a global network: https://www.alliancefr.org/index.php/en/who-are-we/alliance-francaise-paris-ile-de-france
10. 130 years Franco-British friendship in London: www.alliancefrancaise.org.uk/m_history.htm
11. Education minister-councillor Ma Yansheng attended 130 anniversary reception of the founding of Alliance Française (马燕生教育公参出席法语联盟成立130周年招待会): www.education-ambchine.org/publish/portal116/tab5722/info102271.htm
12. Bibliographie: http://doc.sciencespo-lyon.fr/Ressources/Documents/Etudiants/Memoires/Cyberdocs/MFE2001/blaisea/these_back.html
13. Schedule French group classes: www.alliancefrancaise.london/Scheduled-French-Group-Classes.php
14. Alliance Française in Nanjing. 2015 年夏季最新课程: http://afnanjing.org/kcjs.asp?id=1
15. Alliance Française in Beijing: http://beijing.afchine.org/IMG/pdf/06_FILIERE_SEMI_INTENSIVE_AE__VC_1401.pdf
16. Alliance Française in Fiji. The Alliance in Suva offers courses in French, Fijian, and Hindi courses on demand. It organises a free movie night twice a month and other cultural events: https://www.af-fiji.org/
17. Alliance Française in Shanghai: www.afshanghai.org/ch/d/d_12.asp
18. Goethe Institut: www.goethe.de/en/wwt.html
19. Goethe Institut. Organisation: www.goethe.de/en/uun/org.html
20. Goethe Institut. Jahrbuch 2013–2014: www.goethe.de/resources/files/pdf26/Jahrbuch-Goethe-Institut_2014.pdf
21. Goethe Institut in Shanghai. Fast to B1: http://shanghai.goetheslz.com/en/courses/22
22. Goethe Institute. German Language: www.goethe.de/en/spr/unt.html
23. *Hanban*. Confucius Institute Annual Development Report (孔子学院年度报告 2006): http://www.hanban.org/report/index.html
24. British Council "turns into a political tool": http://dblackie.blogs.com/the_language_business/2009/03/british-council-turned-into-a-political-tool.html

3 Studies on Confucius Institute and Language Management

The current study of Confucius Institutes, unlike most others, was conducted within the general framework of language policy and planning (LPP), with reference to its more up-to-date theory of language management. It was the first time that language management was applied in the study of a joint-venture style national language promotion organisation in the international context.

The chapter consists of four sections. The first two sections provide a short review of studies on Confucius Institutes to the time when this study was conducted. Section one gives an overview of studies of Confucius Institutes conducted in China based upon research themes, and the following section presents in a similar fashion, an overview of research completed outside of China on Confucius Institutes. The third section starts with a brief history of the study of LPP and language management theory which deals with LPP from macro (national) and micro (individual) perspectives, both statically (policy statement) and dynamically (policy implementation). Then the section outlines the research design of this study and introduces its ethnographic approach with the two case Confucius Institutes as well as the research instruments. The last section is a summary of the chapter.

Researches on Confucius Institute Conducted in China

The first academic journal article on Confucius Institute can be traced back to 2005 (Liu, C. 2011) in an article titled "Confucius Institute and Traditional Culture", which questioned the use of Confucius as the name of the Institute as the focus of Confucius Institute was on language teaching rather than on Confucius and Chinese culture (Wu, 2005). The research interest steadily grew year by year and culminated in 2014, as shown by the listed entries in the China academic journal database, China National Knowledge Infrastructure (CNKI). The total number of the publications reached 515, consisting of 357 journal articles, 107 postgraduate dissertations and 51 conference papers. The annual number of the listed entries has since remained stable, and the accumulative number of the publications since 2005 reached 3,658 by 2017 as shown in Table 3.1, which also gives an overview of the numbers of publications annually.

While much of the listed literature on Confucius Institute studies came out in the four years between 2014 and 2017, the main themes remain very similar and can be broadly grouped into three strands: (1) strategic and sustainable development of Confucius Institute; (2) roles of Confucius Institute in public diplomacy and soft power building; and (3) Chinese language learning and teaching in Confucius Institute. Most of the research belongs to the first two strands, and in the last strand, few are on language policy.

Confucius Institute and Its Sustainable Development

On the first strand, many studies are about the functions and modes of Confucius Institutes such as those by Zhou and Qiao (2008) and Dai (2012). With the increasing number of the specialist Confucius Institutes, such as those for arts, business, Chinese medicine, martial arts and tourism, relevant studies also follow (e.g. Zhang and Gong, 2013; Chen, 2017). However, much research is about the evaluation of Confucius Institute, with suggested indicators for successful Confucius Institutes (Zhan and Li, 2014) or on strategies for the further development of Confucius Institute (Wu, Y. H., 2009, 2010; Ning, 2017). In his paper "A Strategic Plan for the Sustainable Development of Confucius Institute", Wu, Y. H., (2009) suggested a centralised approach to the development of Confucius Institutes, with a universally accepted syllabus and credit system and joint degree-granting education, as he believes this macro strategic plan would

Table 3.1 Publications on Confucius Institute 2005–2017

Year	Journal Article	PG. Thesis	Conference Paper	Total
2017	299	128	5	432
2016	300	127	8	435
2015	214	212	34	460
2014	357	107	51	515
2013	260	153	50	463
2012	286	70	82	438
2011	214	34	61	309
2010	147	15	48	210
2009	122	7	38	167
2008	78	7	11	96
2007	66	1	4	71
2006	41	1	3	45
2005	16	0	1	17
Total	2,400	862	396	3,658

Source: http://kns.cnki.net/kns/brief/default_result.aspx

help integrate all Confucius Institutes into a super-transnational education group with an efficient vertical managing system. This approach would need input from the government, which Wang and Ning (2016) believe is highly necessary; a certain degree of government intervention, if managed well, can help with the development of Confucius Institutes.

The rapid growth of Confucius Institute naturally comes with some teething problems, and there are studies on such problems that Confucius Institutes are faced, like long-term development and global recognition (Wu and Ti, 2009; Cai, 2012; Wang, 2014), even with suggestion to create Confucius Institute Law to protect the brand (Zhao and Tang, 2014; Cheng and Liao, 2015). Liu (2007) talked about issues associated with the collaborative model of Confucius Institute quite early on, but little further research followed on this until recently (e.g. Zhou, 2017). The interest on Confucius Institute's sustainable development remains high. While there are studies on how to improve Confucius Institutes through innovation (Ning, 2017), funding is one of the major concerns as far as sustainability is concerned. Wu (2010) carefully analysed the modes of funding of Confucius Institute and suggested the best funding model was the mixture of the current three funding channels: *Hanban* project funding, business operation funding, and sponsorship funding, as the prevailing *Hanban* funding mode would be fragile and difficult to survive long unless business operation was introduced and implemented. Chu and Yue (2015) believed that sustainable development would have to depend on market operation of the institutes, an obvious challenge for many Confucius Institutes now.

Confucius Institute and Its Role in Soft Power Building

On the second strand, the focus of early research was mostly on the role of Confucius Institute in promoting and disseminating Chinese culture to increase visibility, understanding and subsequently the influence of China internationally—in other words, its soft power. For instance, in his "A Brief Look at Confucius Institute and Its Role in Soft Power" (2007), Zhang discussed Confucius Institute's function in building China's soft power overseas and argued that Confucius Institute could be an effective tool for this purpose, and its primary role should not focus on promoting Chinese language but on promoting Chinese culture. This view was also echoed by many scholars (e.g. Chen, 2008; Wu, Y., 2009; Gong, 2013). Wu, Y. recommended that Confucius Institute should reflect seriously on its role and strategies in the dissemination of Chinese Culture and that Confucius Institute should ponder what elements of Chinese culture to promote and the challenges it might be faced with. She also suggested that Confucius Institute should not only have channels and mechanism to promote Chinese culture but also methods to assess the performance in this regard, an area that An and He (2017) did some further work on recently.

Promoting Chinese culture was regarded as a most important element to help with soft power build up, and much research were suggestions on which parts of the Chinese culture should be promoted, and their ranking order or further studies on their impact. There were about 40 papers on the promotion of Chinese martial arts in Confucius Institutes, ranging from the analysis of the development strategies, problems, and measures to solve them (Li, 2012) and proposals on operational model with standardised teaching and certification to maximise the impact and the resources (Gao, 2014), to case studies on Confucius Institutes involved in such work, such as those in Norway (Hu, 2012) and in Korea (Piao and Du, 2010), arguing for the importance and effectiveness in using martial arts as a means to promote Chinese culture.

Confucius Institute and Chinese Language Teaching

The research in the third strand are far less in numbers than the first two, not even 5% by a rough calculation, although Chinese language learning and teaching is a key activity for Confucius Institute. Almost half of the research came out only in the last few years, including many postgraduate dissertations. Of all the research in this strand, while they have covered a range of aspects of Chinese language learning and teaching such as course and syllabus design, teaching material development for local users, teaching methodologies, teachers, and learners' motivation, many were reports or surveys about Chinese learning and teaching in Confucius Institute, but few were on acquisition of Chinese language by local learners. A milestone review article on the learning and teaching Chinese in Confucius Institute came out in 2014, on the eve of the 10th anniversary of Confucius Institute, "The Status and Future Prospect of the Chinese Language Teaching in Confucius Institute" by Professor Zhao Jinming. After discussing features of Chinese language teaching in Confucius Institute such as younger learners and diverse courses, Zhao suggested that teaching materials needed to reflect local cultures and teaching methods needed to be flexible to meet the local needs. This was significant in a sense that it indicated that Chinese learning and teaching in Confucius Institute should not be the same as *duiwai hanyu* (teaching Chinese to speakers of other languages in China), and that internationalisation of Chinese meant that Chinese learning and teaching in Confucius Institute needed to be tailored to the local needs.

Of the three key "T" words (teachers, teaching materials, and teaching methodologies) in language teaching, most of the limited numbers of publications seem to have focused on the first two. Of the 16 relevant publications (out of a total 813 on Confucius Institute) found on www.CNKI.net between 2015 and 2017, eight were about teachers, seven on teaching materials, and only one concerning teaching methodology. Much of the discussion was related to how training organised by Confucius Institutes could best meet the local needs (Wan, 2009; Zhang, 2009, Zhang, G. X., 2014).

Advocators for localised training and professional development believed it was the only way for long-term sustainable development of Chinese language teaching in Confucius Institute (Gao, 2014; Wang, 2011; Zhang, 2013). Publications concerning teaching materials were related to these areas: (1) flexible use of the existing teaching materials supplied by Confucius Institute (Liu, 2010); (2) the need for the locally developed teaching materials (Guan, 2012; Li, 2012); and (3) how to compile local teaching materials to meet the local needs (Li and Zhang, 2010). Of the 20 award-winning titles of Outstanding Chinese Language Teaching Materials at the 5th Confucius Institute Conference in 2010 in Beijing, eight were compiled and published abroad with some engagement of local Confucius Institutes.

Features and Trends of Research on Confucius Institute

The first feature of research on Confucius Institute is research topics. As shown in the listed entries in www.CHKI.net, most research is concerned with strategic functions of Confucius Institute and its role in helping with diplomacy, soft power, changing image of China, and since 2015, the Road Belt Initiative, with the means to achieve the goals, usually through the promotion of Chinese culture. Researches on Chinese learning and teaching remain to be scarce. Another feature is a lack of reference to theoretical frameworks (Liu, 2013) or in-depth empirical study for much research, except for some self-declared case studies (Wu, 2011; Long, 2016) and used instruments like surveys and interviews (Yang, 2010; Zhao and Huang, 2010). Comparative study was common, either between Confucius Institutes (e.g. Wan, 2009; Wang and Hao, 2014) or with other language promotion organisations (e.g. Mo, 2009; Tianzhong, 2011; Hisa, 2013; Li, 2017).

There are studies on learning and teaching Chinese, such as Chinese characters (Li, 2013; Yan, 2014); pronunciation and speaking (Zhang et al., 2009; Zhang, J.Y., 2014); vocabulary (Li and Xing 2014); but few on learners and teachers, the real important elements for localisation about their learning styles and motivations (Shi, 2012; Zhao, 2013), and teachers' belief and their behaviour in Confucius Institute classrooms, backed with empirical evidence. This to a certain extent reflects the language promotion policy and mode to spread the language, however, studies on Chinese language policy and Confucius Institute like that by Dong and Peng (2015) are still few, and hardly any on Chinese language policy in Confucius Institute classrooms.

Researches on Confucius Institute Conducted Abroad

Media reports and research on Confucius Institute outside China are increasing in the last ten years, but the former still exceed the latter by far. Today a Google search on Confucius Institute can produce over 600,000 entries in less than a second, though academic research from outside of China remains low in numbers. According to Liu (2011), there were only about 20 publications on Confucius Institute since 2005 listed on EBSCO Information Services. This did not include the relevant conference papers during that period. Some contributed this lack of number to the assumption that most people might not have known about Confucius Institute or cared about it at that time, or China's soft power was still in its initial stage (Paradise, 2009). Most research by 2015 tended to concentrate on the following three areas and many might have been conducted by the overseas Chinese academics and scholars working in institutions of higher education abroad.

The Nature and Role of Confucius Institute

As China's economic and political influence increases, the rapid development of Confucius Institute also increasingly attracts the attention from both media and academic circle outside China, particularly with regards to its role in building up soft power for China, close relationship to Chinese government, and the impact on academic freedom. In "Confucius Institutes and the Rise of China", Hartig (2012b) commented that Confucius Institute in its hundreds around the world helped not only to promote Chinese language and culture but also to enhance and shape the image of China as part of soft power building efforts. Other research papers examined the purposes, nature, features, structure, operation, controversies, and challenges of the Confucius Institute initiative (Ding and Saunders, 2006; Hoare-Vance, 2009; Paradise, 2009; Pan, 2013) through the lenses of soft power theory (Starr, 2009) or cultural diplomacy theory (Hartig, 2012a; Lo and Pan, 2014; Hartig, 2016). Researches before 2010 tended to be more positive towards Confucius Institute—Confucius Institute as a show of Chinese patriotism (Hoare-Vance, 2009) and increased sense of pride (Starr, 2009), as a means to maintain China's own cultural autonomy (Ding and Saunders, 2006), and to form an attractive and new image of modern China (Bolewski and Rietig, 2008; Paradise, 2009; Yang, 2010). Guo (2008) also said that Confucius Institute could help send a message of "harmony" to win goodwill worldwide or as the carrier of new Confucianism (Bell, 2009).

But some media reports and research examined this role of Confucius Institute more critically, especially in north American since 2014 following the closure of a couple of Confucius Institutes there. They questioned China's real intention behind the Confucius Institute initiative[1] (Ding and Saunders, 2006; Zhao and Huang, 2010), warned of cultural conflict (Procopio, 2015) and possible interference with academic freedom (Perkins, 2007; Yang, 2010), and some even suspected Confucius Institute's involvement in espionage or intelligence collecting activities overseas (Hoare-Vance, 2009; Schmidt, 2010; Starr, 2009).

Confucius Institute's close relationship with the Chinese government was often regarded as a weak link or even a threat to academic freedom. Hoare-Vance (2009) argued that it could hardly bring about broader intended outcomes of deepening friendly relationships with other nations, of promoting the development of multiculturalism and creating a harmonious world. Hartig (2012a) used two case studies in Australia and Germany to show that Confucius Institute's engagement with foreign publics was hampered by the connection and links to the Chinese government, as Confucius Institute lacked one essential feature for institutions like Goethe-Institut or British Council: the principle of non-intervention by the government, an issue that Confucius Institute must address (Lo and Pan, 2014; Hartig, 2015). There was also research with focus on Confucius Institute and its relationship with their stakeholders and host countries (Liu, 2011), and how different stakeholders in China and the US perceived Confucius Institute differently with a considerable degree of ambivalence (Wang and Adamson, 2014).

Sustainable Development of Confucius Institute

Sustainability is another issue often discussed or mentioned in reports and research papers on Confucius Institute and its long-term development, usually concerning two aspects. One is about the collaborative nature and relationship between the partners and countries with regards to differences in institutional and social cultures, ideologies, and systems. As far as Confucius Institute system is concerned, the temporary short-term service of Chinese staff, problems with their visa applications, and often ad hoc appointment of local staff are all potential threats in terms of quality control, long-term staff development, and students' learning experience (Starr, 2009; Yang, 2010). This is often exacerbated by more fundamental discrepancies in cultures, intentions, management, and teaching practices in the joint venture between institutional partners, managers, and teachers.

The other aspect of the sustainability issue lies in Confucius Institute's financial status with its income and funding, as only guaranteed financial resources can ensure Confucius Institute's long-term sustainable operation. Currently it over-depends on the Chinese government. According to the constitution and by-laws of the Confucius Institutes, new Confucius Institutes get seed-corn funding plus project funding by *Hanban*, with future annual funding to be shared by institutional partners roughly on a 1:1 ratio.[2] Given that cash is not easily available for many universities in the West and that Chinese is not yet a commodity language like English (Cameron, 2012), a key issue is the overdependence of Confucius Institute on *Hanban* funding and whether this model is sustainable (Yang, 2010; Hartig, 2016). At the same time, some research claimed that the input from the Chinese government with regards to its language and cultural promotion was far from enough if compared with other similar institutions such as Alliance Française and Goethe-Institut (Hoare-Vance, 2009).

Confucius Institute and Chinese Language Teaching

Researches on this aspect are mostly engaged in language policy and its impact, with only a few like that done by Sigley and Li in 2009 on the actual learning and teaching of Chinese and culture. In terms of language policy, research was largely concerned with issues such as why Mandarin Chinese was provided in Confucius Institute instead of other forms of Chinese like Cantonese, Hakka, or Hokkien (Ding and Saunders, 2006; Hoare-Vance, 2009; Zhao and Huang, 2010). There was also research that argued it was only natural that Mandarin should be promoted (Zhao and Huang, 2010), as it emerged as a subject for study with value in educational market. This has also opened a discussion of the implications of the development of the policy of Chinese as a foreign language in diversifying the world's lingua franca and sharing the market of education in the coming era. Some research voiced the concern about overwhelming demand for Chinese language teaching activities in certain Confucius Institute (Yang, 2010) or the relative scarcity of Chinese language teaching in English schools, especially in primary schools (Starr, 2009).

With regards to Confucius Institute's impact in teaching Chinese, Stambach published two sets of qualitative research (2014 and 2015) focusing on selected cases in the US. In her book *Confucius and Crisis in American Universities: Culture, Capital, and Diplomacy in U.S. Public Higher Education* (2014), she reviewed the history of US-China Educational Exchange, presented her qualitative research results, and argued that this Chinese investment in American higher education served as a broad form of global policy and mostly advanced the lives of the already privileged by creating access to overseas labour and markets to the exclusion of middle- and working-class students.

While there is some research about learning and teaching Chinese in Confucius Institute, few studies are significant in terms of their impact.

Features and Trends of Research on Confucius Institute

Several features became apparent in the literature review of the above research on Confucius Institute conducted outside China. First, much research was completed by overseas Chinese living or working outside China. Second, the concept and the scope of soft power tended to be expanded and enlarged. According to Nye (2004), soft power is an ability to achieve what one wants through the appeal of what one has in terms of culture, value, and customary practices rather than by oppressive threat or incentive payment. However, some research mentioned above seemed to have extended soft power to include everything, such as the sports superstar, the celebration of Confucius's birthday, and Chinese Peking opera, so all was linked to soft power building.

Third, much research was based upon literature review or secondary sources, and some could hardly be called research as their evidence was not empirically based. In a study of 20 papers on Confucius Institute, Liu (2013) found that not a single writer had had any personal experience with Confucius Institute and some claims were made only with supporting evidence from local media or hearsay. For instance, some claimed that Confucius Institute had brought a lot of financial benefit to the Chinese partner university (Guo, 2008; Lee, 2010), or Confucius Institute was just a Chinese government propaganda machine simply because some American professor had said so (Schmidt, 2010). Some papers called for their universities not to host a Confucius Institute because they were concerned that Confucius Institute might affect their academic freedom, but failed to quote substantive cases or examples (Liu, C., 2011). Recent research seems to have made impressive progress on this, like the research mentioned above (Procopio, 2015; Hartig, 2016; Gil, 2017).

Confucius Institute's government link will continue to make it a hot topic for research outside China, especially in a time when China is looking for changes in the world order with its increasing influence on the world stage. Confucius Institute will undoubtedly be seen as a vehicle to fulfil the aspiration. What tends to be overlooked is that the Chinese language policy implemented in Confucius Institute results from the interactions of many stakeholders at different levels, and this language management process is worthy of research.

Language Management and Current Study

Language Policy and Planning

Theory of language management is a modern development of the study of language policy and language planning, whose start is often traced back to the late 1950s when Haugen formally quoted and used "language planning" (1959:8). Language policy and language planning are two terms frequently used interchangeably or together (Hornberger, 1994; Ricento, 2006; Johnson, 2013), but debates are unsettled about their relationship since the 1990s when language policy became fashionable. The debates reflect not only the complexity of the relationship between these two, but also the process of development of both the practices and the theories concerning language planning and language policy over the last half century.

Ricento (2000) suggests that the development of the LPP study can be divided into three phases roughly about two decades each, each characterised by "macro-socio-political processes and events, epistemological paradigms, and strategic ends within, by, and for which LPP research has been and is conducted" (Hornberger, 2007:26).

The first phase saw many of Haugen's followers carrying forward the linguistic approach to language planning, regarding the role of linguists as language planners to influence and regulate the linguistic behaviours of the language users, most notably Fishman's *Language Loyalty in the United States* (1966), *Language Problems of Developing Nations* (Fishman et al., 1968) and *Advances in Language Planning* (1974). Language planning in the 1960s was mostly concerned with standardisation of the selected language and was a means to purify the selected language(s) of a state. This was challenged from late 1960s and 1970s as issues of nationalism and conflicts in multilingual societies started to emerge across the world, not only in newly independent countries but also in established and developed countries where more than one language existed. This led to the change and shift in the focus of language planning to providing answers and solutions to problems of multiple languages, with, for example, the trio in the "Language Science and National Development" series (1972)—"The Ecology of Language, Language in Sociocultural Change", and "Language, Psychology and Culture", respectively by Haugen, Fishman, and Lambert. Language planning was no longer just about language issues but was concerned with almost all aspects of a societal life involving the use of language. As Ferguson (1977:9) puts it, "All language planning activities take place in particular sociolinguistic settings, and the nature and scope of the planning can only be fully understood in relation to the settings". The study became more intensified with the birth of the *International Journal of the Sociology of Language*, launched and edited by Fishman in 1974, *Language Planning Newsletter* edited by Rubin in 1975, and *Language Problems and Language Planning* in 1977. These journals played a key role in promoting the applied research in language planning and in building up the study of language planning as a decision-making process concerning languages. Other important publications include Carol M. Eastman's *Language Planning: An Introduction* and J. Rubin and G.H. Jernudd's famous book *Can Languages Be Planned?* (1971), in which they stated expressly that "the study of language planning describes decision making about languages" and "planning is not just a linguistic activity but as a political and administrative activity for solving language problems in society" (Jernudd and Das Gupta, 1971:211).

The second phase marked continued reflective thinking on language planning in the 1980s, with efforts in theorising the study of language planning to provide the vital link between the theory and the actual practice in the field when applied and social linguistic traditions were developing. It was also the time when the scene of language planning was getting more complex with different developments and trends emerging in many countries. Many new models emerged, most notably by Robert Cooper who summarised questions of language planning as all about who plans what for whom, and why and how. In many ways, Cooper is a revolutionary figure in the history of language planning study, and for him, "language planning refers to deliberate efforts to influence the behaviour of others with respect to the acquisition, structure, or functional allocation of their codes" (Cooper, 1989:45). Unlike his predecessors, he felt "to restrict language planning to the work of authoritative institutions is to be too restrictive" (1989:31) due to linguistic diversity and complexity. Cooper also stressed the importance of language teaching by adding the term "acquisition planning", as "a separate analytic category for the focus of language planning seems be justified" (1989:33). This addition was significant as it completed the circle of intention and rules (status planning), uses of intention and rules (corpus planning), and actual users of the stated rules as a result of intention. Thus, language planning was directed "not only towards aggregates at the level of the society or state and larger aggregates which cut across national boundaries, but also at smaller aggregates—ethnic, religious, occupational, and so on" (Cooper, 1989:36). The 1990s saw a heightened awareness of language endangerment (Grenoble and Whaley, 1998; Krausse, 1992; Nettle and Romaine, 2000), with intensified efforts for language revitalisation and stress on language ecology, including linguistic ecology, ecology of language, and ecolinguistics (Fill and Mühlhäusler, 2001; Hornberger, 2002; Phillipson and Skutnabb-Kangas, 1996). LPP also became increasingly linked to other disciplines such as economy, education, culture, and political studies. A most notable change was the spread of multilingualism and plurilingualism in Europe with the birth of the European Union, with its clearly defined and involving multilingual language policies. Language policy, though a relatively new term, soon became very popular. There were fresh examinations of language planning and its close relationship to language policy.

The third phase was characterised with the interest not only in the link between the theory and practice, making LPP study more theoretical, predictive, and explanatory, with potentials as a "set of theories and practices for managing linguistic ecosystems" (Hornberger, 2007:35); but also in the study on the role of human agency, especially the bottom-up agencies (Canagarajah, 2002; Davis, 1999; Freeman, 2004; Ricento and Hornberger, 1996). With critical and emerging emphasis on ideology (Phillipson, 1992; Tollefson, 1991) and postmodernism (Pennycook, 2003; Canagarajah, 2002) in exploring the relationship between language policies and ideologies of power, "the synthesis of elements of critical theory with an ecology of languages approach has led to the formulation of a new paradigm" (Ricento, 2000:206). A number of LPP frameworks were proposed, like Fishman's Graded Intergenerational Distribution Scale (GIDS) for reversing language shift (1991), Kaplan and Baldauf's model of forces at work in a linguistic ecosystem (1997), and Hornberger's continua of illiteracy (2003). According to Hornberger,

LPP offered a conceptual rubric under which to pursue fuller understanding of the complexity of the policy-planning relationship and in turn of its insertion in processes of social change (2007:25).

The relationship between language policy and language planning, particularly by whom and for whom, was central to the discussion and search for answers and solutions to academic and applied research questions. Some scholars considered language policy and language planning are different (Deumert, 2000); some thought one came before the other (Schiffman, 1996; Ricento, 2006); and others believed they were inseparable (Fettes, 1997; Ager, 2001). However, they all showed a growing interest in language policy, with centres and journals emerging because of these interests. But there were two different views on its role (Chen, 2005). One thought that language policy encompassed linguistic culture and language planning and was thus a force for language planning. The other believed that language policy and language planning closely related to each other with the former a concrete manifestation and expansion of the latter. On the question of language policy by whom and for whom, Hall (2002) thought while language policy was usually a statement about what language planning intended to achieve and how to achieve and was an integral part of planning, it was what happened in the implementation of the relevant language policies that determined if and how effectively the stated policy aims were fulfilled.

It is widely acknowledged nowadays that language planning and language policy are closely linked to each other, as seen in the popularity of the term LPP. LPP has evolved from being seen as a tool to address certain language problems to maintain a monolingual state for a society (Li, 2010), typically a top-down, one-way model, to being regarded as process of language management to maintain more varied linguistic sociocultural ecosystems in which languages operate (Fettes, 1997), involving all the relevant human agents with their beliefs, ideologies and practices as elaborated in *Language Management* by Spolsky (2009).

Language Management by Spolsky

The concept of language management was initially developed by J. V. Neustupný and B. H. Jernudd (Jernudd and Neustupný, 1987), labelled as "pre-correction" (Cooper, 1989), when attention was increasingly turning to those linguistic deviations from the norm, which received positive evaluation called "gratifications" (Neustupný, 2003). This version of language management theory involves four stages: noting; evaluation; selection/planning of adjustment and implementation. Neustupný (1994:50) formulates it clearly as follows:

> I shall claim that any act of language planning should start with the consideration of language problems as they appear in discourse, and

the planning process should not be considered complete until the removal of the problems is implemented in discourse.

Language management is seen to perform at two levels—simple (individuals whose language management is as much about varieties of one language as about choices on two or more languages) and organised (directed and systematic interactions and actions concerning language varieties and choices of language). The term "language management" did seem to suggest that it deals mostly with language phenomena, in the narrow sense of the word initially (i.e. the phenomena of linguistic competence), but this is certainly not the case. Language management is also possible to manage communicative phenomena as well as socio-cultural and socio-economic phenomena. In its narrow sense as advocated by Neustupný, language management is about the change of behaviour toward language, and thus this language management theory requires organised management to rely on simple management as much as possible. However, for Bernard Spolsky, who was considered as a follower of this theory, he used the term synonymously with the expression of language planning (Nekvapil and Nekula, 2006), which Spolsky happily accepted, but claimed with a difference—he uses the term "management" rather than "planning" because it more precisely captures the nature of the phenomenon (Spolsky 2009:4).

In Spolsky's view, language policy is all about choices, and "a theory of language policy is to account for the choices made by individual speakers based on rule-governed patterns recognised by the speech community of which they are members" (2009:1). He believes that some of these choices are the result of language management, or conscious and express efforts by language managers to control the choices as all individuals live in a social space as exemplified in a network analysis. In his earlier book, Spolsky (2004) presents a language policy as three independent but interrelated describable components: language practice, belief, and management. Talking about how his language management theory is different from that of Neustupný, Jernudd, and Nekvapil, he points out in a later book that his predecessors' language management starts with the individual that takes all the steps from influencing the policy makers, to initiation and formulation of policy, to implementation and evaluation and subsequent revision of policy (2009:225). It lacks adequate attention to the fact that no individuals live or make choices in isolation, but rather in various social domains relevant to their lives, some concurrently and some successively. Therefore, Spolsky's theory can also be referred to as the domain model of language management.

Domain is a notion first introduced to socio-linguistic by Fishman in 1972 and it is distinguished by three features: participants, location, and topic. The participants in a domain are characterised not as individuals but by their social roles and relationships. So domain is usually named for a social space (Spolsky lists family, religion, work, public signage, schools, legal, health, and military as a few examples), and Spolsky argues that each of the domains has its own policy, with some features managed internally and others under the influence of forces external to the domain (2009:3). Spolsky regards these domains hierarchical in a social structure and interact with government language policies at local, regional, national, and supranational levels, and "language management provides examples of efforts to impose language practices on a lower domain" (2009:7).

Essentially, Spolsky reckons that the regular language courses made by an individual are determined by his or her understanding of what is appropriate to the domain (2009:3), which also seems applicable to managers of organised management actions. Spolsky's domain model pays a great deal of attention to the individuals and organisations, both internal and external forces in managing language change and behaviour. It can be seen that his model was proposed against a background of the apparent failure of the traditional problem-solving approach that was merely by means of linguistic planning. The model reflects his belief in Western democracy that all rights be respected and that only totalitarian governments can bring about swift changes through language planning (organised management).

Language acquisition planning or management consists of two aspects: internal and external (Spolsky, 2009). The first is also referred to as language education, and usually happens within a defined geographical and political area, be it a country, regional or local territory. As discussed above, at the government level, school is often the principal domain in which the organised language planning or management takes place (referred to as the third major activities by Cooper, 1989). The second is referred as language diffusion, and usually takes place outside the statutory geographical or political boundary, defined by Spolsky as "formal efforts by the central government to establish agencies responsible for encouraging people outside the territory to acquire the national language", usually by many large nations (2009:245). This aspect will also include all the relevant agents in the process, such as managers, teachers, and individuals to whom the language policy and planning are intended.

There are a few key features in Spolsky's definition of language diffusion. First, it is a formal effort on the part of the central government, as it is primarily the responsibility of the central government to make the decision and allocate necessary resources to promote its national language. Second, the central government usually establishes some kind of agencies as managers to take charge of its language diffusion policy, managing the policy implementation and evaluation and providing suggestions for policy revision when needed. Third, it is for people outside the territory to learn its national language, usually as a foreign or second language, often in a different linguistic environment in which the named national language operates. A few examples Spolsky cited include British Council, La francophonie and Alliances Françaises, Goethe-Institut, and Japan Foundation. While these institutions have developed at different times with different degree of success, they share the same features of language diffusion. They are the products of the conscious and formal efforts made by the central government, backed with resources to spread their respective national language overseas. Such diffusion efforts focused on language are part of the efforts of former colonial powers to maintain some of the benefits of their lost empires (Spolsky, 2009).

The aims of language diffusion management have largely determined how language acquisition is delivered. Traditionally, language acquisition delivery in such institutions was centred on the relevant national languages and communication was focused on cross-cultural rather than intercultural. The success of these institutions appears to have been determined by factors other than language pedagogies, but by the political and language policies of the language acceptation countries or commercial, cultural, and other affinities between the language diffusion and language acceptance countries. For example, English in some African states remains as the national or official language after they became independent, and English teaching in China is mainstreamed and imbedded in its formal education system.

The importance of the teaching practice and the language users in the language management did not seem to have attracted enough attention until last ten years or so. In some literature on language policy and planning, this factor is often mentioned as human agency with linguistic creativity, which differs from other studies that have downplayed the central role that it plays in the whole process of LPP (Pennycook, 2003). In summarising the fundamental differences between these approaches, Ricento pointed out, "the key variable which separates the older, positivistic/technicist approaches from the newer critical/postmodern ones is agency, that is, the role of individuals and collectivises in the processes of language use, attitudes, and ultimately policies" (2007:208).

Compared with the traditional LPP framework, language management takes a more bottom-up approach and pays special attention to the role of individual agents like language learners and teachers, and societal agents like schools, to examine the dynamic process of language policy and practices of which all the mentioned agents are integral part. It was for this very reason that the current study decided to study Confucius Institutes in the UK in this light and to focus on their Chinese language policies and practices through teachers and students in the classrooms of Confucius Institutes, as they are the best manifestations and results of the interactions between institutional partners at different levels to find out how they reflect and serve the overall Chinese government policy concerning the promotion of Chinese language.

The Current Study: Research Design and Approach

The Research Framework and Design

As discussed earlier, this study has used language management as its theoretical framework because it "is well suited both to the analysis of language macro-planning and language micro-planning, and focuses on the dialectic relationship between these two levels as captured in the concepts of simple management, organized management and language management cycle" (Nekvapil, 2008:344). It would help the study to explore and examine how the international Chinese language policy is "managed" in the entire process of Confucius Institute operations, especially at the grass-roots level on the part of teachers and learners of the language in Confucius Institute classrooms.

Unlike most other studies using this framework, this study transcends the normal local and national levels as the international Chinese policy and Confucius Institute initiative are efforts of outward diffusion over the boundary of home territory in foreign lands of languages and cultures. It applies the domain practice examination to all the three major levels, adding a new perspective to the framework and significance to the research. The research design with its theoretical framework, methodological consideration, and research instruments for the three levels of domains is illustrated in Figure 3.1.

The research has approached the study from two different, yet complementary angles: (1) diachronically from a historical perspective to review the development of the international Chinese language policy and Confucius Institute practices, giving a general background and wider context for this research; and (2) synchronically from the perspective of ethnographic field work to examine two case Confucius Institutes in the UK in

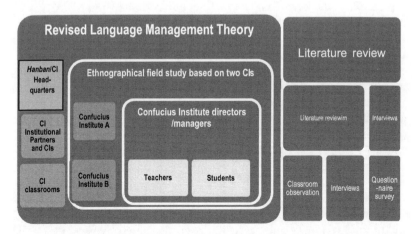

Figure 3.1 Research Methodologies and Research Instruments

detail with regards to international Chinese language policy and practices as experienced by teachers and students in the Confucius Institute classrooms. Initially, the research contemplated a more quantitative approach by conducting a large-scale survey of all 29 Confucius Institutes and follow-up interviews. A preliminary review soon found this would not be able to produce a full and reliable picture of how Confucius Institutes operate concerning the research question of this study as Confucius Institutes were individually different and constantly changing. Subsequently the research design was modified to use mainly qualitative approach based upon an ethnographic field study of two case Confucius Institutes as "in-depth studies of specific 'units'" (David and Sutton, 2011:165), so the study could provide concrete and current data, particularly on the change agents, both at the institutional and classroom levels.

The right part of the figure indicates the instruments to be used at each of the three domain levels to collect relevant data. The ethnographic field study of the two case Confucius Institutes sought data concerning all relevantly important aspects of Chinese language policy and practices taking place at this level. As a qualitative study, the research has also considered how data would be processed in addition to what data and how they would be collected (Brewer, 2000), which is described in the next section.

Ethnographic Study of Two Case Confucius Institutes

Case in ethnography terms is mostly used to "refer to the setting or location of the research" (David and Sutton, 2011:156), and is "crucial to ethnographic understanding of the layers of the LPP onion" (Hornberger and Johnson, 2007). Good case selection should be characterised with both "vertical and horizontal slicing", with the former to build case studies and the latter to identify commonalities and differences across the case studies (Hornberger and Johnson, 2011; Barton and Hamilton, 1998).

The two case Confucius Institutes were selected with regards to relevant criteria and considerations, including the above. They were unique in their own way on the one hand, and representative on the other, and they had key features of all three types of cases in an ethnographical study, intrinsic, instrumental and collective (Stake, 1995). Both case Confucius Institutes had a long history, but with characteristics of their own in what they did and had a sizeable number of learners and teachers of Chinese language. Therefore, the ethnographic study of them may shed new light on and help gain deeper insight into the research question of this study.

CASE 1—CONFUCIUS INSTITUTE A

Confucius Institute A (hereinafter referred to as CI-A) is the first Confucius Institute established in the UK. The host university is a well-established higher education institution in the country with a long history in teaching and researching in Chinese. CI-A was initially housed in the language centre of the host university, a result of many reasons. First, the language centre had already planned to establish a national and regional centre for teaching Chinese, as it predicted the forthcoming increasing demand for Chinese language. Second, the academic department with Chinese language degree programmes was neither keen nor prepared to get involved in the joint venture, partly for fear of potential compromise on its academic independence and impartiality. Third, the language centre was the best place to host CI-A as it had already been doing what Confucius Institute was expected to do, so an additional Confucius Institute could help it further develop and consolidate its teaching operations. At the time when CI-A was established in 2005, the language centre had over 13,000 student registrations on its courses as compared to about 400 in 1999, and the course of Certificate in Teaching Chinese as a Foreign Language, the first Chinese specialist teacher training course, was launched in 2003.

The Chinese partner university of CI-A was a top university in China and appointed by *Hanban* with the belief that the joint venture would be formidable since both universities were among the top 50 universities at that time. The Chinese director arrived towards the end of 2005, but the CI-A didn't start to operate until May 2006 when the initial funding from *Hanban* was finally transferred to the host university. The delay was due to the discussion and negotiation about the form, activities, and financial management of CI-A between the two directors and the partner universities.

In the initial Confucius Institute charter, Confucius Institutes were designated to be joint ventures of independent entity with their own management structure and a separate bank account outside the host university. The Chinese director and the partner university insisted on this first, but this was impossible in any British university as an independent entity with its own bank account and operational management would need to register as a different organisation, with both financial and legal implications. After lengthy discussion, CI-A remained in the host university and was given a separate account, like all other cost centres in the university.

CI-A's governance and management structure were set up as proposed by *Hanban*, with a council responsible for strategic decisions and annual monitoring and two co-directors appointed by their university responsible for day-to-day management. Its council consisted of seven members—four were from the host university, two from the Chinese partner university, and a senior official from the Chinese embassy in the UK representing *Hanban*. However, due to unforeseen circumstances, the Chinese partner university's involvement in CI-A was very limited. Between 2005 and 2012, there had been only two formal council meetings involving the Chinese partner university, and two directors seconded from the Chinese university who were in post only for a very short period of time in the early days of CI-A, one was about nine months, and the other was about three months, leaving CI-A to be run and managed very much by the host university.

This undesirable situation led to the change of the Chinese partner university in 2012, and the new partner university has a constituent college with similar teaching and research interest to the CI-A host university. The Chinese director was in place in 2013. Meanwhile there were some internal changes in the host institution, following the departure of its first Confucius Institute director who was also the director of the language centre. After a couple of temporary appointments, a non-Chinese specialist senior academic took up the Confucius Institute directorship. Meanwhile, Chinese language teaching decreased sharply when CI-A was later moved out of the language centre, though the aims and objectives of CI-A remained very much the same on its website.

CASE 2—CONFUCIUS INSTITUTE B

Confucius Institute B (hereinafter referred to as CI-B) was created in 2006 to specialise in serving business, the first of its kind in the world. The host university was also a well-established institution but had limited Chinese language teaching. Unlike CI-A, CI-B came into being initially as a joint venture between *Hanban* and a syndicate of prominent international companies based in London. As they all had business interest in China, a Confucius Institute was considered to be useful in two ways: to fulfil the needs in their staff development for Chinese language and culture and to create a positive image in China to gain further access and recognition in the Chinese market. *Hanban*, on the other hand, also saw it as a golden opportunity to develop a new model of specialised Confucius Institute by associating with these famous transnational companies and nominated another top university in China as CI-B's Chinese partner. The syndicate was also advised to find a home university for CI-B, and they approached the present host university, also an independent member of the same collegiate university with CI-A's host institution, as it had a high reputation, a good relationship with some companies in the syndicate, and a central location in London. This also meant that CI-B was only a short distance away from CI-A, adding another front to their covert competition.

CI-B also found its first shelter-home in the language centre, and its transition to the host university was gradual. Initially CI-B was an independent organisation with its own operation but housed in the host university on a contractual lease basis. It soon turned out to be an unattainable situation for several reasons. First, CI-B was expected to finance its own operation as a business organisation, with the seed-corn fund provided, but this proved to be very challenging without affiliating to a host university which could at least help cover some operational costs. Second, CI-B's teaching activities in Chinese certainly needed academic input, so having a host university would be an ideal solution. Third, coincidently the pseudo-host university was also planning to develop its Chinese teaching and having a direct involvement in CI-B would not only have access to expertise in China, but also avoid internal competition on its premises. Therefore, the host university soon became a full partner. CI-B relinquished its independent organisational status and was fully merged and housed in the language centre as the latter was responsible for offering all the language learning and teaching programmes in the university.

The governance structure of CI-B was different from CI-A in two ways. Its nine-member council was called Advisory Council, with five company representatives, the director general of *Hanban*, a senior official from the Chinese embassy in London and two senior academics, one from each partner university. The host university also formed an academic steering group with six members of the university to provide guidance on academic affairs of CI-B. With regards to the management structure, in addition to the two directors, CI-B also employed a full-time manager (its title changed over the time) to take care of the daily operation.

Though CI-B always had a business focus, initially both general and business Chinese language courses were developed. The assimilation of CI-B into the host university helped ensure the two units had their own target students so there was no internal competition on the same premises. Like other language centres, the language centre of the host university offered its courses in line with the university language policy, and the courses were general in nature, primarily for university students as part of the institute-wide language programmes, either for credits or certificate issued by the university without CI-B's involvement. The Chinese courses offered by CI-B were designated for business purposes, usually for people from outside the university although they opened to the university students as well, but not for credit and with a preferential discount. CI-B issued certificates of course completion, endorsed by the two partner universities as a symbol of academic assurance. But the increase in the number of students for the university language programme was much faster than that of CI-B classes. CI-B was later also separated from the language centre and continued to offer business Chinese language courses itself.

The Current Study: Research Instruments and Samples

As indicated in the figure, different data collection research instruments were used at different domain levels involving different agents. For the macro level concerning the international Chinese language policy, literature review was the main instrument, which was also partially used for the mezzo level in the case studies. The instruments used for the ethnographic study of the two case Confucius Institutes at the mezzo and particularly the micro levels were varied, including questionnaire survey, semi-structured interviews, and classroom observations, according to the agents from whom the data were to be sought. The agents involved at the mezzo level were mostly directors and managers (in CI-B), and those involved at the micro level were teachers and students. For all the research instruments and subjects in the field study, confidentiality was guaranteed as a matter of research ethics and good practice.

Student Questionnaire Survey

As a key agent, students' views and experience of the Chinese language learning mattered a great deal for the study to learn about how Chinese language policy and practices were managed at the grass-roots level. Both Confucius Institutes had many students on their courses, a combination of instruments of a questionnaire survey and follow-up interviews could yield meaningful and useful data with both breadth and depth.

The initial questionnaire consisted of 36 questions in three sections with about half being Likert scale multiple-choice questions and half open-ended questions. The first nine questions sought information about the students. The next 25 questions focused student experiences and views of their Chinese language learning, ranging from information availability to the learning and delivery of the programme as well as their perceived difficulties in learning Chinese. The final two questions were for their comments and understanding of what kind of organisation Confucius Institutes were for them.

The questionnaire was piloted in two classes, the completed questionnaires were analysed, and some modifications were made. The final questionnaire was a shortened version of 30 questions in two sections with more open-ended questions to gather more individual and qualitative responses. The questionnaire was sent to all the students in the two Confucius Institutes instead of just a sample as originally planned, due to a sharp drop in student numbers in both Confucius Institutes that term, partly because it was so close to Christmas break.

There were altogether 201 students registered on 22 classes in two Confucius Institutes, 152 in 17 classes in CI-A and 49 in five classes in CI-B. The questionnaires were administered with the help of class teachers, but not all teachers distributed the questionnaires in their classes or collected them afterwards. In the end, 156 copies of questionnaires were distributed to 16 classes: 12 classes (113 copies) in CI-A, and four classes (43 copies) in CI-B. Altogether 97 completed questionnaires were collected, with 56 from CI-A (49.5%) and 41 from CI-B (95%), which gave an overall return rate of 62%, a good representation of the students learning Chinese in two Confucius Institutes in number and levels as shown in Table 3.2.

The gender and professional profile of the 97 respondents were: 38 males (39%) and 59 females (61%); 26 were students from the host

Table 3.2 Questionnaire Survey Sample, Its Spread and Return

Level	Total Sample		CI-A			CI-B			Total Return	
	No	%	No	Ret	%	No	Ret	%	No	%
Beginner	99	63.4	68	27	39.7	31	30	96.7	57	57.5
Intermediate	37	23.8	31	18	58	6	5	83	23	62
Advanced	20	12.8	14	11	78.5	6	6	100	17	85
Total	156	100	113	56	49.5	43	41	95	97	62

Table 3.3 Age Distribution of the Respondents

Age Group	Number	Percentage
Under 21	5	6
21–30	51	52
31–40	23	23
41–50	14	15
Over 50	4	4
Total	97	100

universities, 63 professionals including accountant, bankers, civil servants, consultants, engineers, marketing managers, and teachers, and the remaining eight were housewives or retired people. The age spread of the respondents is shown in Table 3.3.

Majority of the students were young professionals and most indicated that they were learning Chinese for career and work (77). This confirmed again that most adult learners would learn for practical reasons. It was therefore very interesting to find out from their perspective if and how the Chinese language courses offered at the two Confucius Institutes met their needs and requirements.

About two-thirds of the respondents (67) had visited China, some as many as three to four times, with reasons like sightseeing, business, study, visiting friends, or volunteer work. Most respondents had only begun to learn Chinese recently, with 39 as ab initio learners and 51 in total learning Chinese for less than a year. 20 had studied Chinese for five years or more, and the remaining 26 had studied Chinese between one to four years. 18 of the respondents were ethnic Chinese, second or third generation overseas Chinese, with most being able to speak Cantonese or Hokkien, and one spoke Hakka.

About two thirds of the respondents (65) had joined the courses that term, so they were new to the Confucius Institutes. 15 students had continued from the previous term, and the remaining 17 were with their institute for over a year. Given both Confucius Institutes had been in operation for a number of years already, the retention of the learners seemed undesirable as a whole. As it was impossible to find out why they had left the courses, the responses to some open-ended questions in the survey, the class observation and interviews might help throw some light on possible reasons for the drop-out.

The answers to the open questions were collated and arranged under different labels where appropriate. Similar or different experiences and views along with any special cases were colour-coded for easy identifications and summary notes were added for possible clarifications and follow-ups in classroom observations and interviews.

Classroom Observations and Interviews

"We place the classroom practitioner at the heart of language policy (at the centre of the onion)" (Ricento and Hornberger, 1996:417). For this research using ethnography as a methodological approach to the research question, classroom observation was a main instrument for collecting relevant data concerning the learning and teaching of Chinese language in the two Confucius Institutes. While the study had hoped to observe classes across a range of courses at different levels over a period of time, like one or two terms, this was found impossible as few teachers were willing to give permission and long-term access to an external observer for various reasons, so observations were all one-off and not longitudinal. Subsequently, 12 classroom observations were conducted in the two Confucius Institutes with a good spread of levels: three and two beginner's classes in CI-A and CI-B respectively; two intermediate class in each Confucius Institute; and two advanced classes in CI-A and one in CI-B.

The observation was non-participatory for being more objective, and the foci (main classifications) of the classroom observations included students and how they were learning, teachers and how they were delivering teaching, the prescribed and additional teaching materials used, and the interactions between the students and the teacher in the classroom. Notes were taken during the observation and later sorted with appropriate sub-classifications and labelling, with a new category for Chinese heritage students and teachers seconded from *Hanban*, as they were different. The relevant details and their implications will be discussed in the analysis and discussions of the research findings in the following chapters.

As interviews were also a main instrument to gather in-depth qualitative data, three sets of interviews were conducted as part of the ethnographic field study during the same time when classroom observations were carried out. Interview with students and teachers were designed to find out their beliefs and views concerning their learning and teaching Chinese, and interviews with directors and managers were to gain their insight and respective about Chinese language learning and teaching and the development of the Confucius Institute concerned. There were two main challenges with the interviews. One was time, as everyone was busy working; the other was many did not want their interview recorded, so sketch notes were made during the interviews and processed afterwards.

The analysis of the early interview data also informed later interviews, so they became more focused with a lot more depth.

The interviews with the Confucius Institute directors went smoothly. As mentioned above, CI-A did not have a Chinese director for a long time, and the other interview was not with the newly appointed UK director (who did not know Chinese) but with its former and first UK director who had just left the job but had previously been in the position for over six years since CI-A was established. The interview of CI-B involved one UK director and one executive director (or institute manager as the role changed title several times), and two China directors. The interview was semi-structured and designed to elicit the views and comments of the directors on their understanding and interpretation of the intention and policy for being part of the joint Confucius Institute as a partner university for which they represented; the development process of their Confucius Institute; and the management and running of Chinese language programmes that their individual Confucius Institute was expected to provide. Each interview lasted about 45 minutes and all the interviews were recorded with the consent of the interviewees.

The interviews with teachers was designed to gather how the teachers, both from UK and from China, understood and viewed the teaching of Chinese in the Confucius Institute, and how and why they were teaching in the way they did. The interview was also semi-structured to allow them to speak freely. There were 10 teacher interviews in total, five from each Confucius Institute, and five employed locally (three in CI-A and two from CI-B), and five from *Hanban* (two in CI-A and three in CI-B). The interviews found noticeable discrepancies in beliefs and views on Chinese and language teaching between the local and *Hanban* teachers, between the teachers who had mostly taught in China and those who had been teaching Chinese abroad, and between the *Hanban* teachers who had attended an induction programme organised by *Hanban* before they came and those who had not. Each interview lasted between 45 and 60 minutes and some were recorded with the consent of the interviewees with the guarantee of their anonymity.

Interviews with the students were all conducted after the questionnaire survey and almost unstructured, tailored to the feedback in the student questionnaires which indicated their willingness to be interviewed if required. The aims were to find out more about their experiences, purposes of learning the language, their views on the learning and teaching of Chinese language, and on the Confucius Institute where they were studying. Nine students were subsequently interviewed, four from CI-A and five from CI-B, with five face-to-face and four over the phone. As with most others, the interviewees were uncomfortable with the use of a recorder, so the researcher had to take some quick simple notes during the interview and wrote up the fuller notes and had them analysed and classified afterwards. The student interviewees were also promised anonymity, and the data gathered helped shed light on the research question, which will be discussed in detail in Chapter 6.

As a multi-instrument approach was used in the field study, interview data were cross-checked with the data from the observations where needed and processed in several stages—transcribe, assign codes, group the data, and identify patterns. Transcribing is not just a straightforward and simple task but involves judgement questions about the level of detail to include (Bailey, 2008). The next three steps took place more or less simultaneously. Since overall categories remained rather stable in three sets of interviews, the processing of the data in terms of data management was relatively straightforward without the needs for such qualitative data software as ATLAS or MAXQDA, as software did not always guarantee the quality of the analysis (Ereaut, 2002). The processed data were then analysed with attention given to look for any salient stories (Chase, 2005), themes (Creswell, 2009), and even issues. Several common themes or tension points emerged across the findings of the field study and will be discussed in the following chapter.

Summary

The study of language policy and language planning has gone through several phases of development over the last half century, from a traditional study with very much monolingual mind-set to a modern discipline in increasingly multilingual societies as the result of globalisation. LPP is no longer a matter of concern just for policy makers well above in the super-structure of society, but involves every stakeholder, especially those at the grass-roots to whom the LPP used to be targeted, as these agents play an increasingly key role in reformulating and implementing the actual policy through their practices. This is how LPP is managed nowadays in most developed societies where multilingualism is a norm.

The current study was one of the few to examine Confucius Institute from the perspective of LPP, and perhaps the very first in the light of language management theory modified by Spolsky. It had also pushed it further since Confucius Institute is in an international setting. The methodological approach of the study was ethnographic, and specific contextual data were collected through the field study of two selected Confucius Institutes with the use of a combination of research instruments including questionnaire, class observations and interviews. As a qualitative study, great attention was paid to ensure the ethics of the research. The findings of the ethnographic study are analysed and discussed in the next three chapters in the light of the theory of language management so as to explore and to gain new insight into the actual process and the working of the international Chinese language policies of *Hanban* through the sampled cases of the two local Confucius Institutes in the UK.

A main contribution of this study lies not only in its first attempt to examine Confucius Institute in the light of language management theory, but also in modifying it to study language being promoted and managed across many borders at the three domains or levels, namely *Hanban* and partner institutions, local Confucius Institutes, and most importantly the Confucius Institute classrooms where the teachers and students acted and interacted as agents of the international Chinese language policies and practices.

Notes

1. China is spending billions to make the world love it: www.economist.com/china/2017/03/23/china-is-spending-billions-to-make-the-world-love-it
2. This is translated from its Chinese version (www.hanban.org/confuciousinstitutes/node_7537.htm). Its English version, however, is somewhat different, stating "The funds for its annual projects shall be raised by individual Confucius Institutes and the Chinese Parties together in a ratio of approximately 1:1 commitment in general". http://english.hanban.org/node_7880.htm

4 Chinese Language Management at the Institution Level

This chapter discusses and analyses the findings of the ethnographic field study of the two Confucius Institutes at the institutional level in terms of the intention, expectation, and commitment of the institutions involved in the three-way partnership of the Confucius Institutes concerned. The chapter consists of four sections. The first section concentrates on the troika of institutional stakeholders of Confucius Institute, namely *Hanban*, Chinese partner institutions, and UK host universities, particularly in terms of their intention in the joint venture. The next section examines the commitments of the troika to the joint venture, and the third section focuses on the resulting policy statements, if any, and the positioning of the Confucius Institute in the host university which may have impacted on the perceived image of the joint venture in the eyes of the local communities. The fourth section concludes with a summary on the analyses and discussions of the chapter concerning the establishment of the two Confucius Institutes by the troika partnership.

Institutional Partners and Their Intentions

Like most Confucius Institutes, both Confucius Institutes in this study involve three institutional stakeholders, *Hanban*, a Chinese partner university, and a local host university in London. This troika created an interesting dynamic between the institutional stakeholders not only in the process of establishing the Confucius Institute concerned, but also in the subsequent operation and management of these joint ventures. This is an area much neglected by existing research, but of critical importance to the study of Confucius Institutes since convergence or discrepancies in the intentions and interests of the institutional stakeholders would subsequently affect the public statement, positioning, operation as well as the management of the Confucius Institutes. This is also one of the main findings from the field study of the two Confucius Institutes.

A main finding of the study is that the three institutions involved have quite different intentions with regards to their involvement and role in the joint venture, even though they all appear to share the common aspiration to provide Chinese language courses to meet the demands and requests from the local communities. In fact, it was becoming increasing clear during the process of the study that they differ from each other in terms of their ultimate goals for the joint venture. The three institutional partners will be examined in turn here, starting with *Hanban*.

Hanban/*Confucius Institute Headquarters*

There are two priorities for *Hanban* concerning the promotion of Chinese language: Putonghua (Mandarin) and simplified Chinese characters, and international Chinese, both of which *Hanban* has always emphasised as integral part of its Confucius Institute initiative. In many ways, this emphasis on Putonghua by *Hanban* can be seen as the natural extension of the Chinese government's language planning policy since the early 1950s. The economic success story of China since 1978 certainly impacted positively on the growing acceptance of Putonghua and simplified Chinese characters abroad too. Apparently, *Hanban* has been very explicit and insistent on this as all Confucius Institutes are expected to promote Putonghua and simplified Chinese characters, though a handful Confucius Institutes teach other spoken forms and traditional characters too. The earlier version of the constitution and by-laws of Confucius Institute stipulated that the Chinese director of the joint venture manages the teaching, so both Putonghua as well as Chinese way of teaching the language would prevail. In addition, some other important factors also contribute to this wide-spread practice. First, Putonghua is the official language of mainland China and thus most host institutions of Confucius Institutes naturally follow the suit in the teaching. Second, the impressive economic growth of mainland China and the generous funding that the Chinese government provided through *Hanban* encourage them to promote Putonghua and simplified Chinese characters. Third, if the Confucius Institute host institution did not have much experience in teaching Chinese, the Confucius Institute would undoubtedly follow the language policy and practice put forward by the Chinese partners.

But for *Hanban*, it is the concept and idea of international Chinese that provides the main drive for the Confucius Institute initiative, which is obvious from the relevant academic research (Chen, 2008; Zhang, Q. H., 2008; Zhang, J. Y., 2014) and available literature in Chinese language, such as official documents from *Hanban* like "Standards for Teachers of Chinese to the Speakers of Other Languages" (*guoji hanyu jiaoshi biaozhun*, 2007), "Chinese Language Proficiency Scales for Speakers of Other Languages" (*guoji hanyu nengli biaozhun*, 2008), and "International Curriculum for Chinese Language Education" (*guoji hanyu tongyong kecheng dagang*, 2008). "International" in the term "international Chinese" means that Chinese language learning and teaching is made available internationally, particularly geographically. Underlining this new concept is the desire of China to build up its linguistic and cultural influence in the world stage compatible to its fast-growing economic and political power, or what is often referred to as soft power (Nye, 2004). Confucius Institute was first mentioned in China's 12th Five Year Plan (2011–2015) and then listed as one of the nine important education modernisation projects in China's 13th Five Year Plan (2016–2020), signifying it has become a project of national importance with guaranteed state funding. Since then Confucius Institute is clearly a vehicle through which China implements its language policy of international Chinese, supported with enormous resources from the government.[1] Therefore, it is not surprising to see such a phenomenal growth in the number of Confucius Institutes and Classrooms across the world in just a decade.

Chinese Partner Universities

As the Chinese partner universities are almost without exceptions public institutions, largely funded and guided by the government, their intentions should not be dissimilar to that of *Hanban* when getting involved in the Confucius Institute initiative. However, there is still a difference. For *Hanban*, Confucius Institute is its main purpose and sole business, but for the Chinese partner universities of the two Confucius Institutes concerned, while they are expected to contribute to implementing this important national strategy, they have the say in determining to what degree. For the Chinese partner institution for CI-A, they

> saw it as an opportunity to extend their excellence in teaching Chinese language and culture into territories over and beyond the walls of the University, which is also fully in line with *Hanban'* policy in the interest of the country.[2]

Therefore, the university went on to forge links with several universities abroad and jointly set up over a dozen Confucius Institutes across all the continents. However, it was clear from the start that while the British partner university of the CI-A seemed to have a good understanding of its Chinese partner institution, this was not the case the other way around. For instance, when the Chinese partner university sent its delegation to the UK to sign the cooperation agreement, the head of the delegation, who was a vice president, was initially very reluctant to do so when he saw the word "school" in the name of the British partner university. To him, this would mean the British partner institution was not at the same level with his university and thus he insisted that he would only sign the agreement with the University of London, which is in fact a collegiate institution. While this may only seem to be a misnomer, it did indicate a clear lack of adequate understanding of the local partner institution, which could lead to disparities in expectations as well as in actions.

The intention of the Chinese partner institution for CI-B appeared to be different. The interview with the Chinese director revealed that while the university supported the Confucius Institute initiative as it was a national strategy, it also had its own considerations. He said:

> The university management recognises that as a leading university in the country, it is our responsibility to contribute to the Confucius Institute initiative as it is an important national strategy. However, the university also knows its limits in terms of the resources, especially with regards to the number of staff currently employed in the Chinese language teaching in the university. The university has a very clear priority. Besides, the university also cares a lot about the quality, not just the quantity, as one would expect from a typical traditional university. So, from the start, the university had made the decision not to expand our involvement in this initiative, but to make sure that we run well our sole Confucius Institute with our partners.

He also said that all the directors seconded from the university were professors from its English or Chinese departments rather than junior staff like many other universities, and its teaching staff from unit of the International Chinese Language and Culture Centre were only seconded to teach in the CI-B in London.

UK Host Universities

By contrast, the intentions of the British partner institutions for CI-A and CI-B appeared very different from those of the Chinese universities. On the institutional level, internationalisation is on the agenda of all the British universities, and many increasingly rely on the number of international students to maintain their financial sustainability. Therefore, language education or teaching is increasingly recognised as a useful instrument for British universities. Some universities have even come up with institutional language policies to demonstrate their commitment to the language learning and teaching in the university. Some universities have made language learning compulsory or integral part of their degree programmes, but an increasing number of universities are making new practical language programmes available to their students as part of electives or an entitlement.

Both Confucius Institute's British university partners have similar language policies and provisions. The host institution of CI-A has a Language Entitlement Programme. The policy states:

> The institution would like all its students to possess at least a basic working knowledge of one of the languages of Africa, Asia, or the

Middle East by the time they graduate. Under the Language Entitlement Programme (LEP), current undergraduate students, regardless of department or degree registration, are entitled to register for one language-acquisition course for free. You do not need to have any prior qualification in or experience of language study to take a language course as part of the LEP. Employers have always welcomed graduates with language skills, so the LEP is a great way to enhance your CV without reducing the number of courses taken on your degree syllabus.

The host institution of CI-B has an Institute Language Policy:

> As part of the institution Language Policy, if you are a UK/EU undergraduate student at the institution, please remember you can claim your entitlement to a free language course during your time at the institution if you do not have a GCSE grade C (or equivalent) in a language which is not your mother tongue.

The commitment of the institutions to the language teaching and learning is clear, and both universities have language centres that offer programmes in many languages to their students and local communities. Therefore, when Confucius Institutes were set up, they were more closely associated with the university language centres. This was why for both Confucius Institutes, the UK director was also the director of the language centre of their university. However, even though what appears in the public domain such as the Confucius Institute website may seem to be in line with *Hanban*'s policy, the interest in and emphasis on China and Chinese language of both Confucius Institute host universities only overlap rather than resonate with the policy intention and objectives of *Hanban*. The UK director of CI-A said the following in his interview:

> As the university is a specialist institution of higher education in the UK, Chinese studies, China and Chinese have always been a key area of research. In fact, the university had been teaching Chinese almost since the inception of the institution in 1916, and ran a whole range of language programmes before it had the Confucius Institute. With the growing interest in China and in Chinese language, the university saw the joint venture a good opportunity to enhance and expand what it had been doing in the provision of the Chinese language. But the university is always clear that while it is very happy to promote the learning and teaching of Chinese, this was not as some Chinese official documents or media said explicitly "for the purpose of spreading Chinese language and culture". As a matter of fact, the university sees it as a source of causing negative responses such as being accused of imperial linguistic and cultural chauvinism or

invasion. So, the university is very careful about the wording in all the official documents to avoid such terminologies and signed a supplement with *Hanban* to ensure that this would not be in any manifestation or any practice of the joint venture.

A similar account was also given by the UK director of CI-B, who revealed how and why his university had decided to get involved in the joint venture which was initially housed on its campus as an independently registered charity in a partnership between *Hanban* and some international companies based in London.

> My university is always interested in China, but the teaching of the Chinese language is relatively underdeveloped. We saw the establishment of a Confucius Institute a good opportunity to make it up. However, the university is always very careful about and concerned with the public opinions and responses of its own academic staff, which is partly why it took the university so long to reach the decision to enter the partnership. Naturally the Language Centre became its home, but it was clear to us from the beginning that the joint venture would not provide any credit bearing programmes as it would compromise and contravene the strict quality assurance code of the British higher education.

Institutional Resources Commitments

Financial Resources

Hanban—As with most other Confucius Institutes, both Confucius Institutes had start-up cash input from *Hanban* when they were launched and then obtained funding for its operations from *Hanban* by applying for project funds on an annual basis. So, regarding financial input, most of the cash fund either came entirely from *Hanban* (for CI-A) or a combination of *Hanban* and other sponsors (in the case of CI-B). *Hanban* also provided funds for the Chinese partner institutions for their involvement in the Confucius Institutes.

Clearly *Hanban* is the drive behind the whole Confucius Institute initiative and its main functions can be seen in two areas: one is to plan for the development and lay down the ground rules on how its objectives can be achieved; the other is to make sure that each Confucius Institute is adequately supported in terms of resources needed for the operation and development. In this aspect, *Hanban* is very much the primary cash funder of all Confucius Institutes. But since *Hanban* doesn't have resources of teaching staff itself, the Chinese partner university is expected to contribute teaching and managerial staff to the joint venture, but the funding of all these involvements also comes from *Hanban*.

Chinese partner universities—Chinese partner institutions are selected and those chosen are required to play an active role in this partnership, particularly in designing and delivering Chinese language courses, as they are usually expected to have expertise in teaching Chinese as a foreign language. As discussed above, while both Chinese partner institutions regarded their involvement in the Confucius Institute as an obligation, the two universities had different intentions and thus differed in their scale of involvement. However, neither needs to make a financial contribution, as evident from the interviews with all the Confucius Institute Chinese directors and seconded teachers. All their salaries and subsidies were financed by *Hanban*, often directly from *Hanban* without even going through their own university or the Confucius Institute where they were seconded during their term. It is therefore an item of expenses that does not usually show as expenditures on the two Confucius Institute's final financial accounts.

Local host universities—As mentioned earlier, financial contribution from the two local host universities was very limited in monetary terms. While there might be many reasons behind the apparent lack of financial commitment, what has emerged from this study appeared to be the following: (1) the financial constraints under which the host university was operating in the current competitive higher education market, and (2) the priority that the host university attached to the teaching of Chinese in the joint venture in its own strategic development. With the government funding for higher education being continuously cut over the last decade, few universities had much spare cash to play with, and resources allocation had to be prioritised, usually for the key activities and areas as regarded by the university. In the case of CI-A, its UK director explained the situation quite frankly in that his university had hardly put any cash into the Confucius Institute, and its main contribution was in kind through the provision of facilities and space, and some staff time as well, like himself.

> Our institution is a specialised HEI based upon languages, culture and social sciences and out of the realm of the perceived practical and useful STEM (science, technology, engineering and mathematics) subject area. As a result, just as our Principal said, the funding from the government had been diminishing over the years and the university had to be more and more reliant on tuition fees and other sources of income. Therefore, there is little fund available from the institution to contribute to this new joint venture. But there are many benefits with the financial and other resources from *Hanban* and Chinese partner university, for example, we can expand what we have been doing, and do things that we were not able to do in the past, such as more cultural events and collaboration with local communities and schools.

By contrast, CI-B had the advantage with about a dozen of high profile international business partners making an initial financial contribution to the establishment of the Confucius Institute. The CI-B UK director said:

> We are lucky with money as we also have support from some high profile firms that put aside a pot of money to support our Confucius Institute. As these sponsors are business firms, they are also keen that we don't lose money and should make enough to survive.

The fact that the host university of CI-B "inherited" this project "with money in the bank from the business partners" meant that the host university did not have to come up with any cash. CI-B came at the right moment as the host university wanted to enhance and further raise its profile on China, including the teaching of Chinese. The Chinese language teaching in the joint venture would not be accredited by the university, so the direct funding from the university was unlikely, though it was happy to get involved in the project as it helped to fulfil some goals of its China strategy. It was clear later that the cash injection from the university on Chinese language teaching was all allocated to the language centre. Likewise, the host university of CI-A channelled its fund to support the teaching of Chinese in the academic department. As a matter of fact, the institutional financial contribution to CI-A was minimal, if not non-existent.

The partnership of the joint venture in both cases was predominantly based upon the perceived mutual benefits in a sense that *Hanban* would have a presence at the highly reputable host institutions in London, while the host universities would have access to financial and other resources to develop or strengthen their Chinese language teaching. Other perceived potential benefits and gains were contributions to relevant cultural activities, scholarships, and opportunities for academic exchange and research. It is also important to point out that financial and resource inputs from *Hanban* did not necessarily guarantee the control or ownership of the Confucius Institutes by the Chinese partners. As a matter of fact, the case Confucius Institutes suggested that activities that had been developed and fostered through Confucius Institutes could become part of the host institution and detached from *Hanban* and Chinese partner, even though the latter provided much of the financial support for the initial launch. This demonstrated how important the local agent was in the making of the language policy and practices from the perspective of language management.

Human Resources

As *Hanban* is very much a sponsor, it relied on the Chinese partner universities for the provision of human resources to work in the two

Confucius Institutes. As the demand is higher than expected and a lot of partner universities could not meet the needs, *Hanban* later set up a central pool of Chinese language teachers and volunteers and dispatched them to local Confucius Institutes when required. CI-A had two teachers, one administrative assistant, and one volunteer over the period of six years from the *Hanban* central pool due to the lack of teachers from its Chinese partner.

It must be pointed out that all the Chinese directors for the Confucius Institutes were seconded full-time directors. If they still had their own roles back home, they would need to travel back and forth. Of the Chinese directors at CI-A, the first director was called back within a year, and the second one was present for a few months as he was badly needed at the home institution. This was partly the problem with the Chinese partner university for CI-A as it had forged links with about a dozen of universities abroad for Confucius Institutes. However, given the personal specifications required for Confucius Institute Chinese directors,[3] it was no surprise that the Chinese partner university soon found itself stretched beyond what it could cope with, which in turn adversely affected some operation and quality of the collaboration with its partner institutions abroad and subsequently the management of the joint venture. One of the reasons was because the Chinese partner university was too ambitious and seriously underestimated the number of key staff required as well as the amount of work needed to make the joint venture work. By contrast, the Chinese partner institution for CI-B only committed itself to one and only Confucius Institute worldwide, although one would expect a university like this should have engaged in more Confucius Institutes. The fact that all its directors seconded were heads of academic departments may also indicate that their university is careful and serious about its commitment with a better understanding of the constraints and limited resources at its disposal, although it may run the risk of being perceived to be lack of enthusiasm in the initiative.

Like the Chinese directors, the UK directors are also seconded from their normal posts as the director of the language centre, but with different institutional practices. The UK director for CI-A was not given any time or financial remuneration for his additional duties in the Confucius Institute, while the UK director for CI-B was awarded an honorarium in recognition of his involvement in the Confucius Institute over and above his job at the language centre. As said above, CI-A host university had no cash to give away and any reduction of workload would mean additional cost. It did, however, consult the Confucius Institute Chinese council member who represented *Hanban* on if the CI-A could factor this cost in its budget, but it was refused bluntly as the host university was expected to come up with funds for paying its director. On the other hand, the involvement of the multinational business in CI-B not only meant that it had the funds to reward its UK director's additional work in the Confucius Institute, but also believed that he should be so awarded in recognition of his work in Confucius Institute above his normal job. This allowance was included in the operating expenses for the Confucius Institute and would have to be recovered from its income generating activities.

In addition to directors, *Hanban* also financed some teachers and volunteers from China to help with the teaching and administration of the two Confucius Institutes. The composition of the teaching team in the two Confucius Institutes was quite illustrative in terms of *Hanban*'s involvement in this regard. For CI-A, which had a team of nearly 30 teachers in all, only two were seconded from China by *Hanban*, with one volunteer who was mostly engaged in administration support with some involvement in tutorial and cultural activities. It was interesting to note that they were all sent by *Hanban* from its pool, rather than from the Chinese partner university as expected. In this case, the Chinese institution remained nearly always dormant in the partnership. The word "volunteer" may be a misnomer if examined in the sense of term in the West, but it is an appropriate description for the Chinese, as they are usually postgraduate students studying how to teach Chinese to the speakers of other languages in Chinese universities and voluntarily sandwich this experience in their study and make it part of their learning and teaching practice in the Confucius Institute. Of the 12 teachers and volunteers working at CI-B, most were from the Chinese partner university—three teachers and five volunteers, with the remaining four employed locally. Unlike the teachers or volunteers from *Hanban*, almost all the locally employed teachers at both Confucius Institutes were working part-time and their workloads depended on the number of the courses running. As most teachers at both Confucius Institutes came from language or social science background, the CI-B-2 China director said that his institute was desperate to get a business postgraduate volunteer from China to join his team as there was such an acute demand for teachers with business background to teach business language courses.

The teachers and volunteers sent from China all worked full-time with sponsorship from *Hanban*, so it did not cost the host university or the Confucius Institutes anything to have them. However, any teaching they did meant a reduction for the teachers employed locally. While the management of the host universities welcomed the cost saving contribution from China, the reactions from their local teachers were not always positive. The UK director of the CI-A said in his interview:

> The teachers and volunteers sent from *Hanban* not only benefit the Confucius Institute, but also the university here. However, the university management only tends to see the financial benefit, as it does help to reduce the staff cost to a certain extent, they are not aware that not all the experienced teachers from China are suitable to teach

in the classrooms here, due to a range of differences between China and the UK. Another important thing is that it can lead to complaints by the local teachers when this affects their workload since most of the local teachers are part-timers. Therefore, it is important for me to make sure that we continue to develop and grow our programme so all the teachers, including the locals, have enough work to do.

This could well explain the reasons why the CI-A only had a very limited number of *Hanban* teachers while running a much larger teaching operation as compared to CI-B. The UK director of CI-A said that he realised that allocation of teaching hours was a sensitive issue and if not well managed might lead to tensions between local and *Hanban* teachers, as sometimes reported in the media elsewhere. Even with just two teachers at a time, he assigned them some teaching in the academic department so that local teacher could teach more in the Confucius Institute/language centre. Despite this awareness and care, there was still an incident in his Confucius Institute, which he talked about quite frankly:

> Confucius Institute can be in a dilemma with regards to its teachers if it runs courses together with the host institution like us. Some local teachers regard the teachers from *Hanban* taking some of their work away as they could have more hours to teach without them. There was already one open incident reported in the media that a local school teacher claimed that she had lost her job because the school had a "free" Chinese teacher sent by *Hanban*. We had an incident too where a local teacher was reported to have shouted to a *Hanban* teacher that she should go back home. Of course, she denied this afterwards, as there was no third party around. The fact was that the *Hanban* teacher was asked to teach a course that this local teacher thought she was appropriate to teach, so it was likely that she believed that that *Hanban* teacher had taken her work, without realising that the *Hanban* teacher was far more qualified and suitable to teach that course, and the allocation was entirely based on experience and suitability in our institute.

The *Hanban* teacher involved in the incident was later interviewed and her story was quite revealing. She was a very experienced teacher seconded from a top university in China specialised in TCFL and had been in the CI-A for two years. This is what she said with regards to her general experience and that incident at CI-A:

> Overall, I enjoy working in the Confucius Institute here. I want to know more about the Chinese teaching here as the university is famous for this, and I have learned a lot. . . . I get on well with most of the colleagues, but I can feel sometimes a kind of unfriendliness

from some teachers as they may think I am taking their work. I am only doing what I am asked to do, and I would like to have more time to do my own research too. . . . About that unpleasant incident, oh, that teacher was rude and terrible, and it is not fair. The management was very kind and supportive, but I do think that there is much that can be done to resolve this.

Other Resources

In addition to financial and human resources, the daily operation of the Confucius Institutes also required other resources such as space, physical equipment, and technical support, which had to be sourced locally. *Hanban* did make available a lot of teaching materials developed in China and other resources such as the "China Experience Multimedia Platform" with both software and hardware as part of its "going international" strategies, but the uptake of these resources was not significant. Neither of the two Confucius Institutes in this study took up *Hanban*'s offer of the "China Experience Multimedia Platform". Although they had each had many copies of the textbooks provided by *Hanban*, neither of them made much use in their teaching, which will be discussed in the next chapter.

For both Confucius Institutes, space had been a serious issue and more so for CI-A than CI-B, especially in the initial stage. With the prime location in the central London and very limited space itself, the host university of CI-A could only manage to squeeze out a small office for the first Chinese co-director, just like what all its other full-time teaching and management staff had. However, this was clearly not what *Hanban* and the Chinese partner university had expected, so the space issue came up time and again when there was a visit from *Hanban* or when partner institutions met. As the British director said, the constant name-dropping techniques used by the Chinese partners that so and so elsewhere had allocated or given a whole building to their Confucius Institute had really annoyed the university management, so much so that the pro-director of the host university once retorted openly in a meeting with Chinese partners that those places mentioned were not in central London. However, the use of space for all CI-A planned activities were usually made available through a central room booking system, just as all other departments in the university did. In 2007 when the language centre was relocated, CI-A was also moved to the new location, with much more spacious offices.

As the host university of CI-B was also located in central London, not very far from that of CI-A, the situation was not dissimilar. A major difference, however, was that CI-B was initially renting space from the host university before the latter took over the joint venture, so the space was larger, but also squeezed out through a lot of shuffling, as very little space was left unused in the university in the central part of London. The CI-B stayed in the same place for many years until a couple of years ago when it was moved to a much larger space in a main tower block, largely due to the fund made available from *Hanban* to refurbish the new venue, with increased office and classroom space dedicated to the use of the joint venture. As its programme grew, CI-B also had a growing number of staff, both seconded from *Hanban* and recruited locally, which also meant that it needed more space. Moreover, the institute was awarded as a Centre of Excellence by *Hanban* a few years ago, and for such honour space was a requirement, which also accelerated the progress for the host university to find more space for the Confucius Institute.

Policy and Position of Confucius Institutes

Institutional Policy on Confucius Institute in the Host University

The disparity in the intentions of having the joint venture was also evident in the fact that neither Confucius Institute had used the term "international Chinese" in their formal policy statement or public documentations. What was in common between the two Confucius Institutes local host universities was that they both emphasised that the newly set-up Confucius Institutes should not operate in competition with their host language centres. The UK director of CI-A said that his university had made sure of this by explicitly including this in a supplementary of their Confucius Institute Collaboration Agreement and integrating the language teaching in its language centre that had already offered both accredited and non-credit bearing courses in Chinese, thus no separate teaching for its Confucius Institute was allowed. The UK director of CI-B accounted the experience of his university as a two-staged process, with his language centre gradually taking charge of all Chinese language courses except those for business purposes, non-credit-bearing and exclusively earmarked for its Confucius Institute. All such policy statements or relevant measures were adopted for the similar intentions and purposes of the local host universities—to develop what the local institutions did not provide, and to enhance what they already had.

An initial look at the available historical documents of the two Confucius Institutes, particularly those in the public domain such as websites, seemed to suggest that the provision of Chinese language teaching at the two Confucius Institutes formed very much an integral part of the two universities' general institutional language policies. These policies and courses in Chinese aimed to give their students a taste of what Chinese language learning was like so that the students could decide if they would like to incorporate it into their degree study where possible or continue to study as an additional course to their degree on a fee-paying basis, usually with a discount. However, the extent to which the Confucius Institute was integrated into the university language provision differed between the two host institutions and changed over time too, which usually was itself an outcome of the institutional policy and practice modification. From the start, CI-A had been an integral part of the host language centre in terms of offering all non-credit-bearing Chinese language courses as the language centre already had a substantive scale of teaching activities in Chinese. Recently the host university moved its Confucius Institute out of the language centre and appointed a new director with higher ranking in the university management but with limited expertise knowledge of China or Chinese language. The Confucius Institute teachers were teaching on the accredited courses of the host institution, but the Confucius Institute activities became limited to auxiliary language activities such as Chinese language speaking corner and cultural events. For CI-B, a similar situation also occurred recently as its Chinese teaching was now only restricted to business Chinese while all the general Chinese language courses had moved away to the language centre of the host university. It was not hard to see from both Confucius Institutes that they were becoming more and more detached from the routine operation of their host universities. What was interesting was that the revised website of the CI-A had quoted directly, without any modification, from the statement of its Chinese partner concerning Confucius Institutes (in Chinese), "Confucius Institute was for promoting the dissemination of the Chinese language and the culture" (*Tuiguang Zhongguo yuyan ji wenhua chuanbo wei mudi*), though there was no such mention in the English version. It is not certain if this was intentional or just an oversight, but it did reflect the paradox of the CI-A in a way as it hardly had any learning and teaching of Chinese language of its own since it had been moved out of the language centre and with a limited amount of cultural activities as seen on the website.

Integration of Confucius Institute Into the Host Institution

Further scrutiny of the publicly available statement of the two host universities revealed that apart from what was on the websites of the two Confucius Institutes, no institutional statements could be found on the website of either host university on how it was related to the Confucius Institute and the support to Confucius Institute activities. This was despite the fact, as the two UK directors confirmed during their interviews, that the universities were very supportive to the joint venture. It could be said that lack of visibility of the host university's association with and engagement in Confucius Institute was one of the key factors that contribute to this apparent absence of knowledge of the students about Confucius Institute, which will be discussed in Chapter 6.

It was found in this study that the degree of integration of the Confucius Institute into its host university was, to a certain extent, an indication of the host university's attitude, positioning, and planning. There were several aspects on which this integration was examined. One aspect was that both the Confucius Institutes was explicitly poised to get involved only with non-credit-bearing Chinese courses on the host university campus, thus regarded as non-academic teaching by the host university. According to the interviews with CI-B UK director, there were two major reasons behind this as far as their university was concerned. One was that the joint venture had a lot of involvement from China which did not conform to the quality assurance procedures as it was not an integral part of the host university with regard to its staff. The other was that some British academics were concerned about the potential interference from Chinese colleagues in their existing or future programmes and about their academic independence. As the CI-A UK director said,

> Initially there was strong resistance from the academic department for the Confucius Institute to get involved in any of its teaching or relevant activities as it was felt that the department had been teaching Chinese for nearly 100 years and did not need any Chinese expertise.

On the contrary, the CI-B British director said that his university was so concerned about political implication with the set-up of the joint venture rather than academic independence. Clearly this reflected how the host universities had positioned the Confucius Institute on their campus and was perhaps the very reason why the two Confucius Institutes were based initially in the language centre of their host university, where most of the non-accredited language courses were offered.

With regards to financial integration, both Confucius Institutes went through a transition period as *Hanban* was originally asking for a separate bank account to be set up for each Confucius Institute and it was what the first Chinese directors were asking for. As the CI-A UK director recalled:

> I can still remember the initial difficult negotiation I was having with my Chinese counterpart who was adamant that the Confucius Institute would have its own bank account as this would ensure the exclusive use by the Confucius Institute of the fund from *Hanban*. He approached this from his Chinese perspective without understanding that such arrangement wouldn't be possible if Confucius Institute was part of the university. All operation units in the organisation are only allowed to have a separate account number under the university's account as stipulated by the university financial regulations. However, after many meetings and consultations with *Hanban*, this was finally sorted as it wasn't just this Confucius Institute that encountered the problem. This was also why our operation didn't start until about eight months after he had been in post when the

Hanban fund arrived at the University. By that time, a few other Confucius Institutes had also been set up elsewhere in the world.

The story with CI-B was slightly different as it was set up as a charity, registered and banked as an independent entity when the host university was only a landlord rather than a partner. This had to change when the university took it over and CI-B became an integral part of the host university's financial management system. However, this integration was more of a result of the requirements of the financial management regulations of the British universities than what was believed to reflect full integration of Confucius Institutes in the local university system. As this study has discussed, academically neither of the two Confucius Institutes became integrated into their host university.

As we all know, a key area for the public to get information nowadays is websites, in this case the presence of the two Confucius Institutes on the host university's websites. For CI-A, the website of Confucius Institute was integrated into the university's website only as a unit of the university just like other similar units. One could not find any clear statement by the university on the website mentioning its link with the Confucius Institute, let alone how it supported or planned to develop it. One may say that this is to ensure that the university treats all the departments on equal terms, but this is a joint venture and it needs the clear message of recognition and support from the host university. Regarding CI-B, its present on the host university website was not easy to locate, and it was not listed as any unit of the host university under its various headings. It could only be found by using the "search" function on the university website or by Google search. As its Chinese director said, such search would direct the reader to the Confucius Institute's website that appeared on the host university website. The logo of the host university did appear alongside with that of *Hanban* and the Chinese partner university, which suggested the association and involvement of the university with its Confucius Institute.

In terms of integration into the host university organisational structure, it seemed that neither of the universities had an explicit long-term plan. All the UK directors pointed out that when the Confucius Institute funding from *Hanban* was allocated on an annual basis, it was difficult to change the still "temporary" nature of the Confucius Institutes in the host university. Therefore, the host university would place Confucius Institute where it felt convenient and fit. The appointment of the director of the language centre as the UK director helped to ensure that the language teaching could be appropriately delivered and there was an effectively and timely communication with the host university management. The change in CI-A with its move into the faculty to become a departmental centre resulted in that the professorial dean being appointed to the UK directorship assisted with a senior language lector as the deputy.

Elsewhere in the UK, Confucius Institute have been placed in different sections and their UK directors were appointed from a range of their internal post holders: pro-vice chancellor, faculty dean, head of department, professors, lecturers, and administrators.

Awareness of Confucius Institute by Its Students

In addition to the above, a most significant contribution from both local host universities was the intangible asset of their reputation, which *Hanban* appeared fully aware of as it always tried to team up with famous universities when and wherever possible. It was through such links that the new joint venture could find a firm footing so soon in such reputable institutions of higher education as the two host universities of the case Confucius Institutes. However, it was surprising to find out from the student survey that many students did not know about the relationship between the Confucius Institute and its host university. The response to the question in the survey was a testimony of this lack of effective communication on the part of the university and Confucius Institute with regards to the nature of this joint venture. The results of the survey have produced a grave cause for concern for the two Confucius Institutes or beyond in this matter. Thirty-two per cent of the respondents thought that Confucius Institute was a "language institute owned by *Hanban* (like British Council) operating in Britain"; 7% respondents believed that Confucius Institute was "a language institute owned by a British agency with Chinese sponsorship"; 15% opted for Confucius Institute as "a language institute of a British university promoting Chinese language and culture"; and another 30% said that they were not sure or didn't know, with 8% simply leaving the question unanswered. Only 8% students knew that Confucius Institute is "a language institute jointly owned and operated by *Hanban* and a British institution". This lack of appropriate understanding of Confucius Institute and its status exposed the lack of right promotional campaign of these Confucius Institutes. If their course participants do not even know what Confucius Institutes are, how can they expect the public to understand who they are and what they are doing? Many of the learners had registered on the Chinese language courses because of the reputation of the universities where these Confucius Institutes were based rather than the reputation of the Confucius Institute themselves. One question asked students why they had chosen the current courses in the first place, the responses to this question (multiple answers allowed) indicated that nearly 80% (76) chose the course because of the reputation of the university with which the Confucius Institute was associated, followed by convenient location (44, or 46%), useful contents of the course (26, or 27%), and competitive price (16, or 17%). It is not difficult to see that apart from the quarter of the respondents who seemed to have really considered if the course could be useful for them or not, most of the respondents had made their decisions predominantly based upon the reputation of the university.

It also showed that it might not be a bad thing that Confucius Institutes kept a low profile intentionally or unintentionally with regards to the Chinese language courses that they were offering, as one student respondent attending a course in CI-A wrote: "I wouldn't have enrolled had I known the course was offered by Confucius Institute". Unfortunately, it wasn't possible to interview this student and to find out why he had such a hostile attitude toward Confucius Institute. He might be influenced by the media and some research as discussed that there were critical and negative views about China's real intention behind pushing the Confucius Institute initiative. This student may represent a group of people who don't like Confucius Institute not because of the language courses they offer but because its status. But in the limited number of interviews held with the students, the general reaction was that they didn't care who organised the Chinese language courses as long the courses met their needs. One interviewee from CI-A said:

> I don't really care who organises the course. I chose the course because its description seems to offer what I have been looking for, and more importantly it is offered by a reputable university that one can trust. I couldn't tell any Confucian element in the course or how the course is associated with Confucius Institute. I did notice different teachers approach their teaching differently, but I suppose that is normal.

Another student interviewee from CI-B working in a financial institution in London said:

> I came because the course is business oriented and offered in a top university in London. The involvement of Confucius Institute is of no concern to me or many of us, I guess, as we are only interested in what we can get from the course with the time and money we put it. The course is very practical. I have heard about Confucius Institute, but I honestly do not know how it operates, except that it is everywhere, a couple of them in London alone. I think that it is like Alliance Française, promoting Chinese language and China.

Nearly all the student interviewees confirmed, their knowledge of Confucius Institute mostly came from the cultural or social events that Confucius Institute organised, such as Chinese New Year, some public lectures, and for some the Confucius Institute scholarship. This shows clearly that both Confucius Institutes appear to face a dilemma in terms of integration into their host university on the one hand and keeping their own identity on the other.

Summary

As analysed and discussed above, the ethnographic field study of the two Confucius Institutes showed that the joint venture nature of the Confucius Institutes was an attractive model to all the partner institutions, at least initially, but the troika of the joint venture approached and embraced the Confucius Institute with different intentions. These different intentions subsequently determined their levels of commitment to and position in the management of the joint venture, even though all the partner institutions shared the seemingly common goal and interest in the provision of Chinese language learning and teaching through the established Confucius Institutes. To a large extent, it was the disparities in intentions and the joint venture nature of the two Confucius Institutes that underpinned the number of issues discovered and discussed above regarding the actual language policy practices of the joint venture. In the light of the theoretical framework of language management, the findings of the field study also affirmed that language policy was not just what was stated on paper, but also the actual practice enacted by various agents concerned. In the case of the two Confucius Institutes, the involvement of multi-agents from the Chinese government agency *Hanban*, Chinese and British local partner universities to the actual Confucius Institutes meant that the joint venture would formulate and implement its own language policy through a dynamic process of interaction and negotiation with all the partner institutions, including all the major participating agents, characterised with constant change both at local and central level.

Each of the troika had its own agendas, expectations, and priorities, as well as interest in the joint venture, and this meant that each partner had a considerable influence and impact on both explicit and implicit Chinese learning and teaching policy statements and practices in the joint venture. Confucius Institute is for *Hanban* a main vehicle to achieve its primary goal to promote international Chinese, hence it is no surprise that *Hanban* provides a lot of support to the joint venture, especially financial support. *Hanban* has also made a good use of China's state education system by mobilising the Chinese universities to be part of this endeavour, with both obligations and financial incentives. For the two top British universities involved in the two Confucius Institutes, they happened to be interested in expanding their provision of Chinese language learning and teaching as it coincided well with their international development strategies concerning China. And not only was the Confucius Institute a readily welcome proposal, the opportunity to be partnered and collaborating with a top Chinese university was much appreciated as such a link would help boost their international profiles in China. Both Confucius Institutes were established in the early days of the Confucius Institute development in the UK, and the host university of CI-A had not expected that the Confucius Institutes would have become such a common phenomenon and had put its institution in the same rank and file with many non-Russell group universities. But it must be said that the host universities were also happy to have cash injection into the joint venture from *Hanban*, along with other direct and indirect benefits such as scholarships and more access to the China higher education market. However, this did not mean that the two host universities were ready to say yes to everything that their Chinese partners had proposed. As British higher education institutions, they both were very mindful of their academic and administrative integrity. As the two host universities had different needs to meet, thus with different agendas and purposes in the provision of Chinese language learning and teaching through the joint venture, they expected, acted, and reacted quite differently from their Chinese partners in the actual operation of the joint venture, ranging from their level of commitment to their roles in the management of the joint venture. As a matter of fact, the disparities in the intentions of the partner institutions were far more deeply rooted than they appeared to be. As Hughes (2014) pointed out in his recent article, a fundamental discord in Confucius Institutes was that the three partner institutions are of completely different institution in nature and incompatible in their missions.

If examined in the framework of language management, *Hanban* can be regarded as a "national" organisation with the role of a super "language agency" working in the "supranational" domain in managing the learning and teaching of Chinese internationally. As a national organisation, it has its mission to promote Putonghua, backed with a steadily increased government fund to support its Confucius Institute initiative, thus a manifestation of Chinese language status planning. As a language agency, while it does not police the learning and teaching, it has published various directives and guides regarding the standards and competence references for TCFL, thus a manifestation of Chinese language corpus planning policy as these standards and references are largely in line with those applied domestically. As a supranational organisation, *Hanban* has its member Confucius Institutes in nearly 150 countries, with 525 Confucius Institutes and 1,113 Confucius Classrooms,[4] and 10 of its 15-member Council (equivalent to the board of directors) come from abroad, thus working in a very international environment.

However, as the Confucius Institute initiative followed a collaborative model that involved at least another Chinese and overseas institutional partner in addition to *Hanban*, the actual working of each of the Confucius Institutes might be different due to the disparities in partner institution's intentions and commitments and subsequent policies and agreement reached for the relevant joint venture. As revealed in the case of both Confucius Institutes concerned in this field study, the details of the policy and agreement reached for the actual Confucius Institute could also change over time, even though the general aims and objectives of the Confucius Institute stipulated by *Hanban* remained the same. While the collaborative model certainly had its advantage in terms of the speed of global development when compared with other major nation-led "international" language promotion organisations such as British Council, some scholars have called for *Hanban* to have more clearly defined and measurable goals for its constituent Confucius Institutes. This and the recognition of different institutional partners having their own agenda and intentions, which would determine their commitment in the relevant joint venture, would allow constituent Confucius Institutes to work more effectively for the realisation of these goals and objectives. The field study of the two Confucius Institutes has again confirmed that this is very much the case. As can be seen, one of the main reasons for the two host universities to have got involved in the initiative was that they were providing Chinese language teaching in their university to meet the local demand, so the initiative came at the right moment. However, it would be a hasty conclusion if one assumed that they completely shared the aims and objectives of the *Hanban* international Chinese language policy. Hughes (2014) talked about this incompatibility between *Hanban* and the host universities overseas in terms of their missions in his article "Confucius Institutes and the University". It was such convergences and differences in the intention that determined, to a large extent, the level of commitment by each partner institution in the two Confucius Institutes, and understandably the actual policy implemented and practised by the various agents on the ground, especially the teachers and students.

The study of the intention, commitment, and subsequent policy for the two Confucius Institutes also exposed a cause for concern in terms of sustainable development of the Confucius Institutes. First, it was about the financial stability, and second, about the actual work borne by the joint staff from *Hanban* and those appointed and employed by the local institutions. As far as financial stability was concerned, the case of CI-A was especially worrying that it seemed to have lost completely the income generating activities by moving out of the language centre and thus would rely solely on *Hanban* funding for its activities and operation. With regard to the working of directors, apart from the uneven workloads between the China and UK directors, the personalities and management style of these directors could lead to friction in terms of the ways they would prefer to manage the joint venture, particularly when the China directors were seconded and changed on a fixed term basis. In addition, there was also the "free" teaching staff seconded from *Hanban* and Chinese partner institutions. This could be seen as a "threat" to the jobs of the local teachers, as illustrated in the case of CI-A above. This would be particularly true when the local part-time teachers were keen to have more work, but the demand was limited, so the use of the "free" human resources would be prioritised at the expenses of the local teachers' job, unless it was carefully and appropriately planned and handled.

It was true that the association with the highly reputable local host universities was a great help for the joint venture to operate so soon in London. However, the involvement of these reputable local institutions also had other implications. On a more general level, the gradual fine tuning of *Hanban*'s policy of international Chinese from a blanket global promotion strategy to one that equally emphasised the importance of localisation in teaching materials, teaching methods, and teacher and teacher training was one of the results of working with such institutional partners, particularly those in the developed countries. But as the local partner institutions increased in numbers and types with regards to their ranking and status in the sector, there was some uneasiness felt in some of the reputable host institutions. The UK director of the CI-A said in his interview that the senior managers of his university were initially very proud when the university hosted a Confucius Institute, but this sense of pride was soon to dwindle as Confucius Institute expanded to include some not perceived to be in the same league as they were. This could well be a reason why the host university had not been very active in promoting its joint venture in the public sphere, which resulted in a rather low awareness of the Confucius Institute by the students, as revealed in the questionnaire survey in this field study. In addition, while *Hanban* funding was always a welcome gift, the amount was not in any sense significant for either of the two host universities in their annual budget. Therefore, both host universities had taken a very pragmatic approach to the joint venture, just to advance and develop their own Chinese language teaching and to expand links with China and Chinese partner institutions where possible via the joint venture without much additional commitment or any obvious long-term development plan. Such attitude and policy could be felt to a certain extent in the actual operation and management of the case Confucius Institutes.

Notes

1. Lu Deping on the significance of Confucius Institute: https://mp.weixin.qq.com/s/9toV4TG23_BGvp5vb5Z4cw.
2. In the words of the first CI-A Chinese director as recalled by the CI-A British director during the research interview.
3. Associate professor and above title; served at least one year as deputy division director or above; having overseas study or work experience and skilfully use of the host country language or English.
4. Liu, Xiaoming. Confucius is a key to China-UK friendship: http://europe.chinadaily.com.cn/a/201806/08/WS5b1999eaa31001b82571ec78.html

5 Language Management at Confucius Institute Level

This chapter first looks at the Confucius Institutes in terms of their organisation and management structure and then the main activities related to learning and teaching Chinese language. The chapter consists of four sections. The first section reports on the study findings on the organisation structure of the two Confucius Institutes and the critical role of their directors. The next section analyses the Chinese language programmes and other related areas such as teaching materials and teacher training of the two Confucius Institutes. The following section briefly discusses other activities of their Confucius Institutes and challenges they faced with for their sustainability. The last section is a summary of the chapter.

The Organisation and Management

Organisational Structure and Directors

While both Confucius Institutes in this study shared the two-tier organisation structure as suggested by *Hanban*, they differed from each other in many aspects. First, at the level of the council, which served like the board of directors and trustees responsible for policy and planning for the Confucius Institute concerned, the two Confucius Institutes had different names and composition. CI-B had its as Advisory Council with members from a varied background, including business partners, *Hanban*, and local Chinese embassy officials, as well as the Chinese and local partner university representatives. It also had an Academic Steering Group along with it, tasked with the responsibility to oversee the academic quality of the courses organised by the Confucius Institute, and was entirely made up by the members from the local host university. By contract, the Council of the CI-A had members from the host university and Chinese partner institution, plus an official from the local Chinese embassy. Unlike the CI-B, the council meeting with CI-A was far less regular, partly due to the absence of the Chinese partner in the Confucius Institute most of the time before this study.

96 *Language Management at Confucius Institute Level*

What the two Confucius Institutes had in common was that all daily management of the operation was left to the directors of Confucius Institutes. However, the two Confucius Institutes had different management set-ups, and even their directors had different titles, which revealed to a certain extent what the partner institutions had agreed on the Confucius Institute management and how each of the two Confucius Institutes was managed. For CI-A, the director seconded from the host university was called a director, while the Chinese partner university initially insisted that the one seconded from them should be on the equal footing, therefore called a co-director (which later changed to Chinese director). Interestingly enough, an additional post of deputy director was created by the host university to take over routine work, not long after the departure of the founding director, as the new director was a member of the senior management with little expertise on China and Chinese language. The Confucius Institute also changed its Chinese university partner, but the new post remained in place even after the arrival of its Chinese director. For CI-B, it had its UK director and an executive director appointed by the local host university and China director from the Chinese partner university. An obvious difference in the management structure between the two Confucius Institutes was that the CI-B also had a post of coordinator for the language programmes which CI-A did not have. While disparities might appear to be minute at the first glance, they, as the study reveals, reflected gaps in expectation and understanding between the two partner universities in the early stage and subsequently between the seconded directors with regards to their roles and positions in the joint venture. In the case of CI-A, the UK director recalled that the Chinese partner university specifically demanded its seconded director to have the title of co-director, thus enjoying equal status and responsibilities:

> I remember that there were a lot of discussions around the management structure of our Confucius Institute in the early days. The Confucius Institute Constitution at that time only suggested that the director from China would usually be responsible for the design and offering of Chinese language courses, while the director from the host university would take the overall management responsibility to oversee the operations of Confucius Institute. It allowed the partner institutions to decide what title they would like to give to the directors seconded from the Chinese partner and the local host universities. For our Chinese partner then, it insisted that its director should be called co-director, so on an equal footing with my role.

It was soon clear to him and the host university that the Chinese co-director very much regarded himself as a formal representative of both his university and *Hanban* and brought with him not only the *Hanban* seeding funds but also apparent advantage and expertise in the learning and teaching of Chinese since his university was well-known in China. He would like the Confucius Institute to have its own teaching, different from those run in the host university. The host university, on the other hand, would like to ensure that its decades of tradition of teaching Chinese to English speakers could continue and there would be no competition between the newly set-up Confucius Institute and its own existing operations. Even though the negotiation over director's title turned out to be only an exercise on paper as the CI-A only had a very short period presence of a Chinese director, what the host university was concerned with before the start of the joint venture did surface even in the short period of time when the two directors seconded from the partner universities were working side by side. When looking back, the CI-A UK director thought it was natural such teething problems had occurred because the Confucius Institute was a new thing for everyone concerned and all parties had their own agenda and interest. His university had a foresight, so the delegation of management responsibilities was necessary and useful at the beginning. He recalled:

> There was a difficult period shortly after the first Chinese director arrived. He insisted that the Confucius Institute should have its own Chinese language teaching courses alongside what was already a full range of provision in the host university. I explained to him that was not possible as the University would not want to have competition on its own campus, which was exactly why the university placed Confucius Institute in the Language Centre in order that the expertise and resources from both top partner universities could be used to enhance and further develop the provision. He wasn't happy with this and tried to fight for it by all possible means because he believed that the Confucius Institute should not benefit the host university. I think he was just doing what he had been asked or expected to do, but the issue was that he didn't seem to understand that he had also to be flexible, adaptable and have an adequate understanding of the local situation, including needs and requirements of the host university.

The apparent neglect of the long-established practice and tradition in the teaching of Chinese language in the host university was not just an individual problem in CI-A but reflected the concept and practice of predominantly China-based *Duiwai Hanyu Jiaoxue* and its extension abroad by the name of international Chinese via Confucius Institutes. This was probably a reason underpinning the clause in the Confucius Institute Constitution that the Chinese director was charged with the design, delivery, and development of the Chinese language courses since they had the expertise and resources. While this might be true with many Confucius Institutes where Chinese language teaching was relatively new, it wasn't the case for CI-A. On the other hand, CI-B was entirely a different experience as the host university very much counted on the Chinese university to design, deliver, and develop the Chinese language courses for the joint venture, which gradually led to the development of its own Chinese language courses. For CI-B, the local director was called UK director and the Chinese one called China director, thus on a rather equal footing. In terms of the division of work, the UK director of CI-B said:

> As I do not know Chinese, I am very happy to leave it to the Chinese director who is an expert in Chinese to take charge of the design and development of the Chinese language courses. Of course, our courses are all business oriented as the name of our Confucius Institute suggests. However, there are always discussions on whether you can teach business language separately from the general language, but for us, it was important to get the courses going. He was a very nice man and soon put in place an operation with the support of the Confucius Institute staff, which we were fortunately to be able to have due to the involvement of the business partners.

This was very much confirmed by the interview with the CI-B China Director (CI-B-1), who said that most of his time had been on the development of Chinese language courses for the institute as teaching Chinese was what he had been doing for many years.

The study found that appropriate candidates for Confucius Institute directors were a key factor that contributed to successful collaboration and operation of the Confucius Institutes. As for the directors from China, it was true that all those who were chosen and sent out were excellent candidates from the point of view of the Chinese partner universities, but their understanding of and adaptability to the local needs and management practices, and moreover their ability to communicate and willingness to learn should also be part of the consideration. As for the teaching of Chinese, they might well be experts in the field of Chinese language teaching in China, but the change of the variables such as location from China to London and more importantly different target learners, could present whole sets of new challenges to them, adding to those policy and management issues. As they usually worked full-time, their engagement in the Confucius Institute operation and management were naturally more extensive than their British counterparts. A real issue revealed from this study was how a Confucius Institute can allocate and determine the amount and scope of work to allow its Chinese director to make full use of the time as well as expertise in the management and operation of the Confucius Institute concerned. The recent separation of general Chinese language courses (moving to the language centre) from the business ones still offered in the CI-B, and similarly the move of CI-A out of the language centre with less involvement in the Chinese language courses, would only add questions rather than answers to this very issue concerning not only the function and role of the Chinese director in the Confucius Institute, but also the scope of the activities of the Confucius Institute concerned.

Teachers' Administration and Professional Development

The interview with the teachers both from *Hanban* and local institutions in the two Confucius Institutes showed that they were generally satisfied with the administration and support of the Confucius Institute. For *Hanban* teachers, CI-B gave the newly arrived a scheduled orientation before their start of teaching since they came in group, while CI-A provided a more individual induction as the number was small. However, one phenomenon was particularly worth noting, which was when *Hanban* teachers were deployed outside Confucius Institute, as the following example indicates.

A young teacher from *Hanban* arrived in CI-A just a few days before the academic term started. As part of her teaching, she was assigned to teach for some accredited courses in the academic department. Such contribution to the teaching on academic programmes in the host university by the Confucius Institute residing on its campus was not uncommon but was rarely mentioned in media or public statements. This errand away from the Confucius Institute could pose potential problem with regards to support and line management. This *Hanban* teacher's comment was very frank as she was clearly frustrated with this dual line management as a "*Hanban* Confucius Institute teacher":

> I have been here for over a year now, and I must say that I have gradually found my way around as there was very little information or induction given as far as the teaching in the department is concerned. I was sent by *Hanban* to work in the Confucius Institute here. But when I arrived, I was told that my teaching time would be divided between the Confucius Institute and the department. The teaching came as a surprise, no warning, no syllabus, no books, nothing. As my time is divided, I feel I am divided too, and fall in between. This is so different from my previous experience in the States where everything was organised to the details. I feel strongly that I am like an unwanted gift, maybe it is not a right metaphor. I don't feel that I can do much here, just to do whatever I am asked to do. I feel very strongly that they should have a good induction to people like me. In fact, the university does have such induction programmes to its new staff, but I am not included or invited, so I remain very much as an outsider.

This feeling of alienation, however, wasn't shared by another *Hanban* teacher in the same Confucius Institute who had been around longer. She said the following in her interview, talking about both her overall experience and some specific ones, including an incident with a local teacher as mentioned above:

> I think that I am happy here in general and the teaching and management of the Confucius Institute and language centre is quite good. The teaching of different courses gives me opportunities to be in touch with all kinds of students. I get on well with all other teachers, but I did have issues with a local teacher. I suppose you have this type of problem in all work places but the management support is very good here.

The interviews with the two *Hanban* teachers in CI-A showed some real and potential management issues if *Hanban* teachers also worked away from the Confucius Institute to which they were seconded, and when taught in the same unit with the local teachers when there was not enough work to share. As all *Hanban* teachers in CI-B worked exclusively for the institute, and a very small number of local teachers employed by the institute (via the host university), there was no such conflict.

Since there was no explicitly specified workload for teachers seconded from *Hanban*, Confucius Institute management and the teachers themselves could have different expectations and in varied practices, as found in this study between the two Confucius Institutes. The interviews with the university teachers seconded from China showed that they used to teach fewer hours a week in China when compared to the teaching load in British universities. Therefore, nearly all the *Hanban* teachers would say that they were over-worked, and some even felt unfairly treated. The directors of the two Confucius Institutes had different approaches in dealing with this.

For CI-A whose *Hanban* teachers were lecturers seconded from Chinese universities other than the partner institution, its UK director regarded them as academic staff who would still need to engage in research and publication for future promotion when they went back to their home institution. Therefore, this research engagement was incorporated in their workload, which proved to be advantageous for several reasons. The teachers concerned were happy, as the Confucius Institute management was considerate for their career development (teaching in the Confucius Institute was part of it anywhere), and the time given would allow them to learn more about the local culture and practices as well as to focus on their research. For the local teachers, this would reduce the competition for work from the seconded teachers. As a result, the teachers got on well and there was close collaboration and frequent sharing of experience and good practices between the two groups. For CI-B, since its *Hanban* teachers all came from the Chinese partner institution, it was much easy to reach an institutional agreement on workload as the partner institution was still the actual line management for the seconded teachers who hardly had any say on this. Instead, they tended to demand more recognition and support from the Confucius Institute management, as one of the interviewee teacher said, "As we will be evaluated for our work here, the support, understanding and appreciation of the line manager in the Confucius Institute is extremely important".

Teachers' professional development was part of the language programme in both Confucius Institutes, but they apparently had different approaches. Under the founding UK director, CI-A organised regular internal seminars, usually twice a term, involving both local and seconded teachers as it provided a platform to share best practices, as well as forging a good bond and working relationship between the two groups. In addition, CI-A also had termly open training programmes and workshops for all teachers of Chinese, and sometimes ran such programmes in conjunction with other institutions, such as British Council, and SSAT. All these events were offered free to the participants, as CI-A regarded it as part of its responsibility to provide teachers such opportunities and to improve their teaching of the language wherever they were teaching. With the language centre, CI-A was also involved in the delivery of the centre's certificated teacher training programmes, for which there was a charge.

CI-B did not provide as many such events, but it focused on two things, as all Confucius Institutes are expected to provide some teacher development opportunities. It had been working on development some online materials on Chinese language for its own teachers as well as those interested from outside after they joined its training events. This was not only an economical option, but also a more up-to-date choice with the use of the internet, as the UK director pointed out. In addition, it organised an annual three-day intensive professional development focusing on the teachers of business Chinese in the last few years, for which there was a charge, and would make it one of its flagship programmes on offer.

The different approaches between the two Confucius Institutes seemed to have been underlined more fundamentally by the different perspectives and understanding by their directors about Chinese language learning and teaching and the purpose of professional development and training programmes, which in turn impacted on the content of such programmes. With the absence of its co-director, CI-A's programmes were mostly guided and organised by its UK director then, who was an English language teacher but now a Chinese language teaching specialist. For him, teaching in CI-A and the UK needed to take into consideration learning and environment as well as the language itself. The following is what he said about his perception of Chinese language learning and teaching in the European context:

> Teaching Chinese here is not like that in China. We have more homogeneous learners here in a sense they all speak English, though many are not first language speakers. Teaching won't be effective

unless you understand how and why your learners learn. London and Europe are also multi-cultural and multilingual, which is obvious if you see how English is used here. So, it won't go down well here if you insist that there is only standard and one requirement with regards to the Chinese language, such as pronunciation and tones. You hear dialects in China all the time, and you will also see how our teachers speak English here. Nobody bothers about these "defects", as long as they can communicate in real life effectively. This also involves intercultural communication skills. For examples, we have colleagues here who speak good English but their language upsets others.

As a result, CI-A's programmes tended to focus more on learners' motivation, their learning characteristics and process. Linguistic contrastive analysis methods were used and the teaching involved both Chinese and English languages. For CI-B, as the UK director did not know Chinese, such programmes were all left to the two China directors, a Chinese professor and an English professor, both with little previous experience teaching language outside China. While they might look at the two languages somewhat differently, the subsequent programmes offered by CI-B and the interview with the Chinese professor director suggested that they both stressed the importance of learning and teaching the standard Chinese in a systematic manner as how it is taught in the home university. When talking about the content and importance of the teacher training programmes, the CI-B China Director (CI-B-2) said:

> The primary function of Confucius Institute is to teach Chinese, and we should make sure that we do that well. Teachers should have a sound knowledge of the Chinese language and culture, or they may mislead their students. Unfortunately, some of our teachers, especially those employed locally without a degree in Chinese language are quite weak in the Chinese language, and we see it a major problem and challenge for our future development. Therefore, we have been developing such remedial materials and we put them online in our system so those who need them can access and learn themselves.

Students' Administration and Support

The question of the administration and support of the learners also reflects the management of the language courses in the two Confucius Institutes. It would be interesting and useful to see what the students' feedback was like on that, both from the questionnaire survey and from the interviews.

The questionnaire survey question on the administration of the language courses at the Confucius Institutes produced a largely positive response. 49 respondents (just over 50%) ranked the administration of the courses as "very well"; 18 (19%) ranked "well", but 24 (25%) reckoned the service was "OK" and six (5%) rated the service negatively. While it can be attributed to the fact that most of the respondents were professionals with higher expectations of service, it would be very useful to find out what were the other reasons that contributed to the making of the less flattering rating. However, the interviews did not shed much light on this as the interviewees were not necessarily those who gave negative feedback on the question. If anything, the problem might have been in some individual cases, as one of interviewees complained about his experience with the long process of a delayed refund for a cancelled course. The Confucius Institute concerned said that it did not have control on this at all, as it was really determined by the financial management system of the host university.

With regards to the question on the course price, the responses were not surprising since the two Confucius Institutes had very different pricing policies. As CI-A offered its courses in the language centre, who was a self-financed unit, its Chinese courses were priced at the market rate, thus much higher than that of CI-B (whose prices are also rising now). So, the responses from CI-A respondents were expected to be "naturally" a bit more negative than those from CI-B. But both Confucius Institutes gave discount to the current and previous students of their own host universities, and such learners counted about a quarter (26%) of the total. Looking at the background of the respondents, their purposes, and expectations of learning Chinese, it was clear that while these professionals were ready to pay for and to invest in what they reckoned as useful and worthwhile, they also naturally had higher expectations of these courses in terms of how well the courses could meet their expectations and how well they were served while learning the Chinese language on the course. In the light of this, the responses to the previous question on course administration and support were in fact very positive.

There was also a question to seek students' views and experiences on the teaching resources and supports available at both Confucius Institutes. The responses, however, were quite surprising. As mentioned before, all Confucius Institutes are relatively well stocked with a lot of resources, mostly provided by *Hanban*, not only books, but also audio and visual materials. However, over half of the respondents (54) said that they had not used such resources at all, the 13 respondents who had used them thought these resources were "good" or "OK", and two reckoned that the resources were not very useful at all. About half a dozen of respondents "complained" that they had no idea that such resources existed, as one student wrote, "These haven't been explained to me so I haven't accessed them at all. It may be useful for me, but I don't have time to use them anyway". The survey result of this question suggested that there might be a lack of communication and consequently a waste of resources at both Confucius Institutes. However, the study also found that much of *Hanban* provided materials were shelved or even in boxes in their office, possibly because some of these resources were regarded not suitable as they could not quite meet the needs of the students. This was why both Confucius Institutes worked hard to develop their own teaching materials.

Teaching and Other Activities

The Chinese Language Courses and Teacher Training

As it is stated in the constitution of Confucius Institute, all the Confucius Institutes are expected to offer Chinese language courses. As far as this was concerned, Chinese and UK partner institutions in the two case Confucius Institutes cherished the same intention. However, what the field study found was that the partner universities and their appointed directors did not always agree on the actual offering and operation with regards to aspects such as what types of courses to offer or what teaching materials and assessment to use, mostly due to the differences between them in terms of their own agenda, their vested financial interest, and their understanding of what Chinese language learning and teaching is and how it should be delivered. All this manifest the actual language policies and practices of the Confucius Institute concerned.

As mentioned before, the language centre was running a full range of Chinese language courses when CI-A was established, from general language courses to those for special purpose such as business and law, as well as bespoke courses on demand. So, an initial problem was the conflict of interest about the ownership of the course offering. The Chinese co-director wanted the Confucius Institute to organise separate courses on the premises of the host university, which the UK co-director resisted as there had already been a decision by the host university that there should only be a single provision of the Chinese language courses, and the involvement of Confucius Institute should help developing the existing programmes further, and separate offerings would create an internal competition and turmoil. Of course, there was also consideration of financial interest. The language centre, as a fully self-financed unit of the university, ran an impressive operation in Chinese on a large scale, which it did not want to lose. The CI-A UK director was very proud about what had been achieved at a time when he was heading both Confucius Institute and the language centre with about 500 registrations per term, and some 1,500 in a year, making it the largest provision of its kind in Europe. However, this initial disagreement, to a certain extent, had overshadowed the collaboration and working relationship between the two partner universities and their first directors.

CI-B was also hosted in the language centre of another local university, but the language centre only had very limited Chinese courses with little expertise when the Confucius Institute set up on its premises. In a sense, it was the CI-B that first brought the Chinese language teaching on a large scale to the host university which clearly had the intention to develop Chinese language programmes. With regards to the course offerings, While CI-B and its courses had special target learners, those with business interest in China, it could not just confine its courses to so-called business Chinese, which was believed to start at a higher level or not to exist by some academics, so general Chinese language courses were also offered at the initial stage in conjunction with the Language Centre, just like CI-A. The interviews with the China and UK directors found that they were both happy about the courses that had been developed and offered at their CI-B-2, as the China director contently mentioned about the figure of some 200 registrations per term at the time of the interview after five to six years' development.

What the field study also found interesting was that both Confucius Institutes once offered courses in Cantonese, which is not what Confucius Institutes are supposed to teach. If CI-A's offer might have been related to the fact that the language centre it was affiliated to always had them, CI-B's offer seemed to have been completely motivated by the market demand and competition as even the course tutor was the same person who taught in CI-A. This is another example of how language policy and practices can be managed differently at the operation level, and competition did exist between Confucius Institutes, which also needs to be properly managed.

Generally speaking, the learners were happy with these courses, as shown in their responses to the specific question in the questionnaire survey on how the course had met their expectations in terms of the progress they had made. Seventy-one respondents gave a positive rating, with 39 for "very well" and 32 for "well"; 17 went for "OK", and there were only two "disappointed" respondents. There were many positive comments in the space provided, such as "1 have learned the basic skills of speaking and reading (from a beginner course)", "I am able to read and speak Chinese now", and "I can communicate with Chinese people in Chinese with confidence" (from intermediate classes). There was also an open question on their expectations of progress to be made through the course. Most beginners expected to learn basic conversational skills ("be able to get by when visiting my wife's family in China"—from a beginner course), while more advanced learners wished to consolidate or further develop their reading and speaking abilities ("can read and understand documents in Chinese and have discussions with Chinese colleagues"—from an advanced class). Some respondents said that they would have to put in more time or repeat the course as they had been too busy to work on the course.

Institutions were changing, and so was the provision. Shortly after the completion of the field study, CI-A was moved out of the language centre by the host university, along with the change of the Chinese partner university. Coincidently, the provision of the general Chinese courses was moved from CI-B to the language centre, so CI-B now only delivered business Chinese courses, focusing on corporate clients and learners. The impact that these changes had on the operation and development of the Confucius Institutes was enormous, even though it was not the whole story of the language policy which obviously also took place in the classrooms, as many scholars had previously argued (McCarty, 2011). This will be discussed and analysed in the next chapter.

Another area relevant to Chinese language teaching was courses for the teachers of Chinese, as it was widely agreed that lack of trained and experienced teachers presented obstacles that restrained Confucius Institutes from a healthy and rapid growth (Wan, 2009). *Hanban* also encouraged all Confucius Institutes to provide such courses. The CI-A UK director said that he had noticed the problem many years ago, as teaching Chinese in the UK was very different from teaching the language in China where most of his experienced and trained teachers had gathered their experiences or received their trainings. This was why he set up the first Chinese language teacher training programme in the country and started to develop teaching materials well before the Confucius Institute was set up. In his view, the concepts and ideas about learning and teaching mattered a great deal in deciding how to facilitate the learning, how to deliver the teaching, and what and how to facilitate and deliver. On the other hand, the CI-B China director, in his interview, seemed to be more focused on the content of the learning and teaching. This, to a certain extent, reflects different approaches in the education and training of Chinese language teachers.

First, it was clear that the Confucius Institutes' China and UK directors tended to have different beliefs and subsequently different approaches with regards to teacher training. Both Confucius Institute UK directors interviewed laid more stress on the importance of the learners in the language learning process, which was very much at the core of the learning and teaching in the UK, rather than on the language and culture even though they both agreed that the latter was also important. What the CI-A UK director thought of this has been mentioned in the previous section, and the CI-B UK director emphasised that "there will be no or little learning taking place if the teachers do not understand their learners and engage them in the learning process". By contrast, the Confucius Institute China directors had different understanding of who the best teachers of Chinese were and what was important in the teaching of Chinese. The CI-A UK director quoted his early China counterpart who reckoned that the teachers trained with teaching experience in China were "real" teaching professionals, so were the teaching materials developed there because

China was where the language was used, while teaching and teaching materials developed abroad were unavoidably somewhat amateurish, particularly in institutions without Chinese departments. The CI-B China Director (CI-B-2) had taught overseas briefly and he realised that teaching Chinese in Chinese departments was different from teaching Chinese as a non-major subject to "foreigner" (in his word) since these teachers would have different foci:

> Teachers from the Chinese department focus more on the research and the depth of the Chinese language, and they tend to think teaching Chinese to foreigners is an easy job. While the teachers teaching Chinese to foreigners tend to think that though the teachers in the Chinese department know a lot about the language, they may not have necessarily good teaching results as they are inexperienced in teaching Chinese to foreigners, which is definitely not an easy job.

His teaching experience overseas proved relevant in gaining this insight, but when it came to what was important to be a proficient and successful teacher of Chinese, he clearly believed that professional linguistic knowledge of the language was the key requirement:

> I think there are two things which are important to the language teaching, one is the linguistics knowledge of the language itself which is the key to the language teachers, and the other is teaching experience which you can accumulate in your teaching. Teaching methodology is important, but through teachers' training and practice, you can get them, the knowledge of Chinese itself cannot be got through intensive training. It requires longer term study. A teacher after three years teaching can master different teaching methodologies such as communicative, comparative and know the theories behind them such as behaviourism etc., but it is difficult for them to master the knowledge of Chinese language itself. This is something once you have missed, it is difficult to catch it up.

What was noticed quite prominent was his choice of words such as "foreigner" and "linguistic knowledge of Chinese". This was a clear example of the impact of *Duiwai Hanyu Jiaoxue* on him and many *Hanban* teachers. First, the word "foreigner" (*Waiguo ren*) is a term still widely used in China to refer to anyone from other countries. However, it rarely occurred to these colleagues from China that this time it was they who were "foreigners" in the UK. The emphasis of linguistic knowledge of Chinese was driven by the understanding in the Chinese cultural tradition of what teaching was—to transfer knowledge from teachers to their students, and thus a thorough grasp and understanding of the subject was critical. While this could certainly work in China, it could run into unexpected problems and challenges when transplanted in Confucius Institutes in London without appropriated heed to the learners.

As mentioned in the above section, the different concepts and understanding of what mattered most for teachers of Chinese were clearly demonstrated in the teacher training programmes that the two Confucius Institutes ran for both in-service and pre-service teachers. CI-A had relatively longer track record in running a range of such programmes, including both the formal and regular university credit bearing ones and informal short and sporadic ones with only Confucius Institute certificates. The guiding principles underpinning these programmes were the awareness of how adult learners learned foreign languages such as Chinese, how the teachers should assist them in their learning, and how to make the content relevant to what they needed. Thus, only limited linguistic knowledge was quoted in the programmes as examples to illustrate how this was done, with an emphasis on the cultivation of the ability with which the linguistic knowledge could be further developed through self-study. Therefore, one would see on CI-A training programme contents such as second language learning for adult learners; how the English speakers learn Chinese; contrastive analysis of Chinese and English; Chinese language as perceived by the English-speaking learners; teaching methodologies and teaching material development to meet the needs of the learners; and those standardised contents in usual teacher training programmes. The teacher training programmes run by CI-B, on the other hand, paid much more attention to the contents, especially the teaching of authentic Chinese language, such as the promoted standard pronunciation and intonation, recognising and writing Chinese characters, business vocabulary, and so on. These programmes were later termed as professional development programmes for teachers of business Chinese. Having said that, it should be pointed out that they also included some shared practices in the teaching of foreign languages, as the CI-B UK director was a German and English language specialist who saw value in getting the teaching of Chinese in line with the teaching of other languages in his language centre.

With regards to the approaches or methods of training, both Confucius Institutes used a mixture of what was called "localisation of teacher education and training", which means that the training was conducted locally and organised based on the local needs, and "professionalisation of the teachers of Chinese", which involves sending the teachers to attend various professional development programmes in Chinese universities sponsored by *Hanban*. In the first aspect and to start with, CI-A was far more active than CI-B. As its UK director had mentioned, it had recognised the significance and value in the development of Chinese language teaching in the UK, especially in schools where there would be a severe shortage of qualified and trained teachers. As a matter of fact, it was one of the initiating institutions for the well-known training programme for 1,000 teachers of Chinese later stamped and supported by the British and Chinese governments. CI-A remained to be partner of the grand teacher training programme till the departure of its UK director and its eventual relocation outside of the language centre.

The Teaching Materials

Closely associated with the question of courses is the question of Chinese language teaching materials. As part of its international Chinese strategy, *Hanban* had the intention to provide all the Confucius Institutes with what it termed as "recommended teaching materials". While this did help those Confucius Institutes that had no such resources, this was not regarded as necessary by CI-A since they had already developed quite a few teaching materials to meet their own needs, including the very first Linguaphone Chinese back in the early 1930s written by the famous Chinese writer Lao She and his British colleagues while he was teaching in the university. Therefore, the free textbooks supplied from *Hanban* were received with mixed feelings. Both Confucius Institutes' UK directors thanked *Hanban* for its generosity in providing teaching materials, but they also felt that some resources and support could have been made better use of if organised more efficiently. The CI-A UK director gave an example:

> Once I was informed by another Confucius Institute down the road that several dozens of boxes had been delivered to her office, but they were actually for my Confucius Institute from *Hanban*. So, I went down to have a look. There in the basement, boxes were piled up and I opened a few and found that they were books on China, Chinese culture and Chinese teaching materials. I was a bit stuck. We had no space in the Confucius Institute to store them. We could not complain as they were free gifts. This was not a one-off thing and it happened from time to time, which was really a waste. I think teaching materials for the overseas market should really be developed locally with the involvement of experts from China, rather than completely developed in China as it would be hard for them to figure out what the local needs are. Fortunately, *Hanban* is now supporting such initiatives.

For CI-B, the China Director (CI-B-1) did use the Chinese textbooks initially but soon found that "they were not adequate for the students in the types of the courses offered at our Confucius Institute". This led to the project of compiling their own teaching materials for their own courses, which was still ongoing at the time of this study, but the first draft had been completed. The CI-B UK director talked about how the teaching materials had been compiled and piloted in his interview:

> Our Confucius Institute has been engaged in the teaching material development for our courses because we hadn't been able to find any adequate textbooks from the existing titles published in China. This is a project led by our former China director with the support of *Hanban*. Many of our teachers are involved in the project, and we have been trying these new materials in class in the last year or so.

It was clear that such efforts to compile local teaching materials were greatly encouraged and supported by *Hanban*. But CI-A UK director expressed his concern during the interview about the quality of such teaching materials as not all the Confucius Institutes had adequate experience and expertise to be able to create good teaching materials. Moreover, as the researcher found during the ethnographic study of the two Confucius Institutes, there was no real collaboration going on between them. He said:

> There doesn't seem to be any coordinated work or collaboration between Confucius Institutes and each Confucius Institute is developing its own materials. This has resulted in waste of lot of useful resources because of the usage of such materials is mostly limited to its own use rather than shared. This is partly because each Confucius Institute is trying to do so to portray an image and claims that it is also developing local materials to meet the needs of its own learners.

Although both Confucius Institutes observed were using their own teaching materials, either compiled or selected and adapted, they were clearly at different stages of material development. CI-B was still piloting its teaching materials while CI-A was using a mixture of published teaching materials compiled by its own or others. The teaching materials supplied by *Hanban* were largely used as reference books in both Confucius Institutes. This signified a nearly full "localisation" in the use of teaching materials in the two Confucius Institutes, as it was clear that more variety in teaching procedures, innovations toward individual student's needs and more creativity in teaching techniques and language use Cunningworth (1995) were of critical importance in any efficient language teaching materials. The CI-B China Director (CI-B-1) said the following in his interview:

> Our Confucius Institute started to develop our own teaching materials for our courses about a year ago, because we found the textbooks from China were not suitable for our courses. This is a project that I am leading as its designer and editor, with financial support from

Hanban as a project of our Confucius Institute. Many of our teachers are also involved in the project. We also provide training for teachers on how to teach business Chinese and share with them this new teaching material.

The CI-A UK director, who was a Chinese language teaching specialist, talked about his views of the teaching materials supplied by *Hanban* and their story of the teaching material development in the interview:

> Language teaching materials should first have their students in mind when being developed. Most of the teaching materials provided by *Hanban* were developed for students from a wide range of language and cultural backgrounds. *Hanban* has put in a lot of resources to develop those books with the involvement of many top Chinese linguists and teachers. However, I do not believe such teaching materials can be used by all the students across the world. You may often hear such comments that "they are good, but we can't really use them here". At this institution, we always use the teaching materials developed by ourselves, and I would say this is the third generation of materials that I started to develop over ten years ago. There are many key features of our new teaching materials. It takes into consideration how English-speaking adults learn Chinese; the contents are relevant to the life of the students and dealt in small and manageable chunks, usually through speech patterns with few jargons; Chinese characters are present from the very beginning, and it follows a progression compatible with the local and European assessment norm as well as Chinese one, such as the CEFR and HSK.

As the two Confucius Institutes had different types of courses and different course structures, subsequently they had different approaches to the development of their teaching materials. For CI-A, its courses were structure grouped in four levels, beginners (A1-A2), lower intermediate (A2-B1), upper intermediate (B1-B2) and advanced (C1 and C1+), each level consisting of three terms over the course of a year. The first two level courses used the teaching materials that it had developed and first published in 2005, which was a winner of the Award for Outstanding International Chinese Language Teaching Materials in 2010 at the Fifth Confucius Institute Conference. The upper intermediate level courses used a set of textbooks with both simplified and traditional characters published in the US. The first two terms of advanced courses also used its own compiled materials adopted and selected from a range of authentic sources, while the materials for the last term were flexible in the sense that the themes were usually negotiated between the teacher and the students. On the other hand, CI-B was specialised in business Chinese and had its course structured in six levels: beginner, improver, lower intermediate,

intermediate, upper intermediate, and advanced, and each level lasted 20 weeks over the course of about six months, but one could only do one level in a year. Its new teaching materials consisted of six trial textbooks being developed and piloted concurrently by six different teachers, each book for one of the six designated levels. It was observed during the field study that the class teacher would hand out the teaching materials in class, usually one week before the lesson as the new materials were still being modified.

Different stages of material development were also reflected in the accuracy of the course descriptions in the two Confucius Institutes. All the classes in CI-A followed a given syllabus, and the referenced objectives were clearly defined and closely related to the content of the textbooks, for instance, number of characters and words. On the contrary, there was often a big gap between what was said in the course description and what appeared in the course book in CI-B, which would make the expected progress from one course to the subsequent higher level quite difficult, due to some huge gaps existing between the course materials in adjacent levels. Part of the problem was the absence of an overall plan and specifications which stipulated what should be included in each book, what progress each lesson would make, and how the six books would be organically interconnected as an integral part of the whole. For example, not only would the students of Book III find that the further reading and super link in Chinese were way beyond their ability, more difficult even than the subsequent books, they would also need far more language knowledge and inputs to deal with the main text than what they used in Book II. However, most of the students were new to the courses—72% in beginners' courses and 14% in intermediate and in advanced courses, respectively—many of whom only joined that term, so most of the students wouldn't have idea of what it was like in the previous term.

As far as the teaching materials for beginners' courses were concerned, both course materials reflected their purposes very well. However, their underlying approaches were different. The most striking difference between them being that CI-A's materials were more focused on getting the students to understand the essential aspects of the language and underpinning cultural bedrock while helping them to learn and use the language, while CI-B's materials were much more function oriented, aiming to equip the students with the language and cultural knowledge that they might need and use in various situations such as living and working in China. For example, when location word was taught, CI-A material would explain how this linguistic element reflected the way the Chinese perceived the world culturally, CI-B's simply treated it as a linguistic component that the students needed to remember in communication. Similarly, when learning about weather, the CI-A materials compared weather in the UK with somewhere in China, CI-B's just talked about the weather in Beijing where the students were supposed to go and work in the future. It was also interesting to note that three out of the four volumes of CI-A materials had their settings in the UK and Europe, while moving to China in the last book, but CI-B moved to China in its Book II with some of the scenario and contents in the previous volume already set in China. While the topics and contexts of the materials by both Confucius Institutes had their students in mind, CI-A had a more locally based intercultural approach to its material development while CI-B had a more function- and language-centred, cross-cultural approach, reflecting to a certain extent how each of the two Confucius Institutes understood and interpreted its mission and tasks as part of the general Confucius Institute initiative.

Finally, CI-A's materials would expose and expect the students to learn Chinese characters from the very beginning. The character-based textbooks were developed to meet the students' needs as a research result showed that students initially learned Pinyin only to find that they had to relearn the language again afterwards, as Pinyin was not the actual written form of Chinese language (Li, 2014). However, as stated by the authors of the textbook (Li and Zhang, 2009), the fact that the textbook is laden with characters does not necessarily mean that the students would have learned all the characters at one go—certainly not like how Chinese children would learn to read, through mechanical copying. Instead, the textbooks aimed to help the students to understand the structure of Chinese characters and the cultural perspective behind them, and then guided them gradually to change their habitual perception in learning European languages to see and read characters as Chinese people would. This approach seemed to be working well, as almost all students in CI-A can follow and read the textbooks being used, though the beginners in the first few sessions would find this quite challenging. The materials being developed by CI-B were also character based, as the teachers also believed that their students needed to learn to read. However, the teachers compiling the textbooks seemed very concerned that their students might not be able to read, therefore, all the main dialogues and texts from Book I to Book IV were annotated with Pinyin, while the rest, including additional reading, was all in characters, thus creating some undesirable disparities with the textbooks themselves.

Feedback From Students and Teachers on Teaching Materials

Generally speaking, the use of the locally developed teaching materials was well received by the students, as was confirmed in the student questionnaire and student interviews.

There were two questions in the questionnaire on teaching materials, with the first one being a choice question on what was used and the second one an open-ended question to seek more detailed and personal views on what they thought about the teaching materials being used. To the first question, a majority of the respondents (63%) was using a serial Chinese language textbook developed by staff in CI-A published first in 2005. This set of the textbooks were widely used in CI-A, from beginners to lower intermediate. Twenty-five per cent of respondents also reported that they were using other materials developed by their own institutions, mostly in CI-B, but also some in CI-A at higher levels. Eight per cent of respondents were using materials published overseas for non-beginner Chinese students in CI-A. Textbooks recommended by *Hanban* were not used, though they have been actively promoted and supported by *Hanban* as key materials for all Confucius Institutes. This showed clearly that even if there was central policy at the Confucius Institute headquarters on the use of teaching materials, the local Confucius Institutes can still choose what they think most suitable for them at their Confucius Institutes, so, the *Hanban* policy could not be enforced and *Hanban* has to heed to the local demands and requirements. That may explain why *Hanban* now is spending a lot of efforts promoting local teaching material development. In its 2013 Annual Report, *Hanban* mentioned that it had supported 18 Confucius Institutes in nine countries in their development of over 20 types of course materials totalling almost 150 volumes (Confucius Institute Annual Development Report, 2013c:5).

The responses to the open-ended question were very positive. This was especially true of the teaching material developed and used in CI-A, which were praised by almost all the respondents and many described the textbooks as "well structured", "easy to use", "contents useful", "well presented, easy to read and good background", and "excellent", with some being as specific as "very good, builds up useful words and concepts, so it feels like we are making progress all the time". Although CI-B was still piloting its own materials, the responses were quite warm and positive. "Relevant" and "useful" were descriptions of high frequency, with some being as specific: "It is very relevant to the course. It has given me a lot of information related to the business terms". Some respondents did mention that the content was a bit too difficult to follow, while others, mostly heritage students, found it fine.

Such positive responses were naturally echoed in the interviews with some students. For example, a respondent from an intermediate class in CI-A, who had learned Chinese a few times elsewhere, spoke very highly of the textbook he was using for the courses in the last years or so at the Institute:

> I have used some other Chinese textbooks, but none of them is as good as the one we have—clear, simple and easy to follow and you learn to speak and read with such an ease. Of course, my previous limited knowledge of Chinese helped me to read, as I know some of my classmates found the characters challenging at the very beginning.

But as we focus more on reading, oh I must say that our teacher loves to teach us how to write, I found it quite doable. My previous experiences showed that if you learn only Pinyin, you may soon get confused as so many Chinese words sound the same.

A student from beginner's class in CI-B made the following remark, both praising the material development efforts and complaining about the experiment nature of the efforts as well as the difficulty to learn how to read:

> I like what we learn in terms of the content. I also understand it is a project in progress. But having handouts every week doesn't give me any idea of the big picture, for example, how we can achieve what is said in the course information at the end of the course at this level. I also hope that they use fewer Chinese characters as this is not what I need nor have the time for. I am quite happy with verbal communication, though I also agree it is useful to learn a few characters, especially the most useful ones such as the sign for toilet, shops, and so on.

As the users of the teaching materials also include teachers, their feedback and views of the teaching materials are highly relevant and useful. The different approaches that the two Confucius Institutes had used in their teaching material development were also reflected in the way they had involved their teachers, and how their teachers regarded the teaching material. For CI-A, its UK director described as a top-down model, with the teaching material centrally planned but based upon the experience and research, then the teaching materials were piloted with feedback from both the students and teachers for several times before it went for print. This was partly because the university had accumulated a lot of experience with expertise in this area, as there had already been a couple of successful textbooks developed before. The following is what a locally employed teacher who had been teaching in the university for well over ten years said in her interview:

> As far as I can remember, we have always used the textbooks developed by our own university. During the time I am here, the one we are using is the third set of the teaching materials we developed, and even this one has already gone through three editions in the last few years. So, there is a constant effort for us to improve and revise our teaching materials, based upon the feedback from students and teachers.
>
> ...
>
> What we are doing is to identify bottlenecks that our students have when learning Chinese and then find ways to help them to get over

these learning obstacles. For example, the Chinese sentence order. Few of the Chinese textbooks can sort it out easily for our students, but based upon the differences between the English and Chinese, we can help students to learn the correct sentence order quite effortlessly as you can see in the textbooks we use.

With regards to what the teaching materials were like, the views as expressed by a very experienced teacher seconded from *Hanban* was quite representative. She had been teaching in CI-A for the past three years. She talked about her experience of using the current textbooks and their characteristics:

> I didn't think very much about the book when I first saw it. It seemed to be very simple and not comprehensive enough from the Chinese language point of view, as compared with most of the other textbooks I had used in the past seventeen years. You know my university is specialised in teaching Chinese to foreign students in China. Our teaching materials are used all over China and in the world. However, after two terms I came to see the strengths of this series. It is best suited to the type of students who study Chinese on such courses here. They are easy to comprehend, and easy to follow. It has clear focus on skills and close link between the language elements covered and Chinese culture. I don't think any materials I have used before could suit the students any better than this.

The other *Hanban* teacher in CI-A also shared a similar view and change of opinion over the time and said the following in her interview:

> When I first used this textbook, I felt a bit uneasy as it was quite different from textbooks developed in China. It seemed to me too simple, and the tasks of exercise were different too. After one year using of this book, I felt it excellent. Now I understand what is students' centred and what is the communicative, functional and cultural approach mean. This book is really prepared for the students with English mother toughen. The textbook uses students exiting linguistic knowledge and compare the speech patterns with English. The sceneries are in UK and the content is practical, so the students can use it immediately after the class.

CI-B approached its teaching materials very differently. The project was led by its former China director, who was a prominent Chinese linguist from the Chinese partner university. As their courses were for business Chinese, he felt that they should have their own teaching materials to reflect this feature. However, as he was very busy, travelling between China and UK on a regular basis, he could only give his overall idea and some direction during the development. Therefore, the way adopted was that a number of teachers were involved on a voluntary basis to draft one book each and pilot them in the classes. Feedback was collected and changes made in the following semester. As the timing was tight, the drafts and their revised versions were handed out only in a week before the lesson. One interviewee teacher said about his experience regarding the need for developing their own textbooks as well as the process of doing this:

> Few of our local teachers were trained as language teachers, so we all rely heavily on textbooks. We used several textbooks published in China before. They may be good for the students in China but none of them was suitable for our students. So, the Confucius Institute finally decided to develop its own materials, which is really hard work, much more difficult than I expected. Fortunately, we have our China director and he is a Chinese language specialist. We have a large team, with six teachers, including half from other universities. We also have some funding from *Hanban*. This is the second year now, and we are experimenting and revising the drafts. We hope to publish it in the future. It still has a lot of problems, but we feel it is our own baby, and we should make sure that it grows up healthily.

One *Hanban* teacher came and joined the CI-B recently from its Chinese partner university. She would stay and teach on a two-year contract. She talked about the need and her involvement in compiling the local teaching materials for their students in the interview:

> I was told that I would be helping with the material development. But this project is nothing like any of what I did before. The lead teacher I am working with has compiled draft lessons that is supposed to cover the language, business related and other necessary skills, but also needed to make sure that it is not too easy or too difficult for the students. As the courses have very limited time, we can't include all the key language elements, at least not in the same way as we would like to include in the textbooks compiled in China. In the Confucius Institute, we need to care more about what the students want. Sometimes I feel awful when I see the face of the students who have difficulty to follow our draft lessons. But overall, the teaching materials are OK with the students. This is what I've learned from other teachers too.

Other Activities and Sustainability

Other Activities at the Confucius Institutes

In addition to Chinese language courses, Confucius Institutes were also expected to organise other activities and events, either to support language learning and teaching or to promote the understanding of Chinese culture. The two Confucius Institutes here were no exceptions. Yet, it was interesting to find that they differed from each other in either how they organised similar activities or what different activities they each organised.

A similar event that both Confucius Institutes organised each year was the Chinese New Year party. However, the two Confucius Institutes did it differently. For CI-A, it was usually an open event of celebration by, for, and of its own teachers and students who prepared and performed at the party on campus. The Confucius Institute would each year invite some external guests and provide some Chinese food and drinks to mark the special occasion. One year, as its UK director recalled, the CI-A even organised the celebration with a Chinese restaurant in the countryside, which not only had a theatre adjacent to the restaurant, but also invited a visiting troupe of professional acrobatic performers from China to join the celebration. By contrast, CI-B tended to organise the celebration differently. It was more of a show for its teachers and students with invited performers from outside the institute, with participation of its own teachers and students sometimes.

Another thing that both Confucius Institutes did was the administration of *Hanban* scholarships, which was created as a measure of incentive to encourage learners to continue with their study of the Chinese language and culture. However, according to the two UK directors, it was good to have the scholarships, but the administration had much room to be improved. Not only was the time framework far too tight—it was usually a last-minute rush—but also the requirement that the learners must be registered on Confucius Institutes courses made it hard to find most suitable for the scholarships. For instance most of those registered on CI-A courses were professionals who did not have the time to join a summer course in China, especially when notified so late. Therefore, scholarships were not fully utilised by the most needed and suitable, with interested learners and their teachers from other institutions feeling quite frustrated at the waste of such good opportunities and resources.

Related to this was the administration of required *Hanyu Shuiping Kaoshi* (HSK) for the scholarship, which now most Confucius Institutes organised. Historically, CI-A and the language centre had offered this for a long time while CI-B was relatively new, and more for its specific audience, Business Chinese Test (BCT). Neither of them had offered Youth Chinese Test (YCT) yet as they were not involved in teaching in schools. Because of its workload and low take-ups, the test was taken only once a year. The number of people taking the test increased in the recent years, mostly in the lower bands of the test, due to the efforts that Confucius Institutes had put it. The test was taken as one of their performance indicators and the scholarship incentive from the headquarters. The simplification of the test made it much more accessible to learners though the references of the test levels to the CEFR remained controversial.

In terms of cultural activities, both Confucius Institutes organised public lectures on China or other related topics as part of cultural activities. These activities were very closely related to the focus of the two Confucius Institutes, with CI-A's more on culture in general, including arts, history, literature, travels, and CI-B's more on business and economic development, partly utilising the internal expertise and resources of the host university. Such events were usually free, and attendance varied. There were also other relevant activities that the Confucius Institutes organised. For instance, CI-A ran a weekly Chinese Corner for the very start of its set-up, staffed to provide platform to meet and speak and to facilitate the learning of Chinese for all. Many other Confucius Institutes modelled theirs on this practice. Nearly all these cultural and language support activities and events were free to attend. CI-A, along with the language centre, was also responsible for organising on its campus the annual university Chinese Bridge competition for many years before it was taken over by the *Hanban* UK Office. The university Chinese Bridge competition is supposed an event for all the university students, but it now appears dominated by Confucius Institutes, from the participants to the panel judges, from the introduction to the competition to the concluding marks, as if all the Chinese teaching in the UK are done by Confucius Institutes and all the contestants are from Confucius Institutes. As most Confucius Institutes only involved in non-credit courses, the contestants are mainly from the degree programmes in the host university where Confucius Institutes locate. Some Confucius Institutes do assign a teacher to supervise the contestants, but that is not the situation for the two case Confucius Institutes. The interview confirmed that the academic departments organised and supervised their own students themselves.

There are also culture visit trips to China for which the participants only need to pay their international airfare, with the remaining costs covered by Confucius Institutes Headquarters. The CI-B UK executive director confirmed that they could send up to two delegates each year to visit China, one for the students and one for the university management or local industries. This was a relative new policy, and the financial supports from *Hanban* were quite generous. But not all students could afford their international airfare, and often some could not find time since the notice was usually quite late. As a result, the CI-B UK executive director said sometimes they called for students from other institutions to join as the students' delegate. This would be more difficult now, as *Hanban* policy requires participants to have been registered with their Confucius Institute for at least two semesters. There were participants who did not meet the requirement joined travel group in some Confucius Institutes, just as some candidates representing certain Confucius Institutes in the Chinese Bridge Competition were not really "the product" of these Confucius Institutes.

Development and Sustainability

It was clear that *Hanban* had long-term plan for Confucius Institutes, with promised resources commitment. For sustainable development, individual Confucius Institutes needed to make sure that they developed products and services that met the local needs and demands as well as generate enough income to ensure the financial security of the institutes and their operations.

The study found that the collaborative model of Confucius Institutes had contributed to or impacted on the change in *Hanban*'s Chinese language policy—from initially a centralised promotional campaign to the current one encouraging localisation. As a result, the two Confucius Institutes had their own say in deciding the types of courses they planned to run, the kinds of teaching materials they would like to use, what teacher training programmes to organise, and what assessment they wished to employ, thus localisation was self-evident. As Confucius Institutes spread all over, their actual development, operation, management, and future would naturally be affected by the influence of the host institution, the local demands for the Chinese language teaching provision, and the individual managers concerned.

But even with adequate courses and materials, sustainable development of Confucius Institutes would ultimately depend on their financial revenue and its stability. For both Confucius Institutes, a most important income stream was their language courses. Yet pricing in expensive and competitive London was not easy, where there had been some formidable growth in the provision of Chinese language learning, including six Confucius Institutes, the highest number in a single city in the world. It was apparent from the interviews with the directors that they all thought their courses were rightly priced, for students and for the institute. CI-B's courses used to be lower than the market rate, but in the recent years, the price was gradually hiking up, now on par with all other similar providers. The cost of the Chinese language courses was certainly a major consideration for many learners. In responding to the question of course price in the survey, about half of the respondents (46, or 48%) thought the courses were too expensive, and particularly those who were on non-beginner courses in CI-A where course prices were tiered in line with the level of the courses, and advanced courses charged considerably more than the ab initio courses. Thirty-four respondents felt that the course fees were reasonable, but quite a few of them were students (26%) who enjoyed a discount, and some were registered in CI-B courses which had a simple one-layer fee structure regardless of the levels.

Both Confucius Institutes seemed to have generated enough to keep the operation going, but there were expenses unaccounted for in the balance sheet of the institute, particularly the human resources supplied by *Hanban*, such as the cost of seconded teachers and volunteers as well as all the project-based operation funding. The CI-A UK director was adamant that his institute could run all the language courses with their own teachers, and only the additional activities would be affected without the *Hanban* fund. For CI-B, which relied heavily on the seconded teachers from China, it would be difficult without that support.

Challenges

The study of the two Confucius Institutes found four major challenges facing their future sustainable development: (1) contradiction between the form of joint venture and disparities in agenda and commitments of the partner universities; (2) the imbalance and disparities in the workload between the directors appointed by the partner universities; (3) tension within and between Confucius Institutes; and above all, (4) disparity between the true operating costs and the income Confucius Institutes were able to generate through its courses and services, i.e. the financial security for the future of Confucius Institutes.

The two host universities were selected because of their reputation in the British higher education sector. But the famous universities had their own agendas and Confucius Institute might not be a top priority; this was evident from their relatively low publicity and visibility in their host universities. The reputation and expertise of the British partner institutions might not always guarantee an expected devotion that the Chinese partner institutions had hoped for. If looked at from the perspective of language management, actual language policy and practices are the result of the consultation and negotiation between the partner universities which had different intention, interest, commitment, and dedication, but ultimately of the daily operations managed by the directors appointed by the partner universities. While all were interested in the facilitation of the learning and teaching of Chinese, the grand goal of international Chinese cherished by the Chinese partners and that of teaching Chinese as a foreign language seen by the host universities would lead to clashes from time to time, manifested in the daily routine management by the appointed directors, exacerbated by different levels of commitment and input, lack of effective and timely communications between partners (as council meeting happens annually), and above all the disparities between the UK and Chinese directors who acted and managed on behalf of their universities.

Confucius Institute as a joint venture meant that individual directors appointed by the partner universities had a huge responsibility in the joint management of the institute, which posed a potential problem with regards to the directors appointed by the partner universities in at least three aspects: their different background and experience, their imbalanced workload, and incompatible terms, with frequent turnover of the Chinese directors. Both Confucius Institutes' initial directors were language professionals, but still with drastically varied experience in teaching and management, especially with regards to teaching Chinese in a non-Chinese but multilingual and multicultural environment. Both local universities appointed a senior managerial staff as the UK director, but in the case of the CI-A director, it was without time allocation or remuneration. This meant that he had to manage the joint venture over and above his "normal" work as the director of the language centre in the host university. A full-time China director and part-time UK director mix was a real issue, as it might give the impression that the host university and its seconded directors were not fully committed to the institute. The relatively short-term service of a Chinese director could also adversely affect the continuity of the work, and the synergies and understanding established between the local directors. The frequent turnover of the Chinese directors also meant that they could bring with them varied experiences, personalities, skill sets, and agendas entrusted by Chinese partners, adding more strain on the delicate management relationship in the Confucius Institute and between the partner institutions.

Another challenge that the study found was internally tensions within the Confucius Institutes and in the host universities. Teachers and volunteers sent by *Hanban* were a great support to the teaching of Chinese language in the Confucius Institutes and its host university, but this had to be managed carefully, as in the case of local part-time teachers in CI-A who saw colleagues seconded from China as potential competitors for work. These two groups of teachers often differed in their concept and approach in teaching Chinese as well. The host university of CI-A welcomed *Hanban* teachers as they could help teaching on other programmes, thus reducing the university staff cost. It remains to be seen how *Hanban* and Chinese partner would react to this as the university had not only excluded its Confucius Institute from any direct involvement in its academic programmes, but also subsequently moved it out of the language centre altogether, leaving the Confucius Institute in the position of just helping the academic teaching in the Chinese department but without any courses of its own. For CI-B, they had to "hand over" their general Chinese courses to the university language centre and confined itself to teaching business Chinese courses only, as both host university did not want to foster internal competition from Confucius Institutes with the course supplied by their language centres.

Externally, there was lack of cooperation and synergies between the two Confucius Institutes in their efforts, as both developed their own teaching materials and ran their own professional and teacher training programmes with a false belief that their audience was different. They were in fact more like competitors partly because of their closeness in distance and sharing pretty much a similar audience pool for Chinese language and cultural activities. For example, CI-A had a corporate client for over two years, and it later switched to CI-B because of its more favourable rate. The UK director of CI-A said:

> We were shocked to learn the news. Well, *Hanban*'s strategic policy is to collaborate with reputable universities, and more geographical

> coverage. But our two Confucius Institutes are almost next to each other; they share the common potential students. We had a large in-company teaching operation for business people and always run advanced evening Chinese classes in business and law. Since the establishment of Confucius Institute B, we have lost major sponsors, who are now on their board, with reduction as much as 50% of our students on those courses.

He had anticipated the problem much earlier and helped to organise a UK Confucius Institute Forum where all the Confucius Institute directors could meet regularly and discuss how they could collaborate and avoid possible conflicts.

> We did meet in the first couple of years when the number of Confucius Institutes was small and everyone found it very helpful and useful. Then it gradually faded away and now with over twenty Confucius Institutes in the country, meetings may become difficult to organise. Having said that, all except one Confucius Institute in London are constituent colleges of the University of London and some of them are very close to each other. So, it is not difficult to imagine the unspoken competition even though few talk about it openly. If you look closely, you cannot find real collaborative work between any Confucius Institutes in a region or in the country.

So the rivalry was real. Both Confucius Institutes needed to do all required to show their engagement and to fight for their survival on two fronts as far as finance was concerned, income and cost-effectiveness in the use of the resources available. The fact that *Hanban* has become an open supporter of local initiatives signified a change in its strategy, but the single promotion effort by the government would require far more resources input and how to effectively use and monitor them (Zhang and Liu, 2006; Wu, 2013).

Both Confucius Institutes seemed to generate enough income through their Chinese language services to cover their teaching operation cost. The study interviewed the directors and asked them where their most allocated funds from *Hanban* were spent. The answers were almost unanimous and much of that budget went on running cultural activities and developmental work such as assisting with teacher training and helping schools with their Chinese language and culture activities. The CI-A UK director confirmed:

> We ran a series of subsidised courses or activities on Chinese calligraphy, Taiji, music and had regular Chinese film show and language activities which we all had to pay. We saw them useful activities to help the participants, some of whom were not our students, to gain a better understanding of China, the Chinese language and culture.

> We also held regular teacher workshops, and they were open to all teachers without charge, a platform for the teachers to meet and discuss issues of concern and to keep up with the development in the field. Theses workshops were often led by experienced teaching professionals. There were also regular cultural activities a few times a year and one year, we staged a Chinese New Year celebration with a local Chinese community in a big restaurant in rural Cambridge with quizzes, traditional Chinese performance and delicious Chinese food. It was well attended as such activities were rare in that part of the country while London was crowded with similar activities.

However, there was often a gap between language teaching and cultural activities that the Confucius Institutes organised as shown in the reply to the question in the survey on attending events organised by Confucius Institutes. Well over half of the respondents (56 in total) said that they had not been to any, and 15 claimed that they had not heard of such events and if had been told that they could attend. However, nine respondents replied that they had participated in such events and most of them found these events "good" or "helpful". The typical responses of non-attendance were "I do not know but I would welcome them" and "not aware, and only aware of the Confucius Institute a month ago". However, most of those who were informed but had not attended such events were largely due to their time constraint, typically response was "I'd like to, but couldn't as I don't have time". The fact that a very small number of the respondents (under 10%) had used opportunities to experience Chinese culture offered by the Confucius Institutes revealed a low-level utilisation of the resource, as the UK executive director of CI-B said:

> We have noticed this problem for a long time as some of the activities we organised hardly had any participants, even though they said that they wanted this. For example, the Chinese film show. In the last three months, the bi-weekly film shows only had handful attendants. But we have to hire the venue and arrange staff for this, and such number cannot justify the cost of the activities. The dilemma is what we do about it in the future, as the cost can be a problem in the future.

The troublesome administration of Confucius Institute scholarships was also example of cost-effective problems. CI-B UK director commented in his interview:

> It is really good of *Hanban* to support students to study in China. But such things need to be planned and there should be clear criteria for selection procedure. You won't get many students if you only give us a couple of weeks' notice as most students plan their activities way

ahead of time. Therefore, sometimes scholarships were handed out to almost anyone and everyone but those who really should have them, which doesn't put our Confucius Institute work in good light either.

Undoubtedly, such cultural events and scholarship all cost money but would help learning and teaching of Chinese language achieve more effective and fruitful results if carefully designed and organised. The cost of running cultural activities was not a problem unique to Confucius Institute, but also for other similar international language and cultural promotion organisations such as British Council, Goethe-Institut and Alliance Française. It was precisely for these reasons that those organisations ran language courses to generate income to support the cultural activities, and they often had separate budget lines like Alliance Française does. But British Council was much more sophisticated in organising its cultural activities, often in conjunction with commercial agents or local partners to increase the leverage of the limited government funding. In fact, the overall financial sustainability remained a question for both Confucius Institutes, CI-A in particular, which did not seem to have any of its own income source but *Hanban* now. As far as the financial operation was concerned, few other similar organisations could achieve the similar efficiency as British Council by generating nearly 80% of its total income through its own activities in the last couple of years.

Summary

The field study of the two Confucius Institutes at the institute level showed, as Spolsky suggested in his language management theory, that the involvement of various university partners and their appointed directors to the Confucius Institutes and the joint management of the institutes meant that the different intentions and interest of the partner institutions did play a role in the forming of the actual language policy and practices in the Confucius Institutes via their courses and other related activities. In the case of the two Confucius Institutes studied here, the disparities in the original institutional intentions were reflected in almost all the aspects of the institutes concerning the learning and teaching of Chinese languages.

The disparities in the original intentions were first reflected in potential conflict of interest, such as who should run the language courses, the local host university or the joint venture; what types of courses that the joint venture should put up, and what materials to be used and so on. The problems did not seem to have gone away with either the case Confucius Institutes with the recent move that both Confucius Institute had out of the original hosting language centre. In the case of CI-B, all the partners' interest seemed to have been taken care of, but this could hardly be said of CI-A. While it seemed to have continued its support for Chinese language teaching on some academic programmes, it would remain as a question regarding what the Chinese partners reckoned they were getting out of this joint venture, as there was hardly any tangible return for all their financial and human resources input.

Different experiences in the provision of Chinese language between the two host universities and the two UK directors also determined that they differed from each other in a quite significant way when managing Chinese language courses. In fact, the two Confucius Institutes were typical in a sense that CI-A represented one extreme scenario where the local host university had taught Chinese for over 60 years, while CI-B represented another extreme scenario with little experience in teaching Chinese before the joint venture was set up. As the study shows, these differences might help set the tone for the working relationship between China and UK directors of the two Confucius Institutes. Clearly it would have been useful if the China directors had had similar background or experience, or at least gone through some practical briefing and training before their posting, which was now a standard procedure that *Hanban* had set up for all the new China directors, another very helpful adaption that *Hanban* had made through the experiences of the joint venture over the last decade, though more attention was needed in intercultural communication skills.

The study also found little or no real coordination and collaboration between Confucius Institutes, resulting in the under-utilisation of the resources available and causing concern for the long-term sustainability of Confucius Institutes. The study could not find any evidence of significant collaboration between the two Confucius Institutes in teaching Chinese, from the course design and course development, teaching material development, to course delivery, activity, or project organisations, including those concerning research of any sorts as one would expect from them as members of a large Confucius Institute family. On the contrary, there was an unspoken competition among them for the local market, just like their host universities. Although the two UK directors knew each other for many years and got on very well, they did not have any plan or intention for long-term win-win collaboration. Therefore, it was observed that there were a lot of duplicated activities and efforts between the two Confucius Institutes, even though they were quite close to each other. As a matter of fact, this was very much the case with the whole of Confucius Institutes in London and in the UK. The CI-A UK director did suggest setting up a Confucius Institute Forum UK in the early years for all the Confucius Institutes in the country to meet, support and work together, but it only ran a couple of years and was then gradually fading out. This may be because all the Confucius Institutes in the same geographical area, like the two Confucius Institutes in this study, were rivals at the end of the day, for they served very much the same target learners interested in learning Chinese language and Chinese culture.

While income was a challenge itself, the study found two areas of ineffective use of the available resources. One was the printed teaching materials sent over by *Hanban*. Neither of the Confucius Institutes used them as their course books, largely because these materials designed, produced, and used in China could not quite meet the learning needs of the courses designed for the local participants. The other area was the low attendance of many activities, usually poorly linked to Chinese language teaching, making these activities extremely uneconomical, and it did not look likely that they would continue for very long if this situation was not going to change unless *Hanban* funding would continue without any heed for the actual effectiveness of such activities.

The intention, understanding, and commitment of the troika partner institutions of the Confucius Institutes affected the subsequent planning and management of teaching activities in the joint Confucius Institutes. They also provided the context and environment for the Confucius Institutes to interpret and implement *Hanban*'s language policies and put them into practice which "fused" all the relevant input from all partners and particularly directors at the institute level. However, the real interpretation and implementation of the newly fused policies occur in the classrooms where the teaching and learning take place, which in turn very much depended on the perceptions and delivery of the teachers and the motivation and learning of the course participants.

6 Language Management at Confucius Institute Classroom Level

This chapter reports major findings of what was observed as learning and teaching in the classrooms of the two Confucius Institutes in conjunction with the relevant data collected through the questionnaire survey and interviews of the field study. It will also analyse and discuss these findings in the light of language management theory that stresses the critical role of the participating "agents" in the practice and process of micro language planning as advocated by scholars such as Jernudd and Neustupný and more recently theorised by Spolsky.

As far as the language practice in the classrooms is concerned, teachers are the main operational agent of language policy (Ricento and Hornberger, 1996). However, students, as the indispensable participants of the process, were the collaborative partners who created the actual policy with their teachers, through their actions in the learning of the language rather than merely being the passive receptive learners as perceived in the traditional language planning studies. So ethnographic observations in the classrooms focused on the three key words starting with "T" for teaching methodologies, teachers, and teaching materials, and one key word starting with "S" for students. The analyses and discussions will look into the beliefs and thinking behind the observed teaching and learning practices, supported with the data collected via the student questionnaire and different interviews.

The chapter consists of four sections. The first section reports on the observed teaching and teaching methodologies in the classrooms as well as teachers and their beliefs. It also examines differences, if any, between the local and *Hanban* teachers. The next section focuses on students, including Chinese heritage students in terms of their motivation to learn Chinese, their classroom performance, and their expectations of the courses. The following section examines assessment, another key area of interest and importance in the teaching and learning of Chinese language, including the forms of assessments, the purposes of the assessments, and their link and reference with external frameworks of standards. The final section sums up what the chapter covers before moving to the last and final concluding chapter.

Teaching and Teachers

Of the classes observed, all the teachers appeared to be confident and experienced in their classrooms: very open and amicable with their students, giving them enough time and communicative tasks to practise the authentic language, particularly in speaking and interacting with one another, and with a variety of exercise forms such as pair work, group work, role play, project, and so on. While all teachers were first and foremost individuals, there seemed to be some identifiable patterns between the teachers recruited locally and seconded from China across both Confucius Institutes. What seemed to be lacking in most of the teachers observed was the possible application of the available technologies in their teaching, apart from a few who made use of simple PowerPoint slides and video clips. It was also observed that *Hanban* teachers were usually well equipped with knowledge of the Chinese language and often better prepared for their lessons, while the local teachers seemed to be more flexible in attending their students' needs or demands, giving them a lot of encouragement. However, with regards to how observed teachers were teaching and why they behaved the way they did in "practising the language policy" in their classroom, some interesting observations are reported below, with analyses, concerning the teachers of the two mentioned groups: those seconded from China and those employed locally.

Teacher and Student Distance

The first and foremost observation in the classrooms of both Confucius Institutes was that many teachers, particularly those seconded from China, perceived their roles primarily as a "teacher" in the sense of the Chinese tradition—to teach by departing knowledge, and to foster by giving their full attention and care, just like a caring Chinese parent as the Chinese tradition would expect them to. Although there was a varying degree to which this attitude and behaviour were displayed as some teachers had taught abroad before, the influence of the Chinese tradition in teaching could still be easily identified in many of the classes observed. Here are a couple of examples.

Observation excerpt 1: A *Hanban* teacher in her late twenties was teaching a beginner class in CI-B. It was the second week of the term, and after revising what had been learned in the previous week, such as simple greeting in Chinese (*nihao*), one's surname *xing* (to be surnamed) and full name *jiao* (to be called), and *Zhongguo ren* (Chinese), *Yingguo ren* (English), she went on to talk about one's profession, with the new vocabulary in this lesson, like *laoshi* (teacher), *xuésheng* (student) and *tóngxué* (fellow student). She started to give a self-introduction.

Teacher: *Lǎoshi* [pointing to herself]. *Wǒ shì lǎoshi* [I am a teacher].
Wǒ xìng Wáng [My family name is Wang]. *Wǒ shì Wang Lǎoshi* [I am Teacher Wang]. *Wǒ búshì xuésheng* [I am not a student].
[Approaching a student.] *Nǐ shì xuésheng* [You are a student]. [Pointing to herself again.] *Wǒ shì lǎoshi* [I am a teacher]. *Wǒ xìng Wáng*
[My family name is Wang]. *Wǒ shì Wang Lǎoshi, nǐ ne?* [I am Teacher Wang. And you?]

Student: *Wǒ shì xuésheng* [I am a student]. *Wǒ búshì lǎoshi* [I am not a teacher]. *Wǒ xìng Brown* [My family name is Brown]. *Wǒ shì Brown xuésheng* [I am student Brown].

Teacher: Very good. But no, we don't say Brown student in Chinese. Student cannot use as a title, student doesn't start with surname, because it is not really a profession, but you can use surname before *tóngxué* meaning fellow students, like *Brown Tóngxué, Philips Tóngxué* [pointing to another student], as I can call you or you call each other. So, what would you say about yourself [pointing back to Brown]?

Student: *Wǒ xing Brown* [My family name is Brown]. *Wǒ shì Brown tóngxué* [I am student, Brown].

Teacher: Very good. In China, students would greet their teacher at the beginning of the class, like "*Nín hǎo, Wáng Lǎoshi*", or simply, "*Wáng Lǎoshi hǎo!*" So next time when we meet, you could say "*Wáng Lǎoshi hǎo*". Say after me. "*Wáng lǎoshi hǎo!*"

[The class repeated after her]

Teacher: *Tongxuémen hǎo! Nǐmen hǎo!* You must have noticed, I use "*men*" here....

...

Teacher: Very good. So, if you have any questions in the future, please raise your hand and *jiào wǒ* (call me) *Wáng Lǎoshi* ...

It was a real demonstration in the use of new vocabulary and to teach authentic language and Chinese culture. The teacher subconsciously or consciously introduced and reinforced the teacher-student hierarchical relationship typical in Chinese cultural environment and education system. By teaching the three words of *laoshi, xuésheng, tóngxué* and their usages, she sent a clear signal to the class about their different identities in class. Moreover, she went on to reinforce this by introducing the typical way of mutual greeting at the beginning of class in most Chinese schools and universities, and suggested that anyone in the class needed to raise their hand to request to speak and address her as "teacher". The teacher was later interviewed and asked about this. She said:

> I think it is important that the students learn something about the Chinese culture when they learn the language. It is important in Chinese culture that students should respect the teacher. Besides, I need to set up some ground rules of the class. This is what all the Chinese teachers would do in a classroom, I think.

What she was conscientiously trying to establish was a Chinese student-teacher "power" relationship. Many British schools may also do that, but it is far less common in adult learning environment such as in universities. For the native speaking teachers of Chinese, such "Chinese teacher talk" did not appear to be an isolated case, and the following was observed in an advanced class with a *Hanban* teacher, also in CI-B.

Observation excerpt 2: A young *Hanban* teacher in her early thirties was teaching an advanced Chinese evening course with five students present when the course started. A couple of others turned up in the next ten minutes or so. The students were supposed to give their individual presentation in front of the class, a project work assigned by the teacher in the previous week. After one student finished her presentation, there was a pause of about half a minute and no one came forward to do the presentation, the teacher said,

Teacher: Next student. Be brave. . . . I'll *diǎnmíng* (make a roll call). [Still silence from the class]
Teacher: Too quiet, *tóngxuémen*. X *Tóngxué*, Y *Tóngxué* (the two heritage students showed apologetic look, but no action). It is your turn next.
Teacher: A *Tóngxué*? [The teacher approached Student A as he sat there with his head bent low.]
Student A: [Raising his head] *I need to think about it.*
Teacher: You should have all been ready for this. Be brave. OK, B, nevertheless, you are brave. You do it.

[Student B came forward and gave her presentation on a film she had recently watched.]
[A few students entered the classroom at that time, smiling at the teacher. She smiled back and said: "sit down".]

Teacher: B *Tóngxué* presented very well. Do you have any questions to ask her?
[One student asked a question, which Student B answered.]

Teacher: Any more questions, *tóngxuémen*? [Then toward one:] C, what about you? Oh, yes. We have three new *tóngxué* today. [Turning towards them.] Can you introduce yourselves?
[The three new students gave a brief introduction about themselves.]

Teacher: OK, let's welcome new *tóngxué*.
[The students didn't seem to be sure what to do.]

Teacher: [To the three new students:] about what B *Tóngxué* talked just now, do you have any questions? Do you want to think it over too? [Turning towards Student A again.] You have been thinking about it for quite a long time, you ask questions next, right? [Student A was shaking his head, appearing to be a bit embarrassed.]

Teacher: OK. Come on, next *tóngxué*, who volunteers? We will *biǎoyáng* [praise] D *Tóngxué*. Excellent! You do it. Your PPT is at the desktop.
[Student D gave her presentation on an article she had read a few days ago.]

Teacher: Very good. D *Tongxué* had a good preparation. We should *biǎoyáng* her. And we have, have E *Tóngxué*, who also had a very very good preparation, sent me the PPT and I put it at the desktop. Especially F *Tóngxué,* she was doing homework at lunch time yesterday. We should praise her. . . . If you are so serious next time, I will put it at the desktop for you.

In this instance, one couldn't help observing her use of the term *tóngxué* to set off her "status" as a teacher, and the word *biaoyang* (praise in public) if anyone in the class followed her instruction, or the word *dianming* (call upon a class member) if the class did not to indicate her "power" as the instructor. She did praise a couple of students, as was observed. Getting people to speak or to write out new words on the board from memory in front of the class were also observed in her class. All this illustrated clearly this teacher's behaviour trying to maintain a formal teacher-student relationship or transplanting some Chinese classroom practice into the Confucius Institute classroom. By comparison, most local teachers were much less formal: addressing the students by their first name, asking them to write on piece of paper, or calling for volunteers to come forward to write on the board rather than calling on someone by name as this might "embarrass those who are unprepared in front of others", as a local teacher in CI-A explained in her interview.

Standard Language and Linguistic Perfection

In addition to the above, this study also found such proof regarding teachers' attitude to the Chinese language and their expectations of their students. Both Confucius Institutes taught Putonghua, and all the observed and interviewed teachers were native speakers. While all were proud of the language they were teaching, the teachers seconded from *Hanban* took the pronunciation and tones much more seriously than the locally employed teachers, and spent a great deal of time drilling and correcting their students.

Observation excerpt 3: It was a beginners' class in CI-B taught by a *Hanban* teacher. The teacher was introducing Pinyin. She was trying very hard to demonstrate, with examples, how to pronounce some individual sounds and get the students to be able to pronounce Pinyin correctly:

Teacher: *Zh-ang*, please read after me. *Zhāng*. [She wrote it on the board.]
Students: *Zhāng*.
Teacher: *Zhang* is a family name in China. *Zh-ong*. Please read after me, *Zhōng*.
Students: *Zhōng*.
Teacher: *Zhōng* can mean many things in Chinese. [She wrote it on the board, below *Zhāng*.] *Zhōng* is middle, like in *Zhōngguó* [wrote it behind *Zhōng*], it means China, middle kingdom, so *guó* means?
[One student said country or state.]
Teacher: Correct. *Zhōng* can also mean clock. *Zhōng*. Let's read together. *Zhōng, Zhōngguó*.
Students: *Zhōng, Zhōngguó*.
Teacher: Now, you have to pay attention to *zh* sound. En . . . It is a retroflex initial, and you need to curl your tongue, *zh . . . zh . . . zh . . . Zhāng, Zhōng*. Very good. Now read after me. *Zhāng, Zhāng kāi . . . Zhāng kāi* means open, like *Zhāng kāi* your mouth. *Zhōng, Zhōngguó*, China. *Zhōngguó* [the class read after her]. Excellent! Now let's read one by one. Let's start from here [pointing to a student on her left].
Student 1: *Zhāng, Zhāng kāi, Zhōng, Zhōngguó*.
Teacher: Very good, *Hěn hǎo. Hao* is good as in *Nǐ hǎo, hen* is very. So *hěn hǎo* is very good. Next [pointing to the next student].
Student 2: *Zhāng, Zhāng kāi, Zhōng, Z Zhōngguó*.
Teacher: Good, but your *zh* sound is not quite right. You have to pronounce *zh* like *Zh-ang, Zhāng, Zh-ong, Zhōng*. . .
Student 2: [A middle aged male student tries after her:] *Zh-ang, Zhāng, Zh-ong, Zhōng*.
Teacher: That is better, but still sounds a bit like English *z-ang*. Your tongue is too . . . front, pull it back, like this *Zhāng . . . Zhōng* [she pointed to the writings on the board and inviting S1 to say again].

Student 1: [Appeared a bit embarrassed and uneasy.] Me again? Zh— Zhāng, Zhāng kāi, Zhōng, Zhōngguó.
Teacher: Better, still not quite. You know it is important to get the pronunciation right in Chinese because we have many words; their pronunciations are the same or similar. People will misunderstand you if you don't pronounce correctly. [Towards S2:] let's try again.
Student 2: Zhāng, Zhāng, Zhōng, Zhōngguó, [trying to relax his tongue] oh, it is difficult.
Teacher: Very good. You will be fine. Now next. . . [individual checking goes on. . .]

The class was dealing with one of the alien sounds [zh] that many European language speakers found difficult to pronounce. A good 20 minutes were spent on this in the class before it moved on. Attention to details, a lot of repetition, and constant interruption were observed in some other classes too. However, when this was done regardless of the types of students, their learning characteristics and motivations could result in not only undesirable learning outcomes but also in discouraging them in the learning of the language. As was in the above observed case, the teacher clearly embarrassed a student by asking him to repeat the correct sound of a mispronounced word again and again. The teacher of course thought it was good for the student, but the student felt embarrassed and a bit annoyed, which you could see through his red face. When I interviewed the teacher and asked if there were other ways of dealing with such an issue, the teacher said:

> As we always say, practice makes progress. In this case, repetition makes progress. I gave him the opportunity to practise in class because I think the error should be addressed immediately. Repetition in class may make him feel a bit embarrassed, but it can help him to remember the correct pronunciation so he would not make the same mistake again in a similar situation in the future.

One might wonder why this teacher would spend so much time on one single sound, and the teacher did not seem to be aware at the same time that most of the students probably did not understand what a "retroflex initial" meant. Similarly, when asked why teachers seconded from China paying a great deal of attention to pronunciations and tones and tended to spend a lot of time on correcting their students, a *Hanban* teacher from CI-A replied with no hesitation:

> I found the students were quite poor at their pronunciation and tones, and they don't speak like Chinese at all. It would be a shame if they go out speaking like that while saying that they learned Chinese at our Institute. I feel it is my duty to at least make their speaking

sound like real Chinese. This is important if they want to learn how to communicate with Chinese people. In China, we would spend at least a couple of weeks at the beginning of a course on practising pronunciation and tones, but this is not possible here.

It also appeared to be a common practice that teachers interviewed did not seem to care about interrupting their students when they found any perceived problems, not only pronunciation and tones but also use of vocabulary. They all seemed to be eager and ready to remedy their students' "problems", as was shown in the following observation by a local teacher in an intermediate class in CI-A. The teacher was observed constantly correcting a student when he was giving a presentation talking about his recent trip to France.

Observation excerpt 4: This was an intermediate class in its fourth week in CI-A. The class started with oral presentations on a topic that students had chosen and prepared before the class. The following was observed when a second student was making his presentation, which is translated into English except those parts given in Pinyin where teacher's corrections were made.

Student: I went to France with my wife this summer. We went to Paris first. There are a lot of *Fǎngwèn rén* in Paris.
Teacher: Should say a lot of *Lǚyóu de rén*, or *Yóukè*. *Lǚyóu* not *Fǎngwèn*. *Lǚ* as in *Lǚxíng*, yóu as in *Yóuyǒng*, *kè* as in *Kèrén*. [Writing the two words on the board in Chinese.] Please go on.
Student: We've been to many places in Paris. Eiffel Tower, Notre Dame...
Teacher: That is *Āifēi'ěrTiětǎ*, *Bālí Shèngmǔyuàn*. Mm... [writing the two place names on the board in Chinese characters]
Student: Where was I? Oh, we had a lot French meal. We like French meal very much, because French meal is *hěn hǎoqī*.
Teacher: It is *hǎochī*, not *hǎoqī*. Read after me, *hǎo chī* (pause).
Student: *Hǎo chī*. [pause], *hǎo chī*.
Teacher: Go on.
Student: I also like very much to drink French wine, but I don't like brandy.
Teacher: *Báilándì*, very easy. (writing the Chinese words on the board). Read after me, *Báilándì*. You don't like to drink *Báilándì*.
Student: *Báilándì*. You don't like to drink *Báilándì*. Is it me who doesn't like to drink *Báilándì*?

The constant interruption by the teacher made it quite difficult for the student to continue. He was clearly lost at the start of the third round after the interruption by the teacher. The teacher was in fact a veteran who had been teaching Chinese for many years, however, it was clear that she did not speak English very well even if having lived abroad for a long while. In the interview with the teacher, she explained her view about the language learning and her teaching philosophy, which was quite representative of many other native speaker teachers. That was, the students should learn to speak like natives:

> Students must learn and speak with correct tones and pronunciation like native Chinese speakers so that they can communicate with them. They also need to learn Chinese characters, and write in Chinese characters. If they have several dozens of characters, they should be able to write many short sentences. Chinese characters are bit difficult, but as long as you work hard and remember a few dozens, it will get easy. The problem is that European students are a bit lazy and won't spend time on this.

The preceding teachers' behaviour of over-correcting their students in the classroom reflected teachers' beliefs about language learning and teaching as well as their expectation of their students. This also showed that teachers' beliefs were shared among teachers from the same cultural and educational background no matter if they were local teachers or seconded from *Hanban*. But on the other hand, *Hanban* teachers observed tended to spend more time on teaching what they saw as fundamentals such as pronunciation and tones in speaking. Time and again they were observed taking painstaking effort, trying to correct pronunciation and tones in most lessons, interrupting their students to make sure that they did it "in the right way". While such practices certainly had their merits, a major drawback on the students in the classroom observed was that it demotivated students and therefore adversely affected their confidence in learning Chinese language, and thus reinforced the widely spread false perception that Chinese was a difficult language to learn. This was clearly felt in one student interview and similar reactions were noticed in some other students towards the overcorrection by their teachers. This interviewed student from CI-B talked about her experience with a substitute *Hanban* teacher once when her own teacher was away:

> The teacher from China was very patient, but she went to great details, seeking perfection and asking us to repeat again and again to achieve prefect tone and intonation. I am sure it must be useful, but very hard to us, and even demoralising as I am tone deaf and could never get some of them right. I am not expecting myself to be able to speak Chinese perfectly. After all, this substitute teacher spoke English with an accent herself anyway. Our own teacher was much more tolerant with us and we had more time to speak and practise the language in class.

As said, similar reactions were found in other student interviewees. Here is an excerpt from the interview with a Chinese heritage student in an intermediate class in CI-A. While she also shared the same view as the above students toward the over-correcting acts of the teachers, she seemed to have a more sympathetic attitude and understanding towards it:

> As a Chinese, it is a bit embarrassing, my Chinese is not good enough to communicate effectively. I should have spent more time learning Chinese when I was a child, but I did not understand its importance, nor did I enjoy my school days. . . . Regarding the current course, I quite appreciate what the teacher did to help me learn all the new words and speak in a right way, but sometimes I did feel a little bit frustrated as I was feeling that I could never be good enough. It was completely different from European language classes. So, I could see why some mates in the class did not like learning Chinese and even stopped coming to class.

Heritage students of Chinese were somewhat different from others as they had had some exposure to Chinese language and culture before they joined course. Therefore, it is not surprised that they tended to be less shocked culturally at some of the teachers' behaviour in the classrooms, and they were quite used to the idea and practice of "striking for the best" at home or in their community. The heritage students will be looked at again in a following section on students.

Language Literacy: Chinese Characters and Reading

Contrary to the above observation on pursuing language accuracy on pronunciation and tones, there was a great deal of "leniency" observed about learning of Chinese characters. Studies on the difficult aspects of learning Chinese show that Chinese characters are perceived to be most difficult to learn by the students (Hu, 2010). But what was the Chinese character learning and teaching like in the observed classrooms?

As Chinese writing system is quite different from that of European languages, it isn't surprising that most European students initially find character recognition and memorisation very difficult. However, the observations found that teaching Chinese characters was slack in both Confucius Institutes, particularly in some beginners' classes in CI-B. Both beginner and intermediate classes in CI-A used textbook series which required the students to learn and live with characters from day one as it was character based. The textbooks were compiled based upon research that students who had initially learned Pinyin would usually find they had to learn the language again as Pinyin was not the actual written form of Chinese language. Of all the CI-B beginners' classes observed, even if the class handouts were laden with characters, hardly any of the observed classes followed the teaching materials teaching Chinese characters, instead Pinyin was used as a main writing system in the teaching. When asked about this, the interviewed teachers gave several reasons. First, like the students, all the teachers believed that Chinese characters were very difficult for their students to learn, therefore should be focus on oral rather than literacy. Second, they thought that there was not enough time for their students to learn all the Chinese characters in the lessons. Third, they did not think that their students were prepared to work hard and do "the boring stuff"—copying in order to master them. The following two extracts from the class observations also confirm the above points.

Observation excerpt 5: This is a term one intermediate class in CI-B, taught by a local teacher who was also a PhD student. The teaching was very communicative with many student activities and task-based interactions on the topic of travel. The whole lesson focused almost exclusively on oral communication, and the main part of the lesson was a class discussion based upon the previously assigned reading from the course handouts which were character based. The teacher spent about ten minutes or so revising new words, explaining the meaning of a few new characters. It was clear that some students were not quite well prepared, and some were very interested in learning characters, with one making comparison of the new ones with what they had learned before.

Student 1: Teacher, *xíng* in *lüxíng* is the same in *zìxíngchē* and the same in *xíngrén*, right?
Teacher: Yes. *Xíng* here means move or walk.
Student 1: We have learned *yínháng*, when to read *xíng* and when to read *háng*?
Teacher: It depends. There are many words like this in Chinese. Just memorise the phrase, then it is OK.
Student 2: *Lǎoshi*, the word *zhǎo*, it means looking for something. It has a hand radical, why? I think it should be eye radical. We use eye to look for something.
Teacher: The radical is useful but not always reliable. There are many other characters like that in Chinese. Just memorise it. OK, let's move on. We shall look at the discussion questions first, and then we can talk about your *lüxíng* experience in small groups.

The above observation shows that the time spent on characters learning and teaching was brief and short, and the teacher did not know the Chinese characters well enough, nor was she aware that the opportunity rose for her to work on characters with the students in the class. Instead she moved away from the topic, which could well give the class an impression that character learning was not very important if one could communicate orally. Moreover, those who could not quite understand the reading were not really heeded, which again might reinforce a false assumption that literacy or reading skills were not important. Even in the observed classes in CI-A whose courses had explicit requirements for their students to learn characters, the teacher did not allocate much time nor give enough attention to learning and teaching characters and reading, as can be observed in the following observation.

Observation excerpt 6: This was an advanced Chinese class of seven students in CI-A taught by a local teacher and the class was almost entirely conducted in Chinese, with some English from time to time, usually to explain some key vocabulary or background information and knowledge. The class was a discussion session on environment based upon a newspaper article in Chinese handed out at the beginning of the class. The article was at an appropriate level and anyone with a repertoire of 2,500 words roughly at level B1 should be able to grasp the gist of the article. The students varied in their levels of character skill and reading proficiency, and some characters and words were obvious obstacles to the reading and understanding of written text. The students were first asked to go over the article, then paired up to help each other for a better understanding of what they had read. There was also opportunity for the whole class to exchange their questions and answers on the article, with the teacher making contribution when and where needed. The teacher did explain some relevant words such as *wuran* (pollution), *paifang* (discharge), and *zaisheng nengyuan* (renewable energy), but attention was more on words rather than their constituent characters.

However, character and reading were also treated in a lighthearted way in this class as in many other lower level classes observed. I went around during the class break and asked the students how long and where they had learned their Chinese characters. Five out of the seven had learned elsewhere: three had studied or worked in China, two had studied Chinese in universities, and the other two had learned Chinese in the language centre over a period of about three years. Nearly all those in the advanced classes observed had learned their reading skill elsewhere. Only a very small number of students progressed to the advanced level. This observed lack of emphasis on character learning in the two Confucius Institute classes was also confirmed in both the student questionnaire results and the student interviews. One of the students interviewed from CI-A said the following on the topic:

> I find reading most challenging . . . but after the university, I went to China to study the language for six months. It was very intensive, but also very rewarding. Now I can understand the general meaning of most of the stuff I read, like newspapers. I want to keep it up and this is why I have been here for the second term now. I am kind of ok with the lessons, but I can see some are struggling a bit sometimes.

I feel that we should have spent a bit more time on reading, as it is a critical skill if one studies Chinese seriously.

The contrast between the highly imbalanced attention by the teachers between pronunciation and Chinese character was very much a result of teachers' belief that the latter was too difficult for European students to learn and most students were only interested in verbal communication competence. While such perceptions may be true to a certain extent, particularly from the students' point of view, the teachers need to understand that much of the perceived difficulty lies in some fundamental differences between many European alphabetic languages that the students are familiar with and logographic Chinese language completely new to them. It is teachers' responsibilities to assist the students to overcome the fear and find ways forward. The apparent interest in oral communication is a primary objective of language learning, but also related to the previous point that it is often an excuse for European learners to avoid learning reading and writing. However, if one asks the question of whether it really fulfils the objectives of Chinese language learning and teaching by working on oracy only, whichever stakeholder is concerned, the answer tends to be negative, particularly from the viewpoint of the Chinese language promotion organisation *Hanban* and Confucius Institutes as oracy with its phonetic Pinyin representation is far from the whole of the Chinese language. It is a clear indication that the language promotion objectives of *Hanban* and Confucius Institutes could be compromised at the classroom level due to the practice by both the teachers and students.

Culture in the Teaching of Chinese Language

There is a widely acknowledged agreement among the language teachers that language learning can be hardly separated from its culture learning. However, there seems not much consensus about what culture is and the purpose of cultural teaching as far as different stakeholders are concerned. The results of this field study have provided further evidence to support this view. While *Hanban* and Confucius Institutes might have a similar view of what Chinese culture would entail through the activities and teaching designed, it was found in the field study that culture was nevertheless understood quite differently by students and teachers in the classrooms.

There were two questions concerning the Chinese culture in the questionnaire. To the question on what the students had learned about the Chinese culture during the course, the overall responses matched well with the course designs. Most of the respondents in CI-A beginner and intermediate courses mentioned "Chinese way of behaviour and thinking" and "Chinese values" as main constructs of Chinese culture which formed an integral part of their language course materials, while the respondents from CI-B courses at all levels often cited more varied range of cultural elements such as "history", "business development", "politics", and " geography", which were stated explicitly in the design of the course materials. Many other aspects were also mentioned, such as "places of interest", "food", "ethnic groups", "Chinese gift giving", "Chinese numbers", and so forth. Not all the students from CI-B were keen on these things, as one respondent from a beginner class noted in the reply, "I have learned a little more about China and Chinese culture through the stories given by our teacher in class, but I'd rather lessons concentrate on language skills, as I can find out most of this by myself". While what this student said might not be representative, it did seem to suggest that these cultural elements did not seem to form an "organic" part of the lesson, so it was seen by students as being "imposed" upon them in their lessons.

Again, it was observed that local teachers and the teachers seconded from China appeared to have somewhat different understanding of and approaches to the teaching of Chinese culture in their lessons. There was also a major difference between CI-A and CI-B due to the textbooks they were using. Most CI-A classes dealt with the Chinese cultural phenomena in a comparative manner, while those in CI-B focused more on China and Chinese. The following is a short moment from a class observation in a CI-A beginner class.

Observation excerpt 7: The observed session was in the late half of the term and the main language content of the lesson was speech patterns talking about how to get to somewhere using different means of transport, including walking. There was a dialogue between two Chinese speakers, with one insisting on offering his bicycle to a friend to go to the library. Some students felt a bit puzzled at this at the beginning. The teacher was observed to take the opportunity to introduce an aspect of Chinese culture in which offering help to each other was considered a virtue, so the Chinese would thus happily and readily do this. The teacher also talked her own experience in the UK where people had also offered her help when she was once in a similar situation. Her landlady offered to lend her bicycle, but when she said she did not really need it, the landlady did not insist as the Chinese would, as such insistence might appear to be imposing in the local culture, as she learned later. In this way, the students were naturally informed of an aspect of Chinese culture while learning the speech patterns. This, however, was not always the case. Some teachers, particularly native Chinese speakers without much intercultural awareness, tended to preach proudly the Chinese culture, as observed in another lesson.

Observation excerpt 8: This was an intermediate class in CI-B taught by a teacher seconded from *Hanban*. She was a very charismatic and enthusiastic teacher, speaking very good English and getting on well with the students. The lesson was about differences in business culture in China. The teacher created a scenario: the foreign expatriate boss was advised by his Chinese associate to meet and entertain a local government official who would pay a casual visit to the company that afternoon while engaged in a business matter nearby. While there was no further explanation in the lesson as to why, it prompted many questions from the students, such as "Is this official a friend of the Chinese colleague?" If not, "Is it common that a government official can just drop in at such a short notice, and what is the real purpose of the potential visit?" The teacher was clearly unprepared and overwhelmed for so many questions and started to give an impromptu lecture on the Chinese *guanxi* culture and how this could help with the interpersonal relationship and business development in China. She emphasised that Chinese were always keen to maintain good relationships with each other, as the Chinese saying goes, "one more friend means an extra way out in time of emergency", and that anyone should do the same in China to show the respect for the local culture and customs. While the advice was "practical", it was obvious that the teacher lacked the necessary knowledge about the local business culture and intercultural competence to handle such questions. The teacher was interviewed later and was asked what she thought of that lesson. She said:

> This is embarrassing. I planned to discuss with the students the taboos and the good ways of treating Chinese official visitors, but the students focused on the procedures and asked why there was no plan for the visit, why it happened at such a short notice. I didn't think much about this when I was preparing my lesson. I found it difficult to decide what to tell and how to tell them. I haven't got time to talk about the gift culture as it is an integral part of *guanxi* building practice. Now looking back, I feel that I should create a different scenario.

For most of the teachers interviewed, Chinese culture as something that characterised everyday life of the Chinese people, such as customs, food, history, places of interest, and so forth. One *Hanban* teacher from CI-B in her interview made a specific point about what she understood as the Chinese culture:

> I often tell my students, "If you are learning the language, you ought to learn the culture". If the students are learning Chinese, they should work hard, like all the Chinese when they learn how to read and write.

For this teacher, learning Chinese culture needs to behave like Chinese and working hard like Chinese. This indicated that the less well-integrated culture factors into the language teaching were closely related to what the teachers understood the culture was. Almost all the teachers from

Hanban tended to present things concerning the Chinese culture and society as a package and expected the students to do exactly the same as the Chinese did. By contrast, the local teachers, particularly those who had tried conscientiously to integrate into the British society, were more considerate about the students and their cultural background. The local teachers, most of them from CI-A, appeared to be better aware of intercultural issues. One of the reasons might be the using of their textbook in which culture was taught during the language teaching. The students were learning both at the same time in an integrated manner without being even aware of it. One local teacher from a beginner class of CI-A said in the interview:

> Some students are very sensitive when we talk about Chinese culture, so I am always very cautious when I talk about it. I would integrate it into my character teaching and text teaching. Fox example, when I teach Chinese brush pen *bi*, I will tell the students it is made of hair and bamboo. I also show to them how to use brush pen to write. In this way, I introduce the Chinese calligraphy to the students. When I teach how to order food in a restaurant, I tell the students that bean-curd is a healthy food and can be cooked in different styles such as spicy bean-curd. In this way, I introduce Sichuan and other styles food to the students. My experience is that one should not teach it separately from teaching the language unless in teaching Chinese major students who take Chinese culture as a separate course.

But not only the teachers viewed and understood culture differently, so did the students. The research found that there was also a question of the relationship between tradition and modern practice with regards to Chinese culture. In addition to the general reply in the survey questionnaire, a student interviewee from an advanced class in CI-A said the following about her perception of the Chinese culture today through a recent session:

> I feel that the discussion on the Chinese modesty in the last session was useful. I have found that Chinese modesty is no longer true in today's China, especially with the young Chinese. They are increasingly like us in the West. You can see that in their job interview performance nowadays. In my university days a long while ago, I was told that Chinese people were usually very modest and would understate their strengths when talking about themselves. I did find that when I was studying in China, but this has all changed. Having said that, one must admit China has changed so much recently, so do Chinese people. China is after all a fascinating place and part of that fascination is its speed of change.

What this student talked about was important in a sense that it was no longer useful, nor possible to present Chinese culture in a stereotyped manner. This interview showed that it was modern China and Chinese people today that students wanted to know. Although stories about history, the data and facts were told in the classes, not much attention had been paid to the inherent linkage between them and contemporary Chinese when presented. This seemed to be a main reason why there was reaction from some students that cultural elements were "imposed" upon them. So how to organically integrate culture which students want to know into the delivery of language courses remains a challenge for all Confucius Institutes.

Professional Knowledge, Professionalism, and Linguistic and Cultural Proficiency

The field study found that the teaching was well accepted by the students, as was evident from some of the comments by the students in their responses to the question of what they were thinking of the teaching methods: "This is the most interactive course I have taken—which suits my learning style more than classes which focus on grammar and reading"; "very effective, my teacher gives us lots of conversation time in class". While such responses were good news, the field study did find some issues in some teachers in terms of their professional knowledge in Chinese languages, in theories concerning language learning and language teaching, and their linguistic and cultural proficiency to work effectively in Confucius Institutes.

A first issue observed was that some teachers did not seem to have sufficient linguistic knowledge of the Chinese language, which clearly showed up when they were dealing with random questions put forward by the students in class. In one observed intermediate class in CI-B, the PhD student-teacher was noticed unable to explain clearly what 下海 *xiahai* meant in response to a student's question. In another advanced class in CI-B, the teacher did not pick up the error in one of the slides that a student had prepared, mistakenly using 按排 *an pai* for 安排 *an pai* (which was also an example that the teacher seemed to have focused more on speaking than on literacy). In an observed case mentioned above, the teacher was trying to brush aside a student's inquisitive question, either subconsciously or even consciously to cover her limited knowledge of the multiple meanings of the character *xing* and *hang* in different word collocations.

Lack of professionalism was another observed issue for some teachers. For the local teachers observed, there was a clear absence of the use of technologies, as only one teacher was observed using power-point slides prepared beforehand, and the rest all relied on the traditional way of teaching, using "chalk and board" plus the textbook with some handouts. By contrast, all the *Hanban* teachers observed used a lot of additional materials and teaching aids as well as ICTs with PowerPoint and video clips. A sign of lack of what was perceived professional behaviours on the part of the *Hanban* teachers, however, was found in the absence of due respect for time and sometimes for classroom management dealing with some late arrivals. In one observed beginner's class in CI-B, the teacher extended the class nearly ten minutes, which made a few students quite edgy and finally said to the teacher that they had to leave as they were concerned about missing the train home. In a beginner 2 class CI-A, the teacher was observed repeating what clearly the class had done in the previous session for the sake of accommodating some students who had missed the previous session. Some students were not happy and this also gave a wrong signal that it did not matter much if one missed a session because the teacher would spend time repeating the content of the previous lessons again. The teacher explained in the follow-up interview that she was also annoyed that there were always students arriving late or missing classes. She had no choice but help them in this way to catch up, otherwise it would not be possible for them to keep up:

> I used to go over with students who were late or missed classes, but I don't do that anymore. There are several reasons for that, the main reason is that I found the students do not appreciate my efforts of coming earlier or staying late for the sake of making up lessons for them. Now I review it in the class. I know it is a bit unfair to the students who came in the previous session, but what can I do? I need to let most students follow the class.

Third, some teachers, especially local teachers, used far too much English than necessary in class, which clearly reduced the exposure of the students to the target language. One teacher explained in her interview that she was speaking a lot of English because she would like to make sure that her students could follow her in class, while the second teacher was clearly not quite aware of how much English she was using in her class as she said in her interview that she completely agreed that the class at that level should be conducted mostly in Chinese. By contrast, one teacher in CI-A was observed only using Chinese regardless of whether the students could follow or not. In the interview with her, the teacher said the following:

> I always use communicative approach in my teaching, which means I should always use Chinese. Students need to hear as much Chinese as possible, and they may not hear Chinese outside my class often. I know it is difficult for the beginners' class, but I am teaching mainly intermediate level students.

Fourth, it was noticed that there was a clear lack of local learning culture as some *Hanban* teachers acted out as if they were teaching in China. The sacrifice of their own time to help their students might not always be appreciated if it was not clearly explained and understood, as this *Hanban* teacher teaching in CI-B said about her experience, which indicated that she had not yet quite fully recovered from "cultural shock" with a student in her evening class last term:

> There was a student in my class who had a poor pronunciation and tone problem. I spent more time with him in class than others, but it didn't work. So, I thought I'd better help him outside the class, so I asked him to come 15 minutes earlier before the start of the class so that I could help him. You know what? He didn't want to and thought I had picked on him. I had done all this for his good, and I used my own time to help him as I felt that was what a responsible teacher would do. My students in China would thank me for that and probably invite me out for a meal, but he apparently didn't appreciate any of this at all.

Indeed, such culturally defined professional attitudes and behaviour were not uncommon among the teachers of Chinese, especially in teachers seconded from *Hanban*. For example, in a beginner class in CI-B, the *Hanban* teacher was observed paying a special attention, trying to help a "weak" student who had made an error in pronouncing the word *Tushuguan*. The teacher asked him to repeat it again and again, more than five times in a row, which clearly made the student quite uncomfortable as his voice became low and low. But the teacher did not seem care about this. The researcher managed to speak to the student during the break and had an informal chat about learning Chinese and his own experience. He said the following:

> I am not a good language learner. I know my pronunciation is not good, and I always feel embarrassed when asked to perform on the spot, let alone repeating something again and again in class, like today. I suppose that I just don't like to have such a special attention on me, and I am much better off to find my own way to progress gradually.

The teacher, on the other hand, defended her behaviour wholeheartedly in the interview, as she believed it was important that her students got the pronunciation right in class, particularly at the beginning of their study, or they will "keep a bad habit speaking". She considered that a responsible teacher should not bow to the students' whimsical ideas or pressure, but stand firm as to what she believed to be the right thing to do. This appeared to be a clear case where the connotation and understanding of professionalism could be different culturally.

Finally, there were cases indicating a lack of cultural and local knowledge in some teachers seconded from *Hanban*. It is a big challenge to

Confucius Institutes as its seconded teachers are usually posted to teach abroad for an average of two years, thus the useful local knowledge gained by those who have been around for a while is soon lost when the replacement teachers come. The local knowledge includes not only the local teaching practice, but also the knowledge about how students learn and why they have the problems. What the *Hanban* teacher from CI-A said about her experience was quite representative, as the teaching in Confucius Institutes differed a great deal from what she was doing in her own university in China:

> It is a real challenge for me when I started to teach this evening class here. There are only two hours a week, I must teach listening, speaking, reading, writing, and translation plus Chinese culture all in one single course. In China, these skills are usually taught in different courses. Moreover, there are many things that I can't do here as they might upset students. Our students in China usually do not leave in the middle of the course, but I am told it is very common here, so we have to please our students.

Her remarks above are a vivid depiction of a journey of gradual discovery about teaching Chinese in Confucius Institutes. The following two excerpts from the student interviews summarised quite well some main differences in teaching that they have experienced and how they perceived in their classrooms delivered by local and *Hanban* teachers. The following was a quotation from an interview with a student in a CI-B beginner class:

> My teacher is an attractive young Chinese lady from China and she speaks quite good English. She is warm and very well organised so we know what we should do. Of course, I didn't always have the time to do what I was asked to do. I know this is just an excuse. She is very strict and I think she would find ways to make you feel guilty if you haven't done your homework. But otherwise I think she is a very good teacher. I think it is important that Confucius Institutes only use experienced and qualified teachers.

Such impressions of the teachers seconded from *Hanban* could also be found in other students interviewed. For example, a heritage student who had been taught by several teachers during the time of his study at CI-A made some comparisons between the teachers employed locally and seconded from *Hanban*:

> I have studied Chinese here for quite a few years now. I've had about four teachers and one of them was a substitute who stood in for our current class teacher when she was ill. Generally speaking, they are

all good teachers, but they are different. The teacher in my first term class was a lady who was a dynamo and would drill us really hard on repeating sounds and words. We didn't quite like that very much at that time, but when I look back later, I feel that it benefited me a lot in my pronunciation. The one I found hard to follow was the second teacher from China who would do dictation almost every lesson, which drove many of us crazy and some didn't come back as they found it too difficult to continue. The teacher we have now is excellent, completely bilingual and keeping our attention and engaged all the time. We enjoy the challenge she gives us. The substitute teacher was just OK.

Discussions and Analyses

From the field study we can see that as far as teaching was concerned, most of the students were very happy, and they also felt that they were learning and making progress. But a number of negative consequences were found as a result of the teachers' behaviour concerning teaching Chinese language and culture.

The findings showed that all the teachers were native speakers of Chinese who were from mainland China or Taiwan. They had received similar education and tended to share similar views on the Chinese language and ways to learn it, regardless of whether they were locally employed or seconded from China. This could be further analysed against the sociocultural background in which they had been brought up as people within a culture shared "primordial values" such as individualist, community, or collectivist orientations (Alexander, 2001). It is interesting to note that almost without exception, there was profound influence of the Chinese cultural tradition on the teachers' beliefs of what teachers were perceived to be and how they were expected to behave in the classrooms, as well as how students should behave as far as learning is concerned.

As most teachers seconded from *Hanban* were first time in the UK, new to the local British culture, they tended to show a clear Chinese cultural influence in their teachings. Imparting knowledge would need the teacher to be very knowledgeable and it would be considered a loss of face if a teacher's authority is challenged. The study found that this manifestation was far more obvious in *Hanban* teachers, for example, the observed behaviour in *Hanban* teachers of maintaining a more formal teacher-student relationship and reinforcing their authority in the classroom. The *Hanban* teachers tended to think that the students were there to learn, both language and culture, which showed the classroom instruction and behaviour, such as *Qing jü shou tiwen* (please raise your hand to ask questions), and *Jiao wo* X *Laoshi* (address me as Teacher X). This was a clear case showing teacher's sense of hierarchy, and the teacher was strongly influenced by the way her teachers teaching and the teachers' training she had received. Most Chinese teacher training programmes nowadays still stress that teachers must be equipped with an excellent and comprehensive knowledge so to be authoritative enough to teach, which can be interpreted as being able to "talk down" in the student-teacher relationship. The teachers should demonstrate care for their students by "praising" the right and "rectifying" the wrong of their students in their class, which in the western value system would be judged as being patronising. This transplant of the Chinese cultural practice into the Confucius Institute teaching might lead to conflict between the teachers and students due to lack of mutual cultural understanding. The Chinese expected an unchallengeable position and a sense of superiority in the interpersonal relationship, but the local students had a more equal and inquisitive mind based on the principle of market economy. This could be particularly tricky when *Hanban* teachers could not proficiently manage the class medium language English and its cultural connotations, as they were the "guests" in a non-Chinese macro socio-cultural environment and acting temporarily as "host" in a micro Chinese linguistic and cultural classroom.

However, even if the Chinese teachers could manage to establish a formal teacher-student relationship in class, their actual influence over the students was rather limited. Baquedano-López and Hernandez's study (2011) found that students' structural subordination to teachers' authority in the institute in US was minimal, because adult students could do whatever they liked and teachers were usually guests staying temporarily in the US institutions where institutes were located. In their view, this more teacher-student egalitarian social field provided an opportunity to examine the classroom dynamics independent of what were often teacher-favouring classroom hierarchies common in diasporic and migration language classrooms and settings.

The Chinese government's language policy of Putonghua and the practice of teaching Chinese as a second and foreign language in China led to a requirement that all the *Hanban* sent teachers must have passed Putonghua test, therefore it seemed that they all have an obligation to seek and strive for linguistic perfection by over-correcting their students so that the students can speak as closely to standard Putonghua speakers as possible. It is the combination of the Chinese teaching tradition and this "monolingual" ideology that underpins the policy and practice that contributed to "zero tolerance" for linguistic deviation as reflected in both the policy and teachers' practice. Some of the local teachers were found not speakers of standard Putonghua. The history and story of English, an undisputable lingua franca shows that if a language is truly international, it is impossible that it is spoken in one format, one voice and one place.

It was observed that the over-correction by the teacher resulted in a rather inefficient use of class time as well. While it was necessary to foster the right habit of speaking Chinese in their students, the amount of time allocated and used was clearly out of proportion to the entire lesson. Moreover, the seemingly caring practice of over-correction dented the confidence of some students, especially the mature students as such an action was demoralising and discouraging the students. In the case of the intermediate class in CI-B, the fact that the student concerned was a young Chinese heritage student made it slightly less tense, as she looked as if she was used to this kind of teaching style. For the same reason, Interferences and interruptions with students were more often observed with *Hanban* teachers too, who were usually eager to "put right" what they feared to be "unauthentic" or "incorrect". Therefore, teaching methods such as "read aloud after me" were observed to be almost exclusively used by *Hanban* teachers.

Many *Hanban* teachers were also prepared to offer to work longer hours, a reflection of the Chinese teaching and learning tradition that the teacher should be diligent and strict in teaching (or spare the rod, spoil the child in the old days for *Jiao bu yan, shi zhi duo*), and be tireless in teaching others (*Hui ren bu juan*), and students should "constantly strive for perfection" (*Jing yi qiu jing*). It was clear that most native Chinese speaker teachers who had been educated in China seemed to try very hard to follow these traditional mottos in their teaching practice as their teachers had done.

For most teachers from *Hanban*, it is very clear that they believed that they had the mission to "teach" Chinese language and culture to the students, and they were the embodiment or representative of relevant knowledge, skills and thus authority of the Chinese language and culture. In this light, all the different and innovative teaching techniques were only employed as the means for the very end—delivering the teaching to the students and make them know the unknown. For them, the question of how students learn seemed of secondarily importance, as it was far more important to get what to learn and teach right. This have been the practice when teaching Chinese in China since the overseas students come from a wide range of social, cultural, and linguistic backgrounds. The research also found that local teachers also shared this, many tended to pay more attention to how their teaching was accepted by their students. It was these different perceptions and understandings of the role of a teacher that underlined the teachers' attitudes to students, principles, methodologies and techniques adopted for teaching, and even the use of English in the classrooms.

The aforementioned findings regarding teaching and teachers have confirmed that teachers' beliefs can greatly influence their classroom practice, teaching instruction, decision making and course planning (Pajares, 1992; Ho et al., 2001). All the aforementioned teaching behaviour and beliefs of the native speaker teachers of Chinese were related to, if not the direct results of, the long reinforced Chinese socio-cultural perception of teacher and of the teacher-student relationship shaped by the Confucian tradition and practice that had influenced the Chinese education and society for thousands of years. For Chinese, "A teacher is one who could propagate the doctrine, impart professional knowledge and resolve doubts", as suggested by a famous Chinese scholar Han Yu (768–824) in the Tang Dynasty (618–907). What was found in the field study were mere manifestations of this Chinese fundamental concept, though to varying degrees.

The findings of the ethnographic study of the teachers discussed above calls for well planned, coordinated, and targeted professional training programmes for all the native speaker teachers of Chinese, both for those employed locally and those seconded from *Hanban*. What appears to be missing in most current training programmes is a key *awareness* that localised language teaching policy of *Hanban* really means different Chinese teaching practices from those in China, and an understanding that students from different cultural and linguistic backgrounds learn Chinese differently. If internationalisation of learning and teaching Chinese is to be achieved through localisation of the policies and practices in the multilingual and multicultural contexts of the world today, it would require very different mentalities, teaching approaches, teaching materials and assessment methods.

Students Motivation and Learning

Motivation for Learning Chinese

Motivation is often regarded as a determining factor for learning performance and results, but the study of Chinese language students' motivation is still relatively few (Ruan, Duan and Du, 2015). However, in the UK, and to a large extent in the world, the need for learning Chinese language was largely driven by economic and political demands, as some studies claim (Wang and Higgins, 2008). This study took the opportunity to gather the feedback from the students on why they were learning Chinese there.

The first set of data came from the student questionnaire. The responses to the open question on the purpose of their study of Chinese were high, with only 3% missing. Apart from eight respondents who were doing the course for interest in Chinese culture, the two most common cited reasons were for work or career development opportunity either now or in the future (56, or 58%), and for personal reasons including having close Chinese friends or relatives (37, or 38%). Such motivations were perhaps best expounded in the interviews with some of the students. A student in Bergner's class in CI-A talked about his decision to learn Chinese as:

> In the back of my mind, I am thinking of potential career change. As China's economy continues to grow, everyone is working with China, and I can see our firm has a rapidly growing business with

Chinese speaking clients. I don't expect to be able to communicate in Chinese as I am not good at languages, and I don't have much time, but some knowledge of the language and the culture will help me if I make any move in the future. This is not something on the immediate horizon, so I am taking it easy.

Another business student from an intermediate 2 class at CI-B had a slightly different motivation and need:

I am thinking of moving to work in China as the bank has more and more business there. My girlfriend is from Shanghai and we have been there a few times. I love the city. In addition, as she is the only child and her parents don't want to live abroad, it will be nice for us to spend a few years close to them. But I am not learning as fast as I wish to. The course is good but Chinese language is very hard. People say I should be speaking better as I have a Chinese girlfriend. As a matter of fact, it doesn't help much at all as my girlfriend speaks very good English. Maybe I will get more practice when I am in China.

The results of the student questionnaire and interviews suggest that while most of the students learning Chinese were doing it for "economic" reasons, as some previous studies indicated, a substantial number of them were not. However, it shows that the underlying motivations for almost all of them are instrumental or practical, which is quite typical of adult students, particularly of the students learning Chinese in institutions like CI-A and CI-B and their host universities (Zhang, 2007, 2012).

The challenges of teaching those students faced by teachers, particularly those seconded from *Hanban* can be very well seen in the word of the following *Hanban* teacher from CI-B, who had years of teaching experience in China, but mostly to students learning Chinese full-time in her home university in China:

Teaching here is very different from teaching in China, and I have learned a lot during the time here about how to teach business Chinese to people like accountants, bankers, and managers. I thought it would be easy to teach these people, but it is not, in fact it is more difficult, or people here say, challenging. You can't just teach them what you want to teach but teach them what they want to learn. It is still Chinese language and culture, but not the same as what I was told or thought was. This is also why we are all supportive to develop our own teaching materials here. I feel that I can be a much better teacher after this experience.

While the above findings were mostly about students' motivation, they also reflected students' attitude to learning and teaching, which were different from those that *Hanban* teachers had experienced in China. In an interview with another *Hanban* teacher who was observed to remind students without doing the homework to remember to do so in class, question was posed to why she was saying things like this in class and her answer was:

> I know that we can't criticise our students and we should make them feel happy, but I have to find ways to make them aware of their problem if they haven't followed my instruction. It is also a way to state that it is your problem not my problem. You can't really teach if they don't do homework. You can't learn Chinese like this and no wonder why they are so slow in their progress. I know some of them are busy, but they don't work hard at all.

Generally speaking, the local teachers, especially those who had been in the UK for a long time, seemed to know their students better as far as their motivation and attitude toward learning was concerned and took measure accordingly. One of the local teachers in CI-A summarised it well:

> I feel that there are several types of teachers here. You have traditional teachers who think they are teachers and native speakers of Chinese and students should simply learn from them without any question. They tended to be senior, usually without excellent command of English and don't really bother about teaching methods or understanding of their students. There are also teachers who understand students' motivation of learning Chinese and try to motivate their students in class by using modern technologies, and English as media language. While some of them are good, some of them don't really teach their students very much. Then there are teachers like myself, somewhere in between, mindfully of how to facilitate our students' learning so that they could find their learning, in our director words, "enjoyable and fruitful", but at the same time, giving students more challenging tasks to do as I know very well why they are here, to learn the language for immediate use.

Difficulties in Learning Chinese

For the sake of language learning and teaching, and studying it as part of language management process, it is important and useful to know what the students find difficult when learning Chinese. One open-ended question in the survey was on this so learner could voice their views as freely as they wished. The results showed that Chinese characters, and pronunciation and tones were the most quoted difficult aspects in their learning of Chinese. They were mentioned 62 and 41 times, respectively, in their responses to the question. For the former, a common problem was in character recognition and memorisation, which had a knock-on impact on reading and writing, while the problem with pronunciation and tones was naturally associated with listening and speaking. There were 15 respondents who stated that they found Chinese grammar and vocabularies difficult to grasp. In addition, there was some mentioning like idiomatic usage of the Chinese language.

The study then sought more detailed explanations from students during the interviews. A student in CI-B who had only learned Chinese in her second term talked specifically about her difficulty in learning the language:

> For me, it is definitely the pronunciation and characters. I just find it sometimes very confusing when some words are pronounced so similar or almost the same, like there are so many "*shi*" in Chinese. It is "ten", it is in the word for teacher "*laoshi*", but it also part of "always". It is amazing that the Chinese can understand each other when sometimes they sound completely the same. Chinese grammar is very simple and straight forward, but characters are certainly not. It is interesting to listen to the teacher and her explanation about the characters such as person and moon, but I just can't remember them when there are so many.

The difficulty that this student encountered was quite representative of other students interviewed too. The following student equally thought that learning to remember and use characters was quite hard even though he felt more confident than before:

> I find it much more manageable than before now that I have learned a couple of hundred characters and I can see how they are formed and structured. However, many of them are still difficult to me, especially when they look similar. Also, I can't remember how some of the characters are pronounced but I can often guess their rough meaning from the context.

All the students interviewed agreed that Chinese characters were interesting, even though they were not easy to learn. Some also said that there were two writing systems in Chinese, Pinyin and characters, rather than simplified and traditional forms of characters, without realising that Pinyin is not a writing system. For those studying at CI-A where the textbooks were character based, the students would have to learn and live with characters from day one. As the CI-A UK director pointed out that adult students did not learn Chinese like Chinese children did with a lot of copying, repetition, and writing without the need of understanding the structures or the grammar of the language. If this approach was imposed on the students, it might well be one of the reasons that so many students stopped learning the language altogether. One critical factor that had impacted on the learning of the Chinese language mentioned by the surveyed students was the time that they spent on learning the language. As most were professionals, time was a rare commodity in their command. This often led to a misconception of them by the Chinese language teachers that they did not work hard.

Chinese Heritage Students

There were quite a large proportion of Chinese heritage students in the total respondents of the student questionnaire survey, 18 (about 19% of the total). This, however, as the researcher learned from the management of the two Institutes, was not a true presentation of the student population in the two Institutes, especially in CI-A where the heritage students only represented about 5% of the total in its annual registrations. The percentage was much higher in CI-B, partly because the host university of CI-B attracted far more Chinese students in its degree programmes than that of CI-A. This was confirmed in the classroom observation that ethnic Chinese students in the intermediate and advanced class were degree students of the host university.

It must be mentioned that the class observation found generally a very distinctive cooperative behaviour in almost all these heritage Chinese towards their teacher and fellow students in the classrooms. They seemed more attuned to the traditional Chinese teacher centred talk method of teaching and always did their homework as requested. Therefore, it was very likely that their cooperation in responding questionnaire survey resulted the larger-than-usual presence of the Chinese heritage students in the survey. In addition to the high respondents for the questionnaire survey, three out of the nine interviewed students were also ethnic Chinese, a third of the total.

The case of Chinese heritage students was first systematically studied by scholars such as Professor Li Wei from the late 1980s, and it has since then attracted a lot of attention in the study of Chinese heritage students and bilingualism, community languages and its role in linguistic ecology of the British society (Anderson, 2008). When Li carried out his research with the Chinese communities and described in his book *Three Generations, Two Languages, One Family* (Li, 1994), the patterns of language choice and shift in many Chinese families seemed to conform to the usual route in which most the new immigrant parents wanted their children to learn the host country's language, often at the expenses of their own heritage language at home or in their community at large. The parents wanted their children to be integrated into the mainstreams of the society first, and then a gradual recovery over the time to a bilingual status in families and communities to maintain their identity. But this study has depicted quite a different picture of their parents and different story of their heritage language learning.

First, most of the 15 ethnic Chinese students were the second or third generation of Chinese and the heritage languages that they knew were mostly Cantonese (ten), followed by Hokkien (four) and Hakka (one). What was interesting was that none of them was from Mandarin speaking families, which tended to be more recent immigrants, mostly since 1980s. Second, it was clear that most of these heritage students had not only learned to speak the variant form of Chinese at home, they had also been sent to study in Chinese community schools in their school days. It is not within the scope of this study to discuss the effectiveness of Chinese learning and teaching in such schools, but the sheer fact that the parents had sent their kids to school to learn Chinese demonstrated that they were far more conscious of the importance of keeping their heritage language and culture in the age of globalisation. And this was almost evident in every interview of the heritage students. A Cantonese-speaking law student learning Chinese in an intermediate class at CI-A described her experience of learning Chinese in the early days, and why she was learning to speak Mandarin and how important it was for her:

> I used to hate it when my parents sent me to Sunday school every week where I was supposed to learn to read and write. But we learned all in Cantonese. I don't speak Mandarin. I feel very embarrassed as I am Chinese. I hope to find a job in an international law firm where I did my intern last summer. It has a lot of business with Mandarin speaking clients, and I know that if I want to join them, I need to learn and be able to speak Mandarin. This is why I am here learning Mandarin now.

While variations such as Cantonese, Hokkien, and Mandarin are all forms of Chinese, and they all follow the same written script, they are, in strictly linguistic terms, different languages phonetically. This was, as mentioned before, a main drive behind the Chinese government promotion of Putonghua, or Mandarin as known in the West. As a matter of fact, a Cantonese speaker may find it just as hard to learn to speak Mandarin as any Europeans, and sometimes it could be even more challenging, particularly the tones and pronunciation. This student studying at CI-B said the following in her interview:

> Some people say that Cantonese has six or seven tones so is more difficult than Mandarin, but I find Mandarin tones much harder. In addition, there are many vocabularies that Cantonese and Mandarin are different. I was disheartened at one stage as I felt I spoke like a country girl entering a big city for the first time. But I am doing fine now and the teacher said that I am making good progress.

For those Cantonese speaking students who could already read, they would have very different needs as compared to other students. It was for this reason that both CI-A and CI-B had developed the course "Mandarin for Cantonese Speakers", where the focus was on how to help these students to learn to speak Mandarin. It was noticed in this study through the interviews that most of the heritage students had a sense of rediscovering their cultural identity while on the journey of learning Mandarin, either consciously or subconsciously.

Discussions and Analyses

The field study of all the students at the two Confucius Institutes yielded a number of findings and observations which would have relevant implications for the learning and teaching of Chinese, and for language practice as integral part of language policy in both Confucius Institutes.

It was clear that the predominant motivation for them to learn Chinese was instrumental, and majority of these leaners were full-time professionals with some university students. This meant that they were likely to have their own expectations, but not necessarily interested in Chinese culture per se while studying on the courses and would probably vote with feet if they did not enjoy or cope with it. The responses to question 14, on how long the respondents had been with the Confucius Institutes, suggested that 67% of the respondents had just joined the courses that term, while 33% had been there a bit longer, with half of them (16%) had continued from the previous term, and the remaining 16 (or 17%) had been with their institute for a year or longer. Given that both Confucius Institutes had been in operation for a few years already, the above set of figures showed a problem with the retention of the students in these institutes. The causes of the problem, however, weren't the courses of Confucius Institutes, as 74% of the responses to the question on how well the courses met their expectations were very positive, with a further 18% "OK", bringing the total to 92%.

The fact that there were so many different courses offered in CI-A indicated the diverse demands and needs of the students, from learning to speak only to studying for specific purposes, such as business, law, and special groups like heritage students. Besides, most of these students were working, some in very demanding jobs with a lot of responsibilities. All this made learning as well as the design and delivery of these courses more challenging. It was for this reason that the teachers' beliefs about their students could have a huge impact on not only the behaviour of teachers themselves, but also on the performance of their students.

The teachers' views on students from the interviews might well shed light on our understanding of the students. First, *Hanban* teachers seemed to feel very strongly about how peculiar it was that the students blamed their teachers and complained when they did not achieve what they expected to. Some teachers felt that the students here did not work hard, and did not appreciate their teachers' help. Some even said that she learned teachers had to praise students all the time because this was how they grew up. As teaching was a market, we had to do everything to keep our students.

However, *Hanban* teachers who had been around longer had different understanding of this. They were more sympathetic with the students on part-time courses. Most of the students were professionals and were very busy with their work and their family as well. The courses were not cheap, and they spent money and time to come and learn Chinese usually after a day's work. These teachers showed more appreciation and were ready to help them achieve what they come here for.

Most local teachers tended to feel more relaxed about their students. They did agree that the students would have made much more progress if they had worked harder, but in the light of the learning environment and culture in the UK, their attention appeared to have focused on what problems that their students often encountered in their learning and how they as teachers could best help them without losing them during the course of the lessons. Needless to say, the teachers' perceptions of the students would have impacted on their behaviour in their teaching, some of which have already been discussed and analysed above in this chapter. However, most of the teachers did understand that the force of the market and the importance of keeping their students. As the CI-A UK director said, "It is the success of the students and their learning that determine the success of teaching". More can be said of this, it is the success of the students and their practice that ultimately determines the success of the language policy.

Assessment

Assessment Methods

Just as how the UK director of the CI-B had described that one cannot discuss about language courses without looking at their assessment, assessment is an important tool to the language learning and teaching as well as a measurable indicator of the extent of success of language learning and teaching of a certain course. The forms and contents of assessment are largely related to the objectives of the course at a micro-level and to the policy at mezzo and macro-levels, as well as to the expectation and needs of the students especially if the courses and policy are created to meet such needs and expectations (Fostaty and Wilson, 2000; Darlaston-Jones et al., 2003). The research found that both Confucius Institutes had their own assessment norms, based upon their course design. For CI-A, the course teachers were required to give regular assignments, both oral and written, which served as formative assessment with feedback during the course. There was a standardised end-of-term exercise for all beginner and lower intermediate courses, which were marked according to a same marking criterion. For upper intermediate and advanced courses, the assessment was a mixture of oral presentation and reading and writing practices during the courses. The participation in the assessments was voluntary as the grades did not have impact on deciding if the students could continue into the following stage since none of these courses carried any credits. As the CI-A UK director explained, the students would decide if the course was at the right level for them, though the teachers would advise their students on this. The focus and the point of the assessment were to give the students constant feedback so that they knew what to do and how to progress in a timely fashion.

CI-B, on the other hand, followed a different pattern of assessment. All the courses conformed to a set norm of 50% for continuous assessment, which was decided by the class teachers, 30% oral presentation in class, and a final test which weighed 20%. But all the assessments rested on the shoulder of the class teacher who set, carried out and marked the assessments. The final grade was important in determining if the student concerned could go on to the next stage or not. However, as the executive director of CI-B explained, since the overwhelming part of the assessment (80%) was subjectively marked by individual teacher, it rarely happened that a student was stopped from continuing if the student attended most of the classes and did homework. The idea of adopting this pattern of assessment was to make sure that the students must attend classes during the course.

In addition to the formal summative measures mentioned above, a range of formative assessment methods were used in the observed classes, more often by *Hanban* teachers than the local teachers, such as dictations, quizzes, and mini-competitions, usually at the beginning of a class to test the students' knowledge and memory of assigned characters, vocabulary, and sentence structures covered in the course. Of all the aforementioned dictation seemed to be most unwelcomed by the students through the observation, and they did not appear to care that much if they could not do well. Quizzes were usually done in small groups, often with some friendly competition going on between them, which the students appeared to have enjoyed with a lot of fun. The locally employed teachers tended to be more relaxed and tolerable about these forms of assessment, but more focused on developing oral communicative competence through assigned tasks, both individual and group.

The responses to the question on assessment were varied, but they did give a rather true reflection of the assessment practices as described above. As mentioned above, there was a uniform end of term test for lower level courses in CI-A. Since nearly two thirds of the students had only joined the courses that term, they had not yet had any test, apart from some summative feedback in the class. The respondents who had joined courses earlier, especially those who were with CI-B, their responses varied a great deal between the courses, from some very uncertain ones such as "no idea", to some more assertive ones like "through attendance", "class presentation" and even "essay writing", or a combination of some. All these assessment methods were obviously employed in different classes at different levels. Generally speaking, the respondents appeared to be happy with the fact that they were given feedback on their progressions by their teachers, and only a few seemed to be interested in the formal course certification as a way to recognise their learning achievements. There was almost no mentioning of HSK as a means of assessment by any respondents in either institute.

HSK

There was a specific question in the questionnaire on HSK (*Hanyu Shuiping Kaoshi*: Chinese Language Proficiency Test) as *Hanban* had been actively promoting this test through its Confucius Institutes. The revised version (New HSK) was another example of the effort that *Hanban* had put in to make it more accessible to Chinese language students and to encourage more students to take up the test. In order to make the test more accessible to students and reduce their fear of learning, *Hanban* had replaced the previous test developed from the later 1980s with a new version of six levels in late 2009 and early 2010. The number of people taking HSK was regarded as a best indicator of the interest in learning Chinese, which was why *Hanban* expected all the Confucius Institutes to encourage their students to take part in the test. But the responses from the survey were more than shocking, as only 7% respondents replied that HSK had been introduced to their Confucius Institute while 93% said that they hadn't been informed of this test, but both the Confucius Institutes had been involved with HSK test for quite a few years, and CI-A was one of the earliest HSK test centres in the UK. When asked if they had taken the test before or planned to, there were only 5% that had taken the test, 18% having planned to, 38% would consider taking the test in the future, and 32% said that they were not interested. *Hanban* expects all Confucius Institutes encouraging their students to sit in the test and both the Confucius Institutes claimed to have done so which was confirmed during the interviews with all the directors. The HSK information was also clearly available on their websites. The CI-A director said that the test information was usually sent to all the students beforehand and there were also relevant test preparatory courses planned. But the enthusiasm and interests had never been very high. The students' responses indicated that neither of the two Confucius Institutes was successful in their effort promoting HSK.

In the interview with a local teacher in CI-A, she said that even with incentives from her Institute with a subsidised fee, the students in the evening classes were never enthusiastic about the idea of sitting in a formal examination like HSK. She did try to encourage her students to take, and some did. But she wasn't convinced that they still would if the examination fee went back to the normal charge, as many of her students simply did not see much use of the test. This was quite true with all the students interviewed on this subject. A student from CI-A said:

> I don't come here for another qualification. The language centre gave an attendance certificate, which was good enough for me when I had financial support from my firm. It made my boss happy to see that I had completed the course. But I am now paying for myself and I am learning Chinese for myself. It is more important what I am learning, so I am not worried about qualification. I can't cope with any formal tests or exams anyway. It is not that I can't do it, but that I am simply too busy to work on Chinese test or exam.

Another interviewee commented:

> I am very busy and do not have time to prepare a test such as this, besides, what is the point of taking it? People say it is a test like IELTS for English and one needs to pass a certain level to study in China. Well, I have no plan to do so, nor take the test. . . . It might help to tell what level I am at, but I don't think my firm understands what it is.

What this student said about HSK was significant not only in terms of its relevance to the students, but also how the test was understood in terms of local framework of standards. As far as language learning and teaching is concerned, the CEFR is now the prevalent framework of standards used in almost all the member states of the Council of Europe. One would find that nearly all language courses and programmes in the UK are described and assessed with reference to the CEFR. Subsequently, almost all the accredited, and increasingly more and more non-credited Chinese language courses in the British universities are linked to the CEFR, including those offered in the CI-A. It was perhaps for this reason that the new HSK also claimed that it was referenced to the CEFR, as can be seen from the link on *Hanban*'s website,[1] with its suggested numbers of vocabularies requested for each of its six levels that matched the similar levels in the CEFR.

However, this association of the new HSK with the CEFR led to heat debates with regards to on what ground this association was established. The Chinese Teachers' Association in German Speaking Countries quickly made an open statement in June 2010, suggesting that the numbers of words required for each of the six levels were in fact much more, and it had come up with their own level descriptors in line with the

CEFR.[2] Meanwhile, there was a collaborative European Benchmarking Chinese Language project (2010–2012) involving universities in France, Germany, Italy, and Britain which intended to come up with adapted level descriptors for Chinese language competences in the European context based upon the CEFR. Although the project only produced the descriptors up to A2 level with seven supporting documents,[3] the vocabulary requirements for the first two level descriptors were more in line not only with the mentioned main European languages, but also with those of the first edition HSK and Chinese language proficiency test administered in Taiwan, thus far higher than those stated for HSK by *Hanban* (Zhang, F., 2014). As a result, while the new HSK, especially the initial level ones were well received by many who took the test, its credibility in terms of its correlation with the CEFR was doubted and questioned. This may be another reason the students are not enthusiastic about the test.

Discussions and Analyses

Assessment is traditionally regarded as a critical part of the language courses, as it helps to evaluate the learning and to a certain extent the teaching, or in language management terms, the effectiveness of language policy as practice. What was observed and revealed in this study with regards to assessment was about how to assess, which obviously include aspects such as what to assess and for what purposes, and the issue was that different stakeholders or agents had their own ideas and expectation.

Hanban would wish to have more students to take HSK and other tests that it had developed, such as HSKK (Chinese Proficiency Speaking Test), BCT (Business Chinese Test) and YCT (Youth Chinese Test), since statistics would provide hard evidence to justify the great deal of efforts and resources put in. In its two recent annual reports, *Hanban* reported a 17% and 16% increase in 2013 and 2014 over the previous year in the numbers of the people taking these tests, from 334,000 in 2012 to 372,000 in 2013 and 430,000 in 2014.[4] The total number of people taking the four tests reached 560,000 in 2016.[5]

For the two Confucius Institutes, their assessment strategies were clearly different from those of *Hanban*, as could be seen from the course descriptions in these institutes. Most of the students that these courses attracted were learning the language for an instrumental purpose, therefore they were not keen on spending more time and effort preparing for formal assessments, as time was a commodity that most of them did not have. As all the teachers in the two Confucius Institutes were native speakers, many, particularly those seconded from *Hanban*, initially could not quite understand why the course assessment was non-mandatory and informal. Some still held the view that all the language courses should be formally, and externally assessed, "How do students know about what they have achieved and their levels if no formal assessment is given?" (a

Hanban teacher from CI-B). But after being in the Confucius Institute for a while, most of *Hanban* teachers agreed that "alternative assessment methods are better in this situation to continuously and informally keep the students interested and motivated". This change of views concerning the assessment of part-time courses was experienced by other teachers too, including the local teachers.

HSK tests preparation classes were offered in both Confucius Institutes, which also had their own assessment strategies. However, while assessment strategies could be different, they should still be able to demonstrate the outcomes of the courses, with references to certain framework of standards. It was found that the two Confucius Institutes differed on this in that CI-A's course descriptions referred to the CEFR, but CI-B's did not. In a way, it indicated that CI-A went for the whole way for the localisation in assessment, while CI-B only halfway. The reference to the widely adopted CEFR would help make the language courses offered in both Confucius Institutes much easier to be comprehended, accepted, and mainstreamed. The link of Confucius Institute scholarship to HSK would certainly promote the test, but only to those interested and able to go and study in China. As most of the adult students on the Confucius Institute courses were full-time professionals or students, its practical appeal to them was still limited, which determines that there would not be a huge surge in the number of people taking HSK from the two Confucius Institutes in the next few years.

Summary

This chapter has reported, discussed, and analysed, in the light of the theory of language management, major findings of the Chinese language teaching and learning practices in classrooms of the two Confucius Institutes, along with opinions and views of the students as reflected in their responses to questionnaire and in the interviews. It also discussed the beliefs and ideas of the teachers and directors on Chinese language teaching and learning which helped to shed light on the relevant teaching and learning practices. These findings indicated to a certain extent the interactive characteristics of language policy and practice, and language learning and teaching that took place in the classrooms of the two Confucius Institutes under study.

In terms of teaching practices, while they were very good and well received, which was evident from the student questionnaire responses and observation in the classrooms, the observation and interviews with teachers showed that the teaching practices varied a great deal as well as teachers' beliefs, particularly between the local teachers and teachers seconded from *Hanban*. While most Chinese teachers were observed to stress the importance of learning to speak authentic and correct Putonghua, those seconded from *Hanban* were noticed paying more attention to the details of pronunciation and tones than the locally employed colleagues. Contrary to this, most of the teachers observed appeared to be quite relaxed about teaching literacy skills to their students, largely because the thought that Chinese characters and reading would be very difficult for their alphabetic language speaking students to learn, a common belief shared by officials, scholars, and practitioners alike. It was clear that such beliefs and teaching practices on the part of the teachers had produced both positive and negative impacts on their students as could be seen in the classrooms observed, but unfortunately more of negative in a number of cases. The students' confidence in learning was dented. It was also observed that there was a wide gap between teachers in using English or Chinese as the medium instruction in the classrooms, again with contrasting beliefs that the students should be immersed in the target language or they should understand the language input in the first instance rather than being thrown into the language to swim or sink. While both practices had theoretical grounds, what was missing as revealed in the teacher interviews was the due consideration of the students, a common phenomenon that can be observed in many of the native Chinese teachers.

Lack of awareness and understanding of how their students were learning Chinese was prevalent among the teachers observed and interviewed, particularly those seconded from *Hanban*. Most of them did not seem to have had any form of formal training on how to teach Chinese in Confucius Institutes abroad prior to their posting. While they all knew that the teaching should be more student-centred, few were aware, at least at the beginning, that a key to the student-centred approach was an adequate understanding of local learners in terms of their expectation, motivation, and their way of learning. So, it often took them a long while before they fully adapted themselves to the local environment and made full use of their specialist expertise. *Hanban* teachers were also more driven by a mission and keen to depart their knowledge to accomplish their mission. They only came to understand after a while that teaching in Confucius Institutes needed to get students interested in learning Chinese, and it was usually more on developing students' practical linguistic competences and skills rather than linguistic knowledge.

Local teachers usually worked part time, and their work depended very much on their own performance and their student feedback. Therefore, it was in their interest to do what they could to meet the needs of their students while following structured and specified course requirements at the Confucius Institutes. Many, especially those with good command of English, were observed to teach from a comparative perspective, using the medium language of English to explain grammar and organise class activities. But for most of the teachers, particularly teachers from *Hanban*, they tended to think that their students in Confucius Institutes did not work hard enough, and they had very little control over their students either in terms of influencing their behaviour or results.

The field study at the classroom level also found that there was room for synergy for Confucius Institute courses to be organically integrated with some cultural activities that the Confucius Institutes organised, and with the methods and purposes of assessment instruments being used. Regarding the cultural element in the cognitive process of language learning, culture is not just a "passenger" in the vehicle of cognitive processes, but can well be the very force that shapes these processes (Nisbett, 2009). It is through the recognition of this that the interest in Lev Vygotsky's socio-cultural insights has been growing in the recent years. Most of the courses would need to make sure that they met the needs in the assessments of their students, who might not be interested in any formal assessment, while the Confucius Institute Headquarters clearly wished to have more students taking up HSK. The tying in of *Hanban* scholarships with HSK results might help to induce more students to take HSK in the future, but the responses to the question in the student questionnaire indicated that there was still a long way to go to achieve the objectives of *Hanban* in this regard.

In terms of learning practices, it was found that most students took a pragmatic approach to the learning of Chinese, and few seemed to really care who offered and taught Chinese there as long as the courses and teaching could effectively meet their needs. The motivation of learning Chinese was mostly instrumental, for jobs and career advancement, or in personal interest, with Chinese heritage students having some of their own requests and learning traits. As their commitment and efforts were closely associated with the practicality and urgency of such needs, rather than some qualification at the end of the course, the students often appeared to be not serious enough about their study in the eyes of their teachers. While they did not seem to have a critical view of the Chinese language teaching at the two Confucius Institutes, they did compare their various learning experiences and would choose an institution with a good reputation even if this meant to be costlier as money did not seem to be their main concern, but time, experiences, and results were.

Most of the students found that tones and characters were most challenging. As most students were interested in learning how to communicate in Chinese, they had a high level of acceptance to the way the language was being taught in classes, though some found the teaching by some teachers was a bit condescending and patronising, and some were also keen to learn how to read as well, especially the heritage students. It was observed that many of the students were working, and qualification was not their main concern. The students appeared to take a very relaxed approach in learning, typically with little time or effort in preparing and revising their lessons, which was one of the reasons why the teachers thought these students did not work hard enough. This also explained the low number of them taking HSK. Their lack of interest in HSK was also partly due to the fact that they could not see much practical use of the qualification, apart from being a Chinese official testimony of their learning.

By comparison, the Chinese heritage students had different attitudes, approaches, and requirements in learning Chinese, and appeared to be much more comfortable with the typical Chinese way of teaching. Most heritage students appeared to be more instrumental in their motivation of learning the language, as they were often expected to be able to speak and use the language since they were Chinese. There were a small number of heritage students whose motivation to learn the language was driven by identity recognition and their needs to be reacculturated into the modern Chinese culture. It was clear that such needs could hardly be met if these heritage students were taught in the same class with non-heritage students. Only special courses could cater for these groups of students and both Confucius Institutes ran special courses for Cantonese speakers who wished to learn and to communicate in Putonghua, and to read both simplified and traditional Chinese characters.

As would be expected from the perspective of language management theory, the impact of the teachers and their teaching on the classroom interactions and the learning of their students were obvious, largely driven by their own beliefs and experiences. It was also clear that the students on the Confucius Institutes were not passively learning what was offered, but influencing the teachers and courses by their behaviour, not only in the classrooms, but also their feedback and above all their decision to continue the course or not to. For the two Confucius Institutes, it was their work to manage their students and teachers' behaviour and subsequently their beliefs as well meeting the objectives of *Hanban*. A key for success, which also remained as a major challenge for Confucius Institutes, was the localisation of teachers, teacher training, teaching methodologies and teaching materials, all of which were related to how to better meet and take into account the learning needs and characteristics of the local students. As Confucius Institutes are running locally, especially in places where education and language teaching well established like in the UK, they have to operate within the local system with due heed to the local practices rather than imposing or transplanting the Confucius Institute headquarters' policies and practices.

In the UK, Chinese is a member of foreign language family, and its syllabi, time schedule, and teaching methods are usually requested to be in line with the other mainstream European languages, even including the standards to be lined up with the CEFR. Such local requirements have led to, in some cases, gaps between the central policies and local agendas and realities, in addition to differences between the Chinese and local staff regarding their practices and beliefs. The offering of Cantonese, a variety of Chinese language not explicitly promoted by *Hanban*, was a typical example. Another example observed and revealed in this research was the fact that both Confucius Institutes were using their own teaching materials that they developed in order to meet the needs of their students.

Notes

1. Hanyu Shuiping Kaoshi (HSK): http://english.*hanban*.org/node_8002.htm
2. A few thoughts from Fach on the new HSK (德语区汉语教学协会对新汉语水平考试的几项说明): www.fachverband-chinesisch.de/sites/default/files/FaCh2010_ErklaerungHSK_ch.pdf
3. European Benchmarks for Chinese Language: http://ebcl.eu.com/
4. *Hanban*. Confucius Institute Annual Development Report: http://hanban.edu.cn/report/
5. *Hanban*. Confucius Institute Annual Development Report: http://hanban.edu.cn/report/

7 Conclusions

This concluding chapter consists of four sections. The opening section recaps the new perspective of this research, the research question and the contributions to the study of Confucius Institutes and management of Chinese language policy. The next section summarises main findings and conclusions of the research. The following section reflects on constraints and limitations of the research, and the last section presents some possible topics for future research on Confucius Institute and Chinese language policy and thoughts on Confucius Institute with regards to Chinese language teaching in the context of an increasingly multilingual Britain.

Research From a Different Perspective

With the rapid development of over 1,500 in 140 countries of the world in just over a decade, Confucius Institutes and Confucius Classrooms are a phenomenon to take note of, and more importantly to understand adequately. It is not surprising that there are increasing reports and research in the recent years on them, but most research completed abroad tends to focus on how China makes use of this initiative as part of the effort to build up its soft power, while most research completed in China concentrates on the needs for them and influence abroad to expand or internationalise the learning and teaching of Chinese language and to promote the understanding of Chinese culture and China overseas. However, few have studied it from the perspective of LPP, particularly in the theoretical framework of language management. This is a gap that the present research set out to fill in by focusing on the actual language policy and practices concerning Chinese in Confucius Institutes in the UK.

While all Confucius Institutes may look similar in name, structure, and their main activity of teaching Chinese language, each Confucius Institute can operate quite differently. Confucius Institutes follow a collaborative joint-venture model by forming partnership with overseas universities or educational organisations, and local environment often differs from one place to another. Therefore, each local Confucius Institutes would undoubtedly be affected not only by the relevant local institutional policies, local needs and requirements, but also by grass-roots level agents like teachers and learners. The impact of the participants was what had underpinned the changes in the study of language policy and planning in the UK and Europe from initially a top-down model to a bottom-up one, and more recently to the one that gives increasing attention to the interactions between institutional policy statement from the above and the actual practices on the ground, or how the language policy is managed (Spolsky, 2004, 2009). So LPP now studies not just what is said, but also what is happening as the language practices of all those concerned at different levels.

The research was designed to examine how the international Chinese language was managed in the implementation process in these local British Confucius Institutes, and to seek answers at three levels: how the Chinese government language policies evolved with regards to the teaching of Chinese language as a foreign language overseas with the initiative of Confucius Institutes; how China's language policies concerning the international Chinese were interpreted by the partner institutions and incorporated into the local institution in terms of services and management; and finally what the actual learning and teaching practices were like in the classrooms of the selected Confucius Institutes with regards to the Chinese language policy.

At the top level, the international Chinese language policy is central to the business of *Hanban*, and the learning and teaching of Chinese is also made central to Confucius Institutes' activities. The initiative of Confucius Institutes for international Chinese can be seen as an extension of the in-China policy and practices of TCFL overseas. However, at the local institutional level, the policy was managed through interactions between all the partners and between the Chinese and local directors. As a result, all Confucius Institutes operate with their own characteristics. This had to a large extent determined the qualitative nature of this research, and subsequent selection of the two Confucius Institutes as case study based upon an ethnographical approach. With the use of a mixed set of data-collection instruments of observation, questionnaire, interview, the research examined in detail at the classroom level, what was taking place in two Confucius Institutes in Chinese language learning and teaching as the local practices of the international Chinese language policy, and how such practices interacted with the relevant central and local language policies and became part of the actual policy being implemented locally. In a way, this is a pioneer piece of research on Confucius Institutes in terms of its theoretical perspective with which the study has been conducted.

Research Findings and Conclusions

The major findings of the ethnographic research based upon the two Confucius Institutes help throw some new light on the dynamic nature

170 *Conclusions*

and interactions between the participating institutional partners and individual teachers and students with regards to the Chinese language policy. From the findings with their analyses of the study, the following conclusions can be drawn.

1. Since Confucius Institutes follow a collaborative joint venture model, conflict of interest exists, and language policy at the level of Confucius Institute is always a process of being negotiated, practised and changing with local influences. It can also be seen as a localisation process of China's international Chinese language policy.

A Confucius Institute involves at least one Chinese and one overseas institutional partner in addition to *Hanban*, and they each may have its own agenda, expectation, priorities as well as interest in the joint venture. Therefore, the actual working of each Confucius Institute is somewhat different due to the disparities in partner institution's intentions and commitments, and subsequent policy and agreement reached. This is shown in the case of the two Confucius Institutes in this ethnographic study in the UK where there is a great deal of autonomy for universities and individuals alike. Both local host universities had taken a very pragmatic approach to the joint venture, just to advance and develop their own Chinese language teaching and to expand links with China via the joint Confucius Institutes without making much additional commitment, nor any obvious long-term development plan. Such an attitude and policy could be felt in the actual operation and management of the two Confucius Institutes.

The local partner seemed to have a considerable influence on explicit and implicit policy statements and practices concerning the content and syllabus of the Chinese courses in the Confucius Institutes after its establishment. Both CI-A and CI-B offered Cantonese courses, clearly not fully in line with the language promotion policy of *Hanban*. So even the policy and agreement reached for a Confucius Institute may change over time too, though the general aims and objectives of Confucius Institute stipulated by *Hanban* may remain the same. When there was conflict of interest, the local host university would do what they could to protect their interest and practice. The clear line drawn for the Confucius Institutes to avoid internal competition and the recent separation of the two Confucius Institutes from the language centres were such examples. In the case of CI-B, at least all the partners' interests seemed to have been taken care of, but this was not quite the case with CI-A, which raised the question on what the Chinese partners reckoned they were getting out of the joint venture for their financial and human resources input.

2. The joint venture model also means the Confucius Institutes follow unspoken competition between their local host universities,

particularly when they are very close to each other in distance and share the same pool of potential learners.

The unspoken competition was obvious in the two Confucius Institutes, which also reflected the rivalry between the two host universities though both are affiliated to the same collegiate university. While the host universities competed for potential students from the similar pool, as the courses offered were similar in many ways, their Confucius Institutes were also competing for learners, especially professionals from the local community, in a very close geographic affinity to each other. Such unspoken competition between them was evident in the lack of coordination and collaboration between them, resulting in not only undesirable competition but also inefficient use of the resources available. This may be true of the relationship between other Confucius Institutes too. While this may appear to be only a management issue now, its future implication can be serious.

The increasing competition between Confucius Institutes raises concern for the long-term development of the institutes as sustainability requires forward business planning and sound daily management to ensure a stable growth and operation of Confucius Institute. This is, however, increasingly a challenge, because while the overall number of learners of Chinese is growing, the average number for each Confucius Institute might not be so. In the two case Confucius Institutes, the number was actually declining due to the increased number of language service providers, including Confucius Institutes themselves. For example, while there are now multiple venues for HSK test in one city, there is only one test venue for the Japanese Proficiency Test (JLPT), once a year, with a high number of candidates as well.

3. Inefficient use of available resources and competition also deepen concerns not only for the current financial operation of Confucius Institute, which seem to be highly dependent upon *Hanban*'s funding, but also the relationship between Confucius Institutes with universities without Confucius Institute and the long-term sustainable development of the institute itself.

While the ethnographic study did not focus on the financial operations of the two Confucius Institutes, it was clear that much of their operational funding came from the head office as the contribution from the local partner institutions was largely intangible or in kind. The under-use of resources such as poorly coordinated and attended cultural and language events like film shows, speaking corners and open lectures drained the limited resources without generating any income in most cases. This was partly because all Confucius Institutes were expected to organise such similar events, even if they were so close to each other in terms of time and distance. The recent requirement for Confucius Institute scholarships often meant that students who really needed scholarships and would better benefit from them could not access them because the students did not register on the courses with a Confucius Institute long enough. However, it was not uncommon that Confucius Institutes often invited students from their host universities to join summer courses in China sponsored by Confucius Institute Headquarters, though the regulations required the students should have registered and studied in the relevant Confucius Institute for at least two terms. They also invited students who learned Chinese well from outside the institute, usually from the host university, to represent it to compete in Chinese Bridge Competition. This might leave out a great number of universities teaching Chinese but without Confucius Institute and make them feel alienated, which was itself a waste of the resources and even income generation opportunities.

It was also clear that while Confucius Institutes were expected to be equally funded by joint partners and to finance themselves in near future, it would be an immense challenge for either Confucius Institute to become fully financially self-reliant and sustainable, generating enough income from the activities and courses they offered to cover all the operational costs, particularly the cost of the directors and teachers seconded from China, which was often not included in the operational cost. In the case of CI-A, the loss of its teaching activities meant it would depend upon *Hanban* funding even more than before. For CI-B, it was making continuous efforts to find new clients and have new businesses. However, as a recent survey indicated, the future number of students learning Chinese would not grow as quickly as in the last ten years, and might even fall for some providers due the reasons discussed.

4. The short-term-based China directors and *Hanban* teachers and part-time appointment of UK directors add uncertainty to stable management and operation of the joint Confucius Institutes.

The model of the Confucius Institute means that individual directors seconded from the Chinese and local partner universities, while sharing the responsibility in jointly managing Confucius Institute's operation, might have huge disparities in management experience, workload, and often agenda entrusted by their own universities. They may also have very different personalities and working styles, which could be further complicated by some underlying social and cultural differences related to their upbringing. In addition, China directors tended to change on a relatively short term, usually every two years a term, or even on an irregular basis as in CI-A where the China director was absent for a long time, and in CI-B where two China directors once had to share the job and often travel back and forth. All this put strain on the working relationship between the China and local directors and thus could affect adversely the management of the joint venture, if not managed conscientiously and properly.

The relatively short-term service of the China directors and *Hanban* teachers often means that they have to get down to work or teach without enough time to know the local culture, local language policy and practices. This could lead to a range of problems as those in the two Confucius Institutes, concerning all aspects of the operation including course design, course delivery, teaching materials and teachers' professional development. This could also alienate Confucius Institute in the local host institution and adversely affect the implementation both central and local language policies and practices of the institute.

5. The Confucius Institutes have two groups of teachers and the differences in their employment status, education backgrounds and teaching experiences not only affect the way they teach, but may also create a potential tension between them.

The study found that there was often an unspoken tension between the teachers sent by *Hanban* and those employed locally in the two Confucius Institutes. While many of the locally employed teachers working on a part-time basis might not have had much formal training in TCFL, most of them had long years of experience in teaching the local learners and they were more attuned to the needs and characteristics of local learners. They were confident in teaching and it was not uncommon that the locally employed teachers regarded the *Hanban* teacher as a rivalry to their work, a threat to their jobs, while the *Hanban* teachers tended to consider some local teachers as less qualified or less well trained to deliver the teaching for the grand goal of international Chinese in the institutes. The short-term contracts of the *Hanban* teachers was also an additional factor for potential inconsistency in the quality of teaching delivery in the classrooms of Confucius Institutes.

6. Most teachers were native speakers of Chinese, and they clearly shared the same cultural and linguistic background. But noticeable gaps were observed between the local teachers and *Hanban* teachers, largely due to individual teachers' beliefs, their education background and their teaching experience.

All the teachers in the two Confucius Institutes were native speakers of Chinese born in and obtaining their first degree in China. Regardless of whether they were employed locally or seconded from *Hanban*, they all shared some similar beliefs and had something in common with their teaching practices. Most teachers still believed that a teacher should be passing on knowledge and strict with students in teaching, and that a student should "constantly strive for perfection". This clearly affected their teaching practices to a great degree. Coupled with the traditional belief and approach in teaching, teachers from *Hanban* tended to focus more on what to teach rather than who to teach and how to teach. They expected their learners to work as hard as they had, as they believed only hard work and strict demand would produce perfect performance (e.g. in pronunciation). While this may be fine when teaching in Chinese in China, it was with no doubt problematic in the Confucius Institutes.

Confucius Institutes needed to provide professional development programmes for both groups of teachers with the emphasis, not just on how to teach Chinese as most training programmes do, but also on how to help them understand their learners and change their perception of their role so that they would be able to better facilitate the learning of their learners, and to strike a balance between being too strict and being too flexible.

7. Most students at the Confucius Institutes seemed to take a pragmatic approach to learning Chinese, not only in terms of their motivation, but also in view of the providers and teachers as long as the host institution was well established and teaching there met their expectations. However, the needs and expectations of the Chinese heritage learners, a significant group in terms of the numbers, seemed to be seriously neglected so far.

It was a surprise that majority of the participants surveyed, adult professionals and students alike, were unaware that their Chinese language course were offered by the local host institution in conjunction with the Confucius Institutes. Few seemed to care who ran the courses and their initial choice tended to have been made based on the status of the local host institution rather than the partnered Confucius Institute.

While this was true of Chinese heritage students, this group clearly had their own needs and requests as they often learned differently from other participants on the course because of their cultural and linguistic heritage and exposure. They were likely to raise questions about Chinese and local culture from their perspectives and keen on learning more about the language and its use, as shown in the field study. There were important implications for the Confucius Institutes with regards to how their Chinese language courses could better meet the needs of these heritage learners in terms of what should be included and how they should be delivered. A real challenge for a teacher was when the heritage learners were mixed with other learners in the same class, particularly when these learners have enormously different exposure to Chinese both culturally and linguistically.

8. The fact that both case Confucius Institutes used their own teaching materials clearly indicated the gap between the teaching materials provided by *Hanban* and what was needed in the local classrooms. The contents and methodologies embedded in these different teaching materials also revealed more fundamental differences in the understanding of language learning and teaching as part of language policy and practice.

The shared experience of the two case Confucius Institutes in compiling their own teaching materials clearly demonstrated the demand for locally developed teaching materials, and part of the necessary localisation process that Confucius Institutes had to go through during the development if they aimed to achieve a sustainable development. The teaching materials *Hanban* provided were often linguistically scientific and culturally abundant in their content to promoting international Chinese, but hardly taking considerations of local learners in the UK whose primary motivation was to learn Chinese as any other foreign languages in a multicultural and multilingual context.

Development of local teaching materials forms an integral part of localisation process Chinese language teaching need to go through before it becomes truly international. Localisation of teaching materials did not just mean that they should just be locally produced, but that they take into consideration how they could best help learners to learn and meet their needs effectively.

9. There was an urgent need and ample room for improved synergy for the Chinese language courses to be organically integrated with other activities of the Confucius Institutes and equally between Confucius Institutes.

The study found that both Confucius Institutes organised many cultural activities independently without much consideration to the language learners' needs, except for Chinese Corner and individual language surgery sessions at CI-A. Most cultural activities were often put on to cater for different audience, and heavily around some significant dates such as Chinese New Year, which again created a kind of competition for the same public or target audience. In addition, it would remain as an issue for a long while to get the teaching, which becomes increasingly localised, in line with the assessment such as HSK that *Hanban* encourages and now forms part of the performance target of the Confucius Institutes.

The study also found that Confucius Institutes needed better coordination and organisation between them in all their activities, as current practices resulted in low efficiency or waste of available resources. Some cultural activities such as paper cutting, tea making, Chinese calligraphy and film shows were repeatedly offered at different Confucius Institutes as all Confucius Institutes were supposed to provide them to promote the understanding of China. The survey results revealed that learners would like to know more about contemporary China rather than the historical cultural heritage. If these activities could have been better planned and organised, they could reach and help more audience and produce better impact.

All the findings are of great importance for sustainable development of Confucius Institute. As the Confucius Institutes involve multiple partners and agents and operate on the premises of local institutional partners, a key process for their success, which also remains as a major challenge for all Confucius Institutes, is their localisation: of teachers, teacher training, teaching materials as well as teaching methodologies. All this were about how to better understand and meet the needs of the local learners, rather than just fulfilling the objectives, especially the short-term quantitative ones of the Chinese language promotion policies set by the Confucius Institute Headquarters.

Reflections on the Research

This study was perhaps one of the very first attempts to study Confucius Institutes in the light of language policy studies. It contributed to the study of Confucius Institutes not only in terms of the focus but also in perspective and methodology. Confucius Institute is primarily a language promotion organisation, but how Chinese language policy is formed, modified, and practised in the institutes has been hardly researched. The perspective of language management theory helped this study to examine the dynamic process of Chinese language policy concerning all the stakeholders at three levels, and the ethnographic case study of the two Confucius Institutes and the mixed instruments enabled the study to produce first-hand data to have an in-depth insight into the process, particularly with regards to the working of the active agents of students and teachers in the classrooms.

It would have been more desirable if a longitudinal study could have been included in the ethnographic study. The current field study only provided a snapshot of what the learning and teaching practices were like in the two Confucius Institute classrooms as observed, and the beliefs and motivations of the participating agents via questionnaire and interviews. A longitudinal research could help to trace changes in the beliefs and practices of both students and teachers at the classroom level over a period, thus demonstrate in a more dynamic manner the interactions between the various agents. At the level of partner institutions, it could help to trace changes in the courses and activities that they offered, and at the macro level of the troika their interactions and subsequent decision and measures. All this was part of the language management process in making and implementing the Chinese language policy in Confucius Institutes. This was not possible this time, primarily due to the time constraint for the researcher, for all the subjects concerned, and it would also need a lot more resources.

Another limitation was associated with time sequence of some of the interviews. Ideally all the interviews with the directors should have been held in the early stage so that the feedback could be used to inform classroom observation, the design of the questionnaires and the subsequent interviews with the teachers and the students. However, this was not possible due to their availability and time constraints as mentioned above.

Possible Topics for Future Research

While the current research has drawn the aforementioned conclusions, it also identified a number of potential areas for further studies during the course of the research. It is hoped that future efforts can be made to follow them up to enrich the research on Confucius Institutes in the light of the study of language policy and planning.

While Confucius Institutes are instrumental in the Chinese government drive to make Chinese language widely available to raise the status of the language in the international arena, Confucius Institutes are now operating in a very different social and political environment if compared with other national language promotion organisations in their early days marked with a clear colonialist thrust. Today when multilingualism and multiculturalism are a main phenomenon in a globalised world, the only way that Confucius Institutes can achieve the goal of making Chinese an international language is through localisation. It is for this reason that ethnographic study is so critical as only such study can throw true light on the working of each individual Confucius Institute whose experience and lessons will not only help us to understand better the dynamic process, but also to manage the process better for those concerned with the institutes.

The first potential areas for further studies is more about research methodology rather than research topics. As each Confucius Institute is different, an ethnographic study is perhaps a best approach in producing a true description of what Confucius Institutes are about. It is felt that in-depth longitudinal study of selected Confucius Institutes could more adequately reflect not only the dynamic changing process of beliefs and practices of the active agents-learners and teachers, but also the changing process of Chinese language policy in Confucius Institutes.

Another interesting topic for further research is the relatively new but rapidly developing school based Confucius Classrooms. Many Confucius Institutes in the UK are involved in this and have their affiliated Confucius Classrooms in schools. Quite a few interesting things are worth noting and studying. One is how well the local university partner is positioned to get involved in school based teaching and how such practices could affect the process and dynamics of the Chinese language policy management since the schools and children's involvement in the language policy is certainly different from the universities and adult students. Moreover, with Confucius Classrooms, *Hanban*'s involvement and influence seem to be more dominant, not only in the large number of Chinese language teachers that it sends over to the Confucius Classrooms, but also in the change of Chinese curriculum and Chinese learning and teaching materials. In a way, it can be viewed as part of the strategy change on the part of *Hanban* to localise the teaching and learning of Chinese and the process seems to be more dominated by *Hanban* and the Chinese partners.

Finally, like Confucius Institutes, sustainable development of Confucius Classrooms appears to be an area that needs more research on even though such localised teaching of Chinese language would have a better chance for long-term development. However, the present localisation is still shallow and superficial in that much of the methods and resources are transplanted and injected by the Chinese partners, and the promised funds to the school by the British government is yet to be realised. A most worrying sign is that there is still lack of enough formal Chinese language teacher training mechanism in the system after so many years' discussion.

Language planning and policy with regards to the promotion of Chinese language through Confucius Institutes are itself an evolving process and have been going through changes since its inception. This demonstrates at least the openness to and readiness for changes of the planning and policy makers to maximise the effectiveness of the relevant policy and planning. This is evident from the shift of the focus at the Seventh Confucius Institute Conference held in December 2012 and has become one of the three key challenges for localisation explicitly marked at the 10th Confucius Institute Conference in December 2015. This shift also signifies that the Confucius Institute development has entered its second phase of internationalising Chinese language, which pays more attention to the adapted teaching and learning of the language rather than a uniform way of language promotion and spread.

It is hoped that this research examining Confucius Institute from the perspective of language management will help to further enhance the study on practical learning and teaching Chinese language in the Confucius Institutes and provide insight into some issues as far as teaching and learning Chinese language in Confucius Institutes is concerned. Findings of this study are also of relevance to the sustainable development of Confucius Institutes. While *Hanban* has become very aware of the importance of localisation of its operation, there is still a long way to go before Confucius Institutes can be truly integrated locally and achieve their overt aims to benefit all the stakeholders concerned, especially the learners, and make them not only effective communicators in Chinese language, but also messengers of world peace with great cultural tolerance and good understanding of Chinese culture.

Bibliography

Adamson, R. (2007) *The defence of French: A language in crisis?* Clevedon: Multilingual Matters.

Ager, D. E. (2001) *Motivation in language planning and language policy.* Clevedon: Multilingual Matters.

Ahmed, K. and O'Neill, J. (2011) China could overtake US economy by 2027. *The Telegraph.* [online] Available at: www.telegraph.co.uk/finance/economics/8901828/Jim-ONeill-China-could-overtake-US-economy-by-2027.html [Accessed Jan. 2013].

Alexander, R. J. (2001) *Culture and pedagogy.* Oxford: Blackwell.

Alliance Française. (2014) *130 years—Alliance Française.* [online] Available at: www.alliantheCEFrançaise. org.uk/m_history.htm [Accessed 10 June 2015].

An, R. and He, G.H. (2017) A preliminary study of establishing a system to assess the cultural promotion impact of Confucius Institutes (孔子学院跨文化传播影响力评估体系建构初探). *Changbai Journal* (长白学刊), 1, pp. 141–148.

Anderson, J. (2008) Towards an integrated second language pedagogy for foreign and community/heritage languages in multilingual Britain. *The Language Learning Journal*, 36(1), pp. 79–89.

Asian Global Impact. (2013) *Australia makes Asian language learning a priority.* [online] Available at: www.agimag.co.uk/australia-makes-asian-language-learning-a-priority/ [Accessed 10 Feb. 2014].

Bach, A. (2011) *Goethe-Institut looks back on 60 years of cultural exchange.* DW [online] Available at: www.dw.de/goethe-institut-looks-back-on-60-years-of-cultural-exchange/a-15277312 [Accessed 16 May 2014].

Bailey, J. (2008) First steps in qualitative data analysis: Transcribing. *Family Practice*, 25(2), pp. 127–131.

Baquedano-López, P. and Hernandez, S. (2011) Language socialization across educational settings. In: B. Levinson and M. Pollock (eds), *A companion to the anthropology of education.* Malden, MA: Wiley-Blackwell, pp. 197–211.

Barton, D. and Hamilton, M. (1998) *Local literacies: A study of reading and writing in on community.* London: Routledge.

Bell, D. (2009) War, peace, and China's soft power: A Confucian approach. *Diogenes*, 56(1), pp. 26–40.

Benesche, S. (2001) *Critical English for academic purposes: Theory, politics, and practice.* Mahwah, N.J. and London: Lawrence Erlbaum Associates.

Black, T. R. (2001) *Understanding social science research*, 2nd ed. London: Sage.

Bolewski, W. and Rietig, C. M. (2008) The cultural impact on China's new diplomacy. *The Whitehead Journal of Diplomacy and International Relations*, Summer/Fall, pp. 83–96.

Brewer, J. (2000) *Ethnography*. London: Open University Press.

British Council. (2015) *Our status*. [online] Available at: www.britishcouncil.org/organisation/structure/status [Accessed 28 May 2015].

Bruézière, M. (1983) *L'Alliance Française, Histoire d'une Institution 1883–1983*. Paris: Librairie Hachette.Cai, H. Q. (2012) Analysis of motivations of Confucius Institute sustainable development (孔子学院可持续发展动因探析). *Southwest Minzu University (Humanities and Social Sciences)* （西南民族大学学报(人文社会科学版）, 3, pp. 213–217.

Cameron, D. (2012) The commodification of language: English as a global commodity. In: T. Nevalainen and E. Closs Traugott (eds), *The Oxford handbook of the history of English*. Oxford: Oxford University Press.

Canagarajah, A. S. (2002) *Reconstructing local knowledge. Journal of Language, Identify and Education*, 1, pp. 243–259.

Chase, S. E. (2005) Narrative inquiry: Multiple lenses, approaches, voices. In: N. K. Denzin and Y. S. Lincoln (eds), *The handbook of qualitative research*. Thousand Oaks, CA: Sage, pp. 651–679.

Chen, G. H. (2008) From the perspective of cultural transmission to see the significance of Confucius Institute (从文化传播角度看孔子学院的意义). *Academic Forum* (学术论坛), 7, pp. 162–167.

Chen, X. (2017) Study on the development and future of Wushu in Bergen—the case of Bergen Confucius Institute (武术在卑尔根的发展现状及对策研究—以卑尔根孔子学院为例). *Chinese Wushu Research* (中华武术研究), 12, pp. 16–19.

Chen, Z. T. (2005) Contemporary language planning in China (当代中国的语言规划). *Applied Linguistics* (语言文字应用), 1, pp. 2–12.

Cheng, T. (2012) On foreign language teaching and research (对外汉语教学研究漫谈). In: *Beijing language and cultural university*. [online] Available at: http://hyjx.blcu.edu.cn/art/2012/7/25/art_7296_1091382.html [Accessed 25 May 2013].

Cheng, Y. L. and Liao, W. W. (2015) Thoughts on the legislation of Confucius Institutes 孔子学院立法若干问题的思考). *Law Science Magazine* (法学杂志), 2, pp. 39–44.

China, Education on Line. (2014) *Study abroad trend report 2014*. [online] Available at: www.eol.cn/html/lx/2014baogao/content.html [Accessed 20 Jan. 2016].

China, National Bureau of Statistics of China. (2014) *GDP*. [online] Available at: http://data.stats.gov.cn/easyquery.htm?cn=C01 [Accessed 19 Jan. 2016].

Chinese Ministry of Education. (2006) *Chinese language situation report*. Beijing: Commercial Press.

Chu, X. and Yue, H. (2015) Analysis of the market operation strategy of Confucius Institutes (孔子学院"市场化"作战略分析). *Taxation and Economy* (税务与经济), 3, pp. 55–60.

Confucius Institute Headquarters/Hanban. (2012) *Standards for teachers of Chinese to speakers of other languages*. Beijing: Foreign Language Teaching and Research Press.

Confucius Institute Headquarters /Hanban. (2013a) *Constitution and by-laws of the Confucius Institutes*. [online] Available at: http://english.hanban.org/node_7880.htm [Accessed 10 Apr. 2013].

Confucius Institute Headquarters /Hanban. (2013b) *About Confucius Institutes/classrooms*. [online] Available at: www.hanban/confuciusinstitutes/node_10961.htm [Accessed 20 Jan. 2013].

Confucius Institute Headquarters. (2013c) *Confucius Institute annual development report 2013*. [online] Available at: www.hanban.org/report/pdf/2013.pdf [Accessed 20 Dec. 2014].

Confucius Institute Headquarters. (2015) *Tell Chinese stories and spread Chinese voice*. [online] Available at: www.hanban.org/article/2015-12/22/content_627909.htm [Accessed 3 Dec. 2015].

Cooper, R. L. (1989) *Language planning and social change*. New York: Cambridge University Press.

Creswell, J. W. (2009) *Research design: Qualitative, quantitative and mixed methods approaches*, 3rd ed. Thousand Oaks, CA: Sage Publications.

Dai, R. (2012) Confucius Institute—the Chinese model of language and culture promotion agency. *Journal of Modern Chinese Studies*, 4(2).

Darlaston-Jones, D., Pike, L., Cohen, L., Young, A. and Haunold, S. (2003) Are they being served? Student expectations of higher education. *Issues in Educational Research*, 13, pp. 31–52.

David, M. and Sutton, C. D. (2011) *Social research, an introduction*, 2nd ed. London: Sage Publications.

Davis, H. A. (1999) The sociopolitical dynamics of indigenous language maintenance and loss: A framework for language policy and planning. In: T. Huebner and K. A. Davis (eds), *Socio-political perspectives on language policy and planning in USA*. Armstead: John Benjamins, pp. 66–98.

Deumert, A. (2000) Language planning and policy. *Introducing Sociolinguistics*, pp. 384–418.

Ding, S. and Saunders, R. A. (2006). Talking up China: An analysis of China's rising cultural power and global promotion of the Chinese language. *East Asia*, 23(2), pp. 3–33.

Dong, X. and Peng, S. (2015) A comparative study of the language promotion policies between China and foreign countries (中外语言国际推广教育的政策比较). *Journal of Foreign Studies* (外国问题研究), 4, pp. 84–88.

The East Asian Bureau of Economic Research. (2013) *Australia in Asian century—white paper*. [online] Available at: www.eaber.org/node/24056 [Accessed 1 Dec. 2013].

Ereaut, G. (2002) *Analysis and interpretation in qualitative market research*. London: Sage Publications.

Ferguson, Charles A. (1977) Sociolinguistic settings of language planning. In: R. J. Björn, H. Jernudd, J. Das Gupta, J. A. Fishman and C. A. Fergusonet (eds), *Language planning processes*. The Hague: Mouton.

Fettes, M. (1997) Language planning and education. In: R. Wodak and D. Corson (eds), *Encyclopaedia of language and education, volume 1: Language policy and political issues in education*. Boston: Kluwer Academic, pp. 13–22.

Fill, A. and Mühlhäusler, P. (eds) (2001) *The ecolinguistic reader: Language, ecology and environment*. London and New York: Continuum.

Fishman, J. A. (1966) *Language loyalty in the United States: The maintenance and perpetuation of non-English mother tongues by American ethnic and religious groups*. The Hague: Mouton.

Fishman, J. A. (1968) Language problems and types of political and sociocultural integration: A conceptual postscript. In: J. A. Fishman, C. A. Ferguson and J. Das Guptas (eds), *Language problems of developing nations*. New York: John Wiley, pp. 491–498.

Fishman, J. A. (ed) (1974) *Advances in language learning*. The Hague: Mouton.

Fishman, J. A. (1991) *Reversing language shift*. Clevedon: Multilingual Matters Ltd.

Fishman, J. A., Ferguson, C. A., and Das Guptas, J. (eds) (1968) *Language problems of developing nations*. New York: John Wiley.

Fostaty, Y. S. and Wilson, R. J. (2000) *Assessment and learning: The ICE approach*. Winnipeg, Canada: Portage and Main Press.

Freeman, R. D. (2004) *Building on community bilingualism*. Philadelphia: Caslon Publishing.

Gao, L. L. (2014) Capacity building of teachers of Confucius Institutes: A case study in Addis Ababa Confucius Institute—on the transformation of English language teachers in the background of language and culture promotion. (孔子学院教师职业能力建设研究: 以亚的斯亚贝巴孔子学院为例—兼谈语言文化推广背景下的英语教师转型问题) *Overseas English* (海外英语), 19, pp. 6–7.

Gil, J. (2017) *Soft power and the worldwide promotion of Chinese language learning: The Confucius Institute project*. Clevedon: Multilingual Matters.

Gong, Z. X. (2013) Dissemination of culture as NGO public debate—A case study of Confucius Institute (文化作为非政府组织公共议题的传播研究—以孔子学院为例). *Contemporary Communication* (当代传播), 3, pp. 49–51.

Grenoble, L. A. and Whaley, L. J. (eds) (1998) *Endangered languages: Language loss and community response*. Cambridge: Cambridge University Press.

Guan, Y. M. (2012) Materials selection and preparation of overseas Confucius institute. (海外孔子学院的教材选择与编写). *Journal of Shenyang Normal University, Social Science Edition*, (沈阳师范大学学报 (社会科学版), 1, pp. 142–143.

Guo, L. S. (2006) The value of language planning in teaching of Chinese as a foreign language and the problems and countermeasures. *The Study of Rhetoric*, 3.

Guo, X. L. (2008) Repackaging Confucius: PRC public diplomacy and the rise of soft power. *Asia Papers Series*. 1. [online] Available at: http://www.isdp.eu/images/stories/isdp-main-pdf/2008_guo_repackaging-confucius.pd [Accessed 18 June 2012].

Hall, K. (2002) Asserting 'needs' and claiming 'rights': The cultural politics of 'minority' language education in Britain. *Language, Identity and Education*, 1(2), pp. 97–119.

Hartig, F. (2012a) Cultural diplomacy with Chinese characteristics: The case of Confucius Institutes in Australia. *Communication, Politics & Culture*, 45, pp. 256–276.

Hartig, F. (2012b) Confucius Institutes and the rise of China. *Journal of Chinese Political Science*, 17(1), pp. 53–76.

Hartig, F. (2015) Communicating China to the world: Confucius Institutes and China's strategic narratives. *Politics*, 35(3–4), pp. 245–258.

Hartig, F. (2016) *Chinese public diplomacy: The rise of the Confucius Institute*. London: Routledge.

Haugen, E. (1959) Planning for a standard language in modern Norway. *Anthropological Linguistics*, 1(3), pp. 8–21.

HEA (Higher Education Academy). (2014) *UCML-AULC survey of institution-wide language provision in universities in the UK (2013–2014)*. University Council of Modern Languages, University of Southampton. [online] Available at: www.ucml.ac.uk/languages-education/he-languages [Accessed 20 June 2015].

Heller, M. (2011) *Paths to postnationalism: A critical ethnography of language and identity*. Oxford: Oxford University Press.

Hisa, C. H. (2013) The joint promotion of teaching Chinese as a foreign language on cross strait: A study of aspects from the Confucius Institute and the Taiwan Academy. *Research on the Development of Confucius Institute*, 2, pp. 52–69.

Ho, A., Watkins, D., and Kelly, M. (2001) The conceptual change approach to improving teaching and learning: An evaluation of a Hong Kong staff development programme. *Higher Education*, 42(2), pp. 143–169.

Hoare-Vance, S. J. (2009) *The Confucius Institutes and China's evolving foreign policy*. Master's dissertation, University of Canterbury.

Hornberger, N. H. (1994) Literacy and language planning. *Language and Education*, 8, pp. 75–86.

Hornberger, N. H. (2002) Multilingual language policy and the continua of biliteracy: An ecological approach. *Language Policy*, 1(1), pp. 27–51.

Hornberger, N. H. (ed) (2003) *Continua of biliteracy: An ecological framework for educational policy, research and practice in multilingual settings*. Clevedon: Multilingual Matters.

Hornberger, N. H. (2007) Biliteracy, transnationalism, multimodality, and identity: Trajectories across time and space. *Linguistics and Education*, 18(3/4), pp. 325–334.

Hornberger, N. H. and Johnson, D. C. (2007) Slicing the onion ethnographically: Layers and spaces in multilingual language education policy and practice [Special issue]. *TESOL Quarterly*, 41(3), pp. 509–532.

Hornberger, N. H. and Johnson, D. C. (2011) The ethnography of language policy. In: T. L. McCarty (eds), *Ethnography and language policy*. London: Routledge.

Hu, B. (2010) The challenges of Chinese: a preliminary study of UK learners' perceptions of difficulty. *Language Learning Journal*, 38(1), pp. 99–118.

Hu, N. (2012) The study of the status and strategies of national traditional sports courses in the Confucius Institute in Bergen, Norway (挪威卑尔根孔子学院民族传统体育课程开设现状与对策研究). Beijing Spots University. (北京体育大学), 9.

Hughes, C. (2014) Confucius Institutes and the university: Distinguishing the political mission from the cultural. *Issues & Studies*, 50(4), pp. 45–83.

Hymes, D. (1964) Introduction: Toward ethnographies of communication. *American Anthropologist*, 66(6), pp. 1–35.

Internet Live Stats. (2014) *Internet users by country (2014)*. [online] Available at: www.internetlivestats.com/internet-users/#trend [Accessed Sept. 2015].

Jernudd, B. H. and Das Gupta, J. (1971) Towards a theory of language planning. In J. Rubin and B. Jernudd (eds), *Can language be planned? Sociolinguistic theory and practice for developing nations*. Honolulu, HI: University of Hawaii Press, pp. 195–216.

Jernudd, B. H. and Neustupný, J. V. (1987) Language planning: For whom? In: L. Laforge (ed), *Proceedings of the international colloquium on language planning*. Québec: Les Press de L´Université Laval, pp. 69–84.

Ji, H. and Zeng, D. (2009) *Conference paper: On the special feature of French Confucius Institute teaching resources development* (法国孔子学院特色教学资源的开发). Conference on digital Chinese language teaching. La Rochelle, France: Association of Modernization of Chinese Teaching 中文教学现代化学会.

Johnson, D. C. (2013) *Language policy*. London: Palgrave Macmillan.

Kaplan, R. B. and Baldauf, R. B. (1997). *Language planning: From practice to theory*. Clevedon: Multilingual Matters.

Krausse, M. (1992) The world's languages in crisis. *Language*, 68(1), pp. 1–42.

Language Policy Research Network (LPReN). (2013). *About LPREN*. [online] Available at: www.cal.org/lpren/about.html [Accessed 3 Dec. 2013].

Lee, K. (2010) Towards a new framework for soft power: An observation of China's Confucius Institute. *Inter Faculty*. University of Tsukuba. [online] Available at: https://journal.hass.tsukuba.ac.jp/interfaculty/article/view/3/5 [Accessed 26 Nov. 2012].

Li, B. G. (2017) Cultural interactions: A comparative study of Motifs for Confucius Institutes and Russian (文化互动中的孔子学院与俄语中心:办学理念的比较研究). *Journal of Northwest Normal University (Social Sciences)* (西北师范大学学报 (社会科学版)), 1, pp. 121–127.

Li, H. L. and Xing, X. (2014) The continuum model and implication of vocabulary teaching at French Confucius Institute (法国孔子学院词汇教学连续统模式及其启示). *China Paper Work*. [online] Available at: www.xzbu.com/1/view-5139154.htm [Accessed 7 Sept. 2015].

Li, L. (2014) Chinese characters teaching in non-Chinese major courses in the UK universities. In: L. Li and M. J. Xing (eds), *Chinese language teaching and learning: Theories and practice -applied Chinese language studies*. London: Cypress Books Co UK Ltd, 5, pp. 110–120.

Li, L. and Zhang, X. (2009) A common framework of standards for non-major Chinese courses in British universities. In: X. Zhang (ed), *Chinese language teaching and learning: Theories and practice -applied Chinese language studies*. London: Cypress Books Co UK Ltd, 2, pp. 143–151.

Li, L. and Zhang, X. (2010) Chinese language teaching in the UK: Present and future. *Language Learning Journal*. London: Routledge, 38(1), pp. 87–97.

Li, L. Y. (2013) Confucius Institutes is inseparable from the Chinese *Pinyin* ("孔子学院" 离不开汉语拼音). *Applied Linguistics (*语言文字应用*)*, 1, pp. 41–42.

Li, W. (1994) *Three generations two language one family: Language choice and language shift in a Chinese community in Britain*. Clevedon: Multilingual Matters.

Li, Y. (2012) Strategy of Wushu development of Confucius Institute (孔子学院武术发展策略研究). *Sports Culture Guide (*体育文化导刊*)*, 9, pp. 123–126.

Li, Y. M. (2010) *On Chinese language planning (*中国语言论*)*. Beijing: Commercial Press.

Liu, C. (2011) A review of domestic research on Confucius Institutes and its prospect (孔子学院国内研究现状及走向). *South China University of Technology Intercultural Communication Studies*, 1, pp. 193–207.

Liu, H. (2013) A review of domestic research on Confucius Institutes (国内孔子学院研究的现状与分析). *Journal of Chongqing Socialist College* 《重庆社会主义学院学报》, 5, pp. 38–41.

Liu, L.H. (2007) Problems and solutions for collaborative model of Confucius Institutes (中外合作创建孔子学院的问题与对策). *Journal of Shenyang Normal University (Social Science edition)* (沈阳师范大学学报 (社会科学版)), 3, pp. 145–147.

Liu, L.P. and Jiang, X.X (2011) From Goethe Institute to see the path of sustainable development of the Confucius Institute (从歌德学院看孔子学院可持续发展之路). *Contemporary Education and Culture* (当代教育与文化), 3, pp. 83–87.

Liu, Q.G. (2010) *Discussion on the use of the Confucius Institute teaching materials (*孔子学院教材使用问题刍议*)*. The Conference proceedings of symposium of 10th international Chinese teaching. 第十届国际汉语教学研讨会论文选. Shenyang: Wanjuan Publisher.

Liu, X.P. (2011) *Research and promotion patterns of Korean from Chinese international promotion perspective (*汉语国际推广视角下的韩国语推广模式研究*)*. MA dissertation, Shandong University.

Lo, J.T. and Pan, S. (2014) Confucius Institutes and China's soft power: Practices and paradoxes. *Compare: A Journal of Comparative and International Education*, pp. 1–21.

Long, Z. (2016) *A study on the teaching approaches in Italian cultural setting: The case of Pisa Confucius Institute* (意大利文化背景下的汉语教学策略研究—以比萨孔子学院为例). MA dissertation, Chongqing University.

McCarty, T.L. (2011) Introducing ethnography and language policy. In: T.L. McCarty (ed), *Ethnography and language policy*. London: Routledge, pp. 1–28.

Mo, J.L. (2009) A comparative study of Confucius Institute and other international institutes of language and culture promotion (孔子学院与世界主要语言文化推广机构的比较研究). *Yunnan Normal University Press* (云南师范大学学报(对外汉语教学与研究版), 5, pp. 21–27.

Nekvapil, J. (2008) Language cultivation in developed contexts. In: B. Spolsky and F.M. Hult (eds), *The handbook of educational linguistics: Planning to language management. Sociolinguistica: International yearbook of European sociolinguistics*. Tubingen: Niemeyer, 20, pp. 92–104.

Nekvapil, J. and Nekula, M. (2006) On language management in multinational companies in the Czech Republic. *Current Issues in Language Planning*, 7(2 & 3), pp. 307–327 [online] Available at: http://citeseerx.ist.psu.edu/viewdoc/download?doi=10.1.1.493.8342&rep=rep1&type=pdf [Accessed 3 Mar. 2014].

Nettle, D. and Romaine, S. (2000) *Vanishing voices: The extinction of the world's languages*. Oxford: Oxford University Press.

Neustupný, J.V. (1994) Problems of English contact discourse and language planning. In: T. Kandiah and J. Kwan-Terry (eds), *English and language planning*. Singapore: Academic Press, pp. 50–69.

Neustupný, J.V. (2003) Japanese students in Prague. Problems of communication and interaction. *International Journal of the Sociology of Language*, 162, pp. 125–143.

Ning, J.M. (2017) New status quo: Improving and innovating Confucius Institutes (新常态: 孔子学院的完善与创新). *International Chinese Language Education (*国际汉语教育*)*, 3, pp. 10–15.

Nisbett, R. E. (2009) *Intelligence and how to get it: Why schools and cultures count*. New York: Norton.
Nye, J. (2004) *Soft power: The means to success in world politics*. New York: Public Affairs.
Pajares, M. (1992) Teachers' beliefs and educational research: Cleaning up a messy construct. *Review of Educational Research*, 62, pp. 307–332.
Pan, S. Y. (2013) Confucius Institute project: China's cultural diplomacy and soft power projection. *Asian Education and Development*, 2(1), pp. 22–33.
Paradise, J. F. (2009) China and international harmony: The role of Confucius Institutes in building Beijing's soft power. *Asian Survey*, 49(4), pp. 647–665.
Patton, M. Q. (2015) *Qualitative research and evaluation methods*, 4th ed. London: Sage Publications.
Pennycook, A. (2003) Global Englishes, Rip Slyme, and performativity. *Journal of Sociolinguistics*, 7(4), pp. 513–533.
Perkins, D. (2007) China's soft power. *Harvard International Review*, (Fall), pp. 82–83.
Phillipson, R. (1992) *Linguistic imperialism*. Oxford: Oxford University Press.
Phillipson, R. and Skutnabb-Kangas, T. (1996) English only worldwide or language ecology. *TESOL Quarterly* (special topic issue Language Planning and Policy), pp. 429–452.
Piao, Y. Z and Du, S. S. (2010) On Wushu culture international spread based on Confucius Institute model: A case study of South Korea (基于孔子学院模式的武术文化国际传播研究—以韩国为例). *Journal of Shenyang Sport University* (沈阳体育学院学报), 1, pp. 125–128.
Procopio, M. (2015) The effectiveness of Confucius Institutes as a tool of China's soft power in South Africa. *The China Monitor*, 1–2. http://aeaa.journals.ac.za/pub/article/view/155
Ricento, T. (2000) Historical and theoretical perspectives in language policy and planning. *Journal of Sociolinguistics*, 4(2), pp. 196–213.
Ricento, T. (2006) *An introduction to language policy: Theory and method*. Malden, MA: Blackwell.
Ricento, T. (2007) Models and approaches in language policy and planning. In: M. Hellinger and A. Pauwels (eds), *Handbook of applied linguistics*. Berlin: Mouton de Gruyter, 9, pp. 211–240.
Ricento, T. and Hornberger, N. H. (1996) Unpeeling the onion: Language planning and policy and the ELT professional. *TESOL Quarterly*, 30(3), pp. 401–427.
Ruan, Y., Duan, X. and Du, X. (2015) Using tasks to enhance beginners' orientations for learning Chinese as a foreign language. *International Journal of Research Studies in Language Learning*, 4, pp. 41–55.
Rubin, J. and Jernudd, B. H. (eds) (1971) Can language be planned? In: *Sociolinguistic theory and practice for developing nations*. Honolulu: University of Hawai'i Press.
Schiffman, H. F. (1996) *Linguistic culture and language policy*. London and New York: Routledge.
Schmidt, P. (2010) At U.S. colleges, Chinese-financed centers prompt worries about academic freedom. *Chronicle of Higher Education*, 57(9), pp. A8–A10.
Shi, X. (2012) Thailand students' Chinese learning motivations and relevant teaching strategies—a case study of Confucius Institute at Khon Kaen university (泰国大学生的汉语学习动机与教学策略—以孔敬大学孔子学院为例) 剑南文学

Jiannan Literature. [online] Available at: www.freedocuments.info/5682691735/ [Accessed on 20 Apr. 2015].

Sigley, G. and Li, J. (2009) Challenges and opportunities in overseas Chinese language teaching and cultural challenges—a case study of Confucius Institute at university of Western Australia. (开展海外汉语教学和文化交流的挑战与机遇—以西澳大学孔子学院为个案). *Yunnan Normal University Press.* 云南师范大学学报 (对外汉语教学与研究版), 1, pp. 32–36.

Silverman, D. (2004) *Qualitative research: Theory, method and practice*, 2nd ed. London: Sage Publications.

Spolsky, B. (2004) *Language policy.* Cambridge: Cambridge University Press.

Spolsky, B. (2009) *Language management.* Cambridge: Cambridge University Press.

Stake, R. E. (1995) *The art of case study research.* London: Sage Publications.

Stambach, A. (2014) *Confucius and crisis in American universities: Culture, capital, and diplomacy in U.S.* New York and London: Public Higher Education Routledge Series, Education in Global Context.

Stambach, A. (2015) Confucius Institute programming in the United States: Language ideology, hegemony, and the making of Chinese culture in university classes. *Anthropology and Education.* [online] Available at: http://onlinelibrary.wiley.com/doi/10.1111/aeq.12087/full [Accessed 14 Dec. 2015].

Starr, D. (2009) Chinese language education in Europe: The Confucius Institutes. *European Journal of Education*, 44(1), pp. 65–82.

Tollefson, J. (1991) *Planning language, planning inequality.* New York: Longman.

Tianzhong, X. M. (2011) *Comparative study of Chinese and Japanese international promotion* (汉语国际推广与日语国际推广的比较研究). MA dissertation, Liaoning Normal University. [online] Available at: www.taodocs.com/p-16581016.html [Accessed 20 Oct. 2013].

Tinsley, T. and Board, K. (2014) The teaching of Chinese in the UK. *British Council.* [online] Available at: www.britishcouncil.org/sites/default/files/alcantara_full_report_jun15.pdf [Accessed 25 Sept. 2015].

UK, Financial Times. (2015) China to become one of world's biggest overseas investors by 2020. [online] Available at: www.ft.com/cms/s/0/5136953a-1b3d-11e5-8201-cbdb03d71480.html#axzz3xNwDpvPQ [Accessed 21 Dec. 2015].

UK, The Guardian. (2015) VisitBritain aims to attract Chinese tourists with new names for landmarks. [online] Available at: www.theguardian.com/uk-news/2015/feb/16/visitbritain-mandarin-names-uk-landmarks-chinese-tourists [Accessed 3 Nov. 2015].

Wan, X. Z. (2009) Localization of Confucius Institute and Chinese language teachers abroad (孔子学院与海外汉语师资的本土化建设). *Yunnan Normal University Press* (云南师范大学学报 (对外汉语教学与研究版), 7(1), pp. 27–31.

Wang, D. P. and Adamson, B. (2014) War and peace: Perceptions of Confucius Institutes in China and USA. *The Asia-Pacific Education Researcher*, 24(1).

Wang, J. (2014) On sustainable development of the Confucius Institute (试论孔子学院的可持续发展). *Journal of Capital Normal University* (Social Sciences Edition) (首都师范大学学报 (社会科学版)), 1, pp. 164–167.

Wang, L. and Higgins, L. T. (2008) Mandarin teaching in the UK in 2007: A brief report of teachers' and learners' views. *Language Learning Journal*, 36(1), pp. 91–96.

Wang, H. L. and Ning, J. M. (2016) Appropriate intervention: Government action and choice in the development of Confucius Institutes (适度干预:孔子学

院发展中的政府行为选择). *Journal of Yunan Normal University (Humanities and Social Sciences Edition)* (云南师范大学学报 (社会科学版)), 1, pp. 54–61.

Wang, M. (2011) *Past, present and future of the French overseas cultural transmission network* (法国海外文化传播网络的历史、现状和未来). [online] Available at: www.culturalink.gov.cn/portal/pubinfo/001001/20120618/5834b3022f354fb4bea1ce1e12894466.html [Accessed 5 Jan. 2013].

Wang, Z. P. and Hao, L. Y. (2014) The role of the Confucius Institute in Chinese and foreign cultural exchanges: A case study of Confucius Institute for Ireland (孔子学院在中外人文交流中的作用：以爱尔兰孔子学院为中心). *Academic Forum* (学术论坛), 2, pp. 163–166.

Wu, X. L. (2005) Confucius Institute and traditional culture (孔子学院和传统文化). *Zhongguancun* (中关村), 1, pp. 82–85.

Wu, X. P. (2011) Enhance the image of China: Inspiration from the Confucius Institute teaching—based on the empirical study of UMass Boston and Bryant University Confucius Institute (中国形象的提升：来自孔子学院教学的启示——基于麻省大学波士顿分校和布莱恩特大学孔子学院问卷的实证分析). *Foreign Affairs Review* (外交评论), 1, pp. 89–102.

Wu, Y. (2009) Reflection on strategy of promoting Chinese culture by Confucius Institute (对孔子学院中国文化传播战略的反思). *Academic Forum*. [online] Available at: http://wenku.baidu.com/view/404c36edaeaad1f346933fa7.html [Accessed 15 Mar. 2013].

Wu, Y. and Ti, W. J. (2009) Development status and problems of the Confucius Institute (孔子学院的发展现状与问题分析). *Journal of Yunnan Normal University* (Teaching and research on Chinese as a foreign language edition) (云南师范大学学报 (对外汉语教学与研究版)), 5, pp. 28–33.

Wu, Y. H. (2009) A strategic plan for the sustainable development of Confucius Institutes (关于孔子学院整体可持续发展的一个战略设想). *Journal of Yunnan Normal University* (Teaching and research on Chinese as a foreign language edition) (云南师范大学学报 (对外汉语教学与研究版), 1, pp. 23–26.

Wu, Y. H. (2010) On operational models and the sustainable development of Confucius Institutes (孔子学院经营模式类型与可持续发展). *China Higher Education* (中国高等教育), 2, pp. 30–32.

Wu, Y. H. (2013) *Theory and methods of Chinese international spread* (汉语国际传播理论与方法). Beijing: China Minzu University Press.

Wu, Y. Y. (2012) Confucius Institutes and international Chinese education in foreign diplomacy (孔子学院与国际汉语教育的公共外交价值). *Journal of Xinjiang Normal University (Edition of Philosophy and Social Sciences)* 新疆师范大学学报(哲学社会科学版), 4, pp. 100–105.

Yan, M. M. (2014) *Study on classroom activities design for Chinese character teaching in Confucius Institute—a case study of Confucius Institute at the University of St. Thomas in Chilly* (孔子学院汉字教学课堂活动设计研究——以智利圣托马斯大学孔子学院为例). [online] Available at: http://116.213.76.141/p-1227189199.html [Accessed 29 July 2015].

Yang, R. (2010) Soft power and higher education: An examination of China's Confucius Institutes. *Globalisation, Societies and Education*, 8(2).

Ye, Y. (2015) Images abroad of Confucius Institutes from the perspective of media reports oversea (从外媒报道看孔子学院的海外形象). *Journal of Sichuan University (Philosophy and Social Science Edition),* 四川大学学报 (哲学社会科学版), 3, pp. 48–57.

Zhan, C. Y. and Li, M. N. (2014) Sustainable development of the Confucius Institutes: Indicators, mode and future perspective (孔子学院的可持续性发展: 指标、模式与展望). *Journal of South China Normal University* (Social Sciences Edition) *(华南师范大学学报* (社会科学版)), 5, pp. 78–82.

Zhang, D. X. (2000) Fifty years for teaching Chinese as a foreign language.—Reviewing and thinking at the turn of the century (对外汉语教学50 年--世纪之交的回眸与思考). *Applied Linguistics (应用语言学)*, 1, pp. 49–59.

Zhang, F. (2014) Confucius Institutes get new Latin American hub. *China Daily USA*. [online] Available at: http://usa.chinadaily.com.cn/epaper/2014-05/13/content_17503832.htm [Accessed 9 Feb. 2015].

Zhang, F. and Wang, H. M (2006) The power of culture: The German Goethe Institute's history and revelation (文化的力量: 德国歌德学院的历史和启示). *Comparative Education Review (比较教育研究)*, 11, pp. 23–27.

Zhang, G. X. (2009) Chinese language teachers training. In: *Chinese learning and teaching*. London: Cypress Books Co UK Ltd.

Zhang, G. X. (2012) Language policy of European Union and universities' foreign language teaching [欧盟语言政策和大学外语教学]. In: L. Hong (ed), *International Chinese Teaching in HE in the Context of Globalisation (《全球语境下海外功效汉语教学》)*. Shanghai: Xuelin Publishing Press, pp. 3–20.

Zhang, G. X. (2013) The localisation of the training of school teachers of Chinese in the UK (英国的中小学汉语教师培训的本土化). In: M. Jiang (ed), *Chinese international education: The current state and strategies of teacher training (汉语国际教育：人才培养现状与对策)*. Beijing: Language and Multimedia Press, Open University of China, pp. 156–167.

Zhang, G. X. (2014) The standards for teachers of Chinese to speakers of other languages and the localisation of teachers' education (国际汉语教师标准和汉语外语师资培训本土化). *Chinese Language in the World (国际汉语)*, 3, pp. 47–51.

Zhang, J. Y. (2014) *The application and reflection of situational teaching in the intermediate oral class at Confucius Institute in Munich* (情境教学在慕尼黑孔子学院中级口语课上的应用及反思). MA diss, Beijing Foreign Studies University. [online] Available at: www.qianluntianxia.com/lunwen/487/1881767.html [Accessed 8 Sept. 2015].

Zhang, Q. H. (2008) Japan plan to add substantial overseas Japanese teaching points to counterbalance the Confucius Institute. *China News*. [online] Available at: www.chinanews.com/gj/ywdd/news/2008/03-18/1194549.shtml [Accessed 27 Aug. 2009].

Zhang, X. H. and Gong, Q. (2013) How Confucius Institutes should realize development with unique features (孔子学院特色发展的解读与例证). *International Chinese Education (国际汉语教育)*, (1).

Zhang, X. P. and Liu, Y. (2006) Study the overseas language promotion policy and promote Chinese overseas (研究国外语言推广政策, 做好汉语的对外传播). *Applied Linguistics (应用语言学)*, 1, pp. 39–47.

Zhang, X. P. (2007) On Confucius Institutes and its role in soft power (简论孔子学院的软实力功能). *International Chinese Teaching (世界汉语教学)*, 3, pp. 25–27.

Zhang, Y. C. Yuan, G. J. and Ouyang, X. F. (2009) Pinyin teaching in overseas cross-cultural context – second case study of Chinese teaching and promotion in US Confucius Institutes (跨文化语境中的海外汉语拼音教学——美国

孔子学院汉语教学与推广研究之二). *Yangtze River Academic* (长江学术), 2, pp. 112–117. [online] Available at: http://www.docin.com/p-799297084.html [Accessed 07 Feb. 2017].

Zhao, H. Y. (2013) *Chinese learners' grammar Learning strategies in Korea Confucius Institute—A case study of Confucius Institute at Dongseo University* (韩国孔子学院汉语学习者语法学习策略调查研究——以东西大学孔子学院为例). MA dissertation, Shandong University. [online] Available at: www.docin.com/p-1096519739.html [Accessed 29 June 2014].

Zhao, H. Q. and Huang, J. B. (2010) China's policy of Chinese as a foreign language and the use of overseas Confucius Institutes. *Educational Research for Policy and Practice*, 9(2), pp. 127–142.

Zhao, J.M. (2014) Status and prospects of Chinese language teaching in Confucius Institutes (孔子学院汉语教学现状与教学前景). *Journal of South China Normal University* (华南师范大学学报), 5, pp. 67–72.

Zhou, Y. (2017) Analysis of interest in jointly run Confucius Institute between Chinese and foreign universities (中外大学合作建设孔子学院的利益分析). *International Chinese Language Education* (国际汉语教育), 3, pp.16–20.

Zhao, Y. and Tang, Y. Q. (2014) The legal issues and its construction in the development of Confucius Institute (孔子学院发展中的法律困境与建构). *Journal of Political Science and Law* (政法论丛), 3, pp. 136–144.

Zhou, Z.G. and Qiao, F. Z. (2008) Explore the modes of overseas Confucius Institute of cooperative education (海外孔子学院合作办学模式探析). *Jiangsu Higher Education* (江苏高教), 5, pp. 32–35

Index

academic freedom 52–55
accredited course 41, 42, 86, 99
acquisition planning 57, 60
administration 99, 102–103, 118, 124
agenda 76, 91–93, 121
agent 16, 21
Alliance Française 31–34, 44–45, 125
analyses 148, 157, 162
annual report 10, 25, 36, 114, 162
approach 63, 91, 113, 165, 174
assessment 29, 33, 36, 158–160
awareness 57, 89, 141, 151

background 103, 136, 148, 151, 173
British Council 25–30

Cantonese 68, 105, 156–157
case 51, 53, 54, 63
CEFR 118, 161–163, 166
certificate 30, 37, 64, 66, 108, 161
challenge 3, 49, 69, 121–122, 146, 166, 171–172, 174
China Director 106, 112, 126, 172
Chinese character 137, 154, 164
classroom observation 69, 155
collaborative model 10, 92, 120
commitment 77–78, 120, 170
competition 85, 100, 126, 170–171, 175
conclusion 19, 93, 169
conflict 42, 52, 100, 104, 123, 125, 149, 170
Confucius Classroom 11, 38–40, 92
Confucius Institute 9–10, 44–45
Confucius Institute Headquarters 11, 38, 74
Confucius Institute initiative 10–12, 74, 92
constitution and by-laws 10, 15, 53
Cooper 56–58
corpus planning 57, 92

course 29, 33, 36, 41, 104
cultural activities 26, 31, 43, 119–125, 175–176

development 37–38, 48, 120
difficulty 153
discrepancy 53, 70, 73
disparity 85, 121
domain 59–62, 72, 92
Duiwai Hanyu Jiaoxue 2, 17, 107

ethnography 20–21, 63, 69, 71
evaluation 58, 60
excerpt 129–135, 137–147
expectation 73, 105, 132, 157–158, 164, 174
expertise 41, 79, 86, 96, 110, 121, 164

feedback 103, 113–115, 117, 158–159
Ferguson 56
financial recourses 78
Fishman 56, 57, 59
focus 101–102, 106–107, 116, 119, 138, 144, 158
framework 20, 61–62, 92, 161
funding 28, 32, 35, 43, 45, 49, 53, 78

Goethe-Institut 34–37
Guoji Hanyu 7–8, 74

Hanban 2, 10, 11, 74
Hanban teacher 83, 99–100, 129, 136, 144–152, 173
Hartig 52–53, 55
heritage student 38, 137, 155–157, 166, 174
Hornberge 58–59, 63, 69, 128
host university 63–80, 85–98, 122
HSK 118, 160–166
human resources 33, 35, 80

Index

ideology 57, 149
impact 12–13, 30, 44, 73, 91, 106, 120, 157–159, 166, 169
influence 43, 49, 56–57, 59, 90, 129, 148, 165, 166, 170, 178
institutional policy 15, 85–86, 169
instrument 17, 20, 51, 66, 67, 69, 71, 165, 169
integration 42, 86–88, 90
interference 42, 52, 87, 150
international Chinese 8, 16, 62, 74, 94, 169
internationalisation 50, 76, 151
interview 69–71, 76–77, 99–105, 116–124, 134, 142, 154, 163–164

Japan Foundation 11, 61
joint venture 91–94, 121, 170

language diffusion 60, 61
language management 17, 19–21, 58–61
language spread 6–8, 20
learning style 51, 144
lingua franca 27, 28, 54, 149
linguistic knowledge 107
Li Wei 155
localisation 2, 3, 12, 15, 51, 94, 108, 110, 151, 163, 166, 170, 175, 176
local teacher 83, 93, 100, 129, 132, 143–145, 149–150, 153, 158, 163, 173
LPP 19, 47, 55–58, 61, 63, 71, 169

media 8, 13, 18, 51–52, 55, 77, 90, 99, 153
mission 19, 35, 42, 92–93, 113, 150, 164
model 10, 44, 49, 53, 56–60, 115, 120, 169, 170–172
motivation 7, 20, 50, 102, 127–128, 134, 151–153, 157, 164, 166, 174–176

native speaker 34, 133, 148, 153, 162, 173
nature 42, 45, 52, 53, 56, 59, 66, 88, 91, 169

obstacle 106, 116, 139
online 4, 5, 10, 12, 28, 29, 30, 101, 102
organisational structure 95, 88

participation 118, 159
partnership 1, 12, 28, 44, 73, 78, 80, 82, 168
perception 9, 13, 42, 101, 113, 127, 136, 140, 143, 150, 158, 174
Pinyin 113, 115, 133, 137–138, 140, 154
position 18, 70, 85, 91, 122, 149
priorities 74, 91, 170
professional development 37, 51, 99, 101, 108, 173, 174
professionalism 144, 146
proficiency 5, 7, 21, 27, 37, 74, 139, 144, 160, 162, 171
pronunciation 51, 102, 108, 133–136, 140, 146, 153, 154, 156, 164, 174
Putonghua 2, 5, 7, 74, 92, 133, 149, 156, 163, 166

qualification 7, 34, 37, 77, 161, 165
quality 12, 15, 41, 76, 78, 81, 87, 95, 110, 173
questionnaire 21, 66–70, 105, 113, 140, 151, 155, 160, 163, 165

resources 78, 84, 103, 123, 162, 171–172
response 77–78, 89, 103, 105, 114, 124, 140, 144, 151, 154, 157, 159, 160, 165
Ricento 19, 55–58, 61, 69, 128
role 3, 7, 19, 32, 35, 39, 48–52, 56–59, 125, 129, 150

sample 66–68
scholarship 26, 80, 90, 92, 118, 124–125, 163, 172
seed-corn funding 53
soft power 54–55
special Confucius Institute 12
Spolsky 19, 45, 59–61, 169
sponsorship 37, 49, 82
Stambach 54
standardisation 7, 56, 108, 159
status planning 57, 92
strand 26, 48
strategy 5, 49, 162, 163
support 45, 55, 82, 88, 99, 102, 114, 119
sustainable development 48, 53, 93, 120–121
syllabus 7, 37, 48, 50, 112, 170
synergy 33, 122, 165, 175

Taiwan Shuyuan 1, 24–25
TCFL 2, 6–7, 92, 169, 173
teachers' beliefs 136, 148, 150, 163, 173
teacher training 13, 27, 34, 43, 64, 101, 104, 122, 149, 176, 178
teaching materials 109–117, 175
teaching method 94, 144, 150, 153, 155, 166
teaching methodology 50, 107–108, 128, 166, 176
textbook 84, 109, 112–117

tone 133, 136, 153, 156, 165
trend 51, 54, 56
troika 73, 91, 127, 176

UK Director 70, 77, 81, 88, 105–106

volunteer 13–14, 81–82, 120, 122

Wu, Y. H. 2, 48

Zhang, G.X. 4, 50
Zhao Jinming 50